Crimes of Democracy

versus

Crimes of Communism

Results of Real Experiment in Slovakia

and

in the World

Karol Ondrias

To Elena and Jurko

Personal logo: Rats' tails as a symbol of confusion. From Children's Book Illustration, F. Pocci, 1846

One may send comments to: karol.ondrias@savba.sk

Note for Librarians: A cataloguing record for this book is available from Library and Archives Canada at www.collectionscanada.ca/amicus/index-e.html
ISBN 1-4251-2162-4

Trafford
PUBLISHING™

Offices in Canada, USA, Ireland and UK

Book sales for North America and international:
Trafford Publishing, 6E–2333 Government St.,
Victoria, BC V8T 4P4 CANADA
phone 250 383 6864 (toll-free 1 888 232 4444)
fax 250 383 6804; email to orders@trafford.com
Book sales in Europe:
Trafford Publishing (UK) Limited, 9 Park End Street, 2nd Floor
Oxford, UK OX1 1HH UNITED KINGDOM
phone +44 (0)1865 722 113 (local rate 0845 230 9601)
facsimile +44 (0)1865 722 868; info.uk@trafford.com
Order online at:
trafford.com/07-0564

10 9 8 7 6 5 4 3 2 1

Content

Introduction

This book, which I wrote for the common people, is divided into three parts. The first part presents data from the real experiment of socialism versus capitalism in Slovakia. This is taken as an example of a country that transitioned from socialism to capitalism. It is an example in which one can easily compare the crimes of democracy vs. the crimes of communism. The second part presents global data on the same issue. It presents evidence of the criminality of capitalist society and deterioration of human rights based on recent capitalistic democracy versus the "totalitarianism" of a socialist society. It presents evidence of the crimes of democracy, which are several times higher than the crimes of communism. The third part discusses the rules of global capitalistic democracy leading to high inequality, modern democratic serfdom and the crimes of democracy, which are based on the rules of the capitalistic democracy coupled with unlimited private property. Some parts of the book are English translations from my books published in Slovak [1-3]. I drew all the data presented in the figures from the sources referenced at the bottom of the figures.

I am using the terms 'capitalistic democracy or democratic' to describe a practice of the state or multi-state system having political pluralism and multi-party elections based on unlimited private property, which is generally called a democratic state or democratic system. Similarly, I am using the term 'communism' to describe a practice of the state socialist system in the former socialist countries (FSC) and recent communist countries, based mostly on collective property. This book is not against the principles of democracy; it describes the negatives of recent capitalistic democracy based on the unlimited power of private property. Capitalistic democracy means that the owners of unlimited wealth have the power to govern through democratically elected representatives. On the other hand, socialist democracy means that democratically elected representatives have real power to govern the owners of property.

I have lived in Slovakia for nearly forty years during socialism and now for more than ten years under capitalism. During socialism I did not pay much attention to politics, but I started to be interested in the competition between socialism and capitalism during my six years of postdoctoral studies in the field of biophysics in the USA. This took place between the periods of 1988-1999, when I shuttled between the USA and Slovakia. I observed that these economically and politically different systems each produced a different kind of society.

After the transformation of socialism to capitalism in 1989, I was surprised by the unexpected changes (most of them negative ones) that capitalism had brought into our daily life. Most importantly, I found that capitalism changed people's behavior (some of it negatively), formed a new culture (mostly negative), and formed a new capitalistic society that is, according to the data I present, far less humane and civilized than the previous socialist society. As a result, I joined the Communist party of Slovakia and started to be even more interested in the discussion of socialism versus capitalism.

Many books and articles present theories and conclusions criticizing real socialism in former socialist countries by emphasizing the crimes of communism. Interestingly, many of the book's authors never lived under socialism or lived in countries under the transition of socialism to capitalism. Instead of a real discussion about socialism versus capitalism, many of them presented limited facts and repeated myths about the totalitarian communist regime, the crimes of communism and the failure of socialism. I had a feeling that they were trying to hide real evidence about socialism or did not know the real facts. It is highly probable that the recent global capitalistic aristocracy realizes the possible advantages of real socialism over real capitalism, i.e. the danger socialism presents to them. Therefore, we are subjected to a massive amount of propaganda slandering real socialism in the FSC. Simply put, the recent global aristocracy may have realized that socialism can take away their privileges based on the rules of a capitalist democracy.

Now when former socialist countries are transformed into capitalist ones, it is easy to compare how the transition affects the economy, human rights, freedom, happiness, satisfaction and the whole economic, cultural and social life of the people. It is easy to compare the crimes of communism with the crimes of recent democracy. As I found out, there are many studies criticizing socialism. However, I do not know of studies comparing the result of a real socialist experiment in the former socialist countries versus real capitalism in the same countries, in spite of fact these data now easily available.

Usually when I read books describing socialism in the former socialist countries as a "criminal, totalitarian and inhuman communist regime, under which people were living without freedom, human rights, or democracy", I am very surprised and cannot understand the descriptions. I cannot find statistical data or use my personal experience to support this general view.

It is unbelievable that still nearly all respected scholars from abroad and at home are repeating the myths about the bad, totalitarian and criminal socialist society. They tell us how the capitalist democratic society liberated us from the evils of communism. Nearly every day some person or respected organization condemns the crimes of communism, but nobody is mentioning the crimes of democracy, to which we, the people in the FSC, were subjected to for the last 17 years.

These myths provoked me to write this book. I would like to present the real data to those who believe in the crimes of communism. The real data show that socialism was a more humane society in comparison to recent capitalism and that the crimes of democracy are several times higher than the crimes of communism.

As I said, the purpose of the myths is to bury socialist or communist ideas because they are very dangerous for the recent global "democratic" world, which is convenient for very few. I will present data supporting the view that the purpose of the myths is to glorify recent capitalistic democracy because it is the base for exploitation, increased inequality, modern democratic serfdom and legalization of capitalist crimes convenient for the few who rule over the capitalistic democracy.

As a scientist trained in natural sciences (working in the field of biophysics), I always try to have a scientific point of view and to study a problem using scientific methods. I do not know whether I will succeed in using these methods to compare socialism vs. capitalism and the crimes of democracy versus the crimes of communism. I am going to try by presenting the effects of the transition from socialism to capitalism on the real life of society, comparing several parameters of economic and social development. It is my hope that the data presented will contribute to a better understanding of the advantages or disadvantages of real socialism versus real capitalism.

To compare the crimes of democracy vs. the crimes of communism, I will make conclusions based on measured data only (at least I will try), and not on ideology, religion or personal feelings. For example, if somebody says that it is cold outside, because he felt cold outside; or because it is winter, so it should be cold outside; or because somebody told him that it is cold outside, I would use a scientific approach to investigate the claim. My approach would be to take three thermometers and measure the temperature outside. According to the measured temperature I would say for example: According to three thermometers, the measured temperature is 17.2±0.1º C.

Of course, to write a book summarizing only the data is easy, but to answer the following questions is challenging. Is socialism better than capitalism? Is recent capitalistic democracy better than "communist totalitarianism"? Is socialism an indispensable next step forward for our civilization in order to solve the present global capitalist problems? Was socialism the wrong way to improve our civilization? Is socialism dead forever, as nearly all respected scholars suppose? Can I present evidence that socialism, as an economic and political system, is better for the people and for the progress of our civilization?

Even more challenging questions: Why are the crimes of recent capitalistic democracy several times higher that the crimes of communism? What are the bases of criminal acts of recent capitalistic democracy? Who rules over the rules of democracy?

This is a challenge. Looking for the answers to these questions is also the purpose of this book.

The data in this book demonstrates the decline of Slovak society and societies of former socialist countries in most 'humane' parameters after the transition from socialist to capitalist societies. After comparing the data, I have come to the conclusion that the capitalistic transition of the former socialist country after 1989 was nothing but a democratic-colonization of the few over the many. This event brought along the deterioration of society. This was achieved by the uncompromising introduction and practice of totalitarian rules of capitalistic democracy.

The data clearly indicates that socialism, as an economic and political system in the former socialist countries, was something new, and in many aspects better, for people when compared to recent capitalism. Simply, the result of capitalistic democracy in the former socialist countries is worse than the result of "communist totalitarianism". This may imply that socialism may be a next step in the organization of our society and civilization. It may be the base for a new, better and united world civilization set on socialist principles.

Bratislava, Slovakia
February 18, 2007

Abbreviations:

FSC: former socialist countries in Central Europe and former Soviet Union
C-S-C: capitalist-socialist-capitalist
Demoserfdom: democratic serfdom based on the rules of the capitalistic democracy
WWII: World War II.
Mill: million
Bill: billion
GDP: gross domestic product
GDP$_{PPP}$: gross domestic product in purchasing power parity
GNP: gross national product
HDR: Human Development Report
HDI: human development index. UN publication - Human development report ranks countries according to human development index (HDI), which is a composite index measuring average achievement in three basic dimensions of human development—a long and healthy life, knowledge and a decent standard of living. The country that ranks first place has number 1 in HDI. The lower the HDI, the better quality of life.
EU: European Union
RVHP: The Council for Mutual Economic Help (of FSC)
CSSR: Czechoslovakia

1. Crimes of democracy vs. crimes of communism
Real experiment in Slovakia – myths, facts and mysteries

The debate over which politico-economic system is better, capitalism or socialism, has been going on for many years. Which system is superior? Today, capitalism is the superior politico-economic system. In industrialized nations, like America, capitalism is in place. We see low unemployment, low interest rates, high standards of living, and efficient companies that are implementing technology in high quality consumer products

This website is created to explain the Superiority of Capitalism over Socialism.

http://www.srsd.org/search/studentprojects/2001/communism/

During forty years of socialism (1948-1989) the people of Slovakia were subjected to both a domestic communist propaganda and a foreign capitalist one. For the most part, the people did not believe the domestic communist propaganda, even though, as I found now, it was mostly true. On the other hand, they believed the myths, the mostly biased foreign propaganda received from Radio Free Europe, the Voice of America, BBC, Austria's TV and foreign radio broadcasts, or from articles and books smuggled from abroad. Some of the foreign propaganda information was simply lies, and it was easy obtainable for those interested in it. Generally, the domestic propaganda was amateurish in comparison to the foreign.

I present facts documenting how the capitalist propaganda (during 1948-1990) was not telling the truth about our form of socialism and glorified our future under the capitalist system. Today's propaganda in Slovakia and abroad is not telling the truth about our real life under capitalism in comparison to socialism. I present facts that the development of socialist Slovakia was relatively positive when compared to the recent capitalist one. The crimes of communism and the humanity of capitalism in Slovakia were and continue to be myths.

The data presented in this part of the book are not a comprehensive review of Slovak development during the last 70 years, but they should give an opinion on the transition changes of Slovak socialism to Slovak capitalism. The data were mostly obtained from the Historical statistical Yearbook of Czechoslovakia 1985; Statistical Yearbook of the Czech and Slovak Republic 1990-1991, Statistical Yearbook of the Slovak Republic 1994-2006 and yearbook statistics of different Slovak organizations. In most cases, where it was possible, I put citations in the figures or in the text. In some cases I have to connect data from different publications. To simplify the text, I will not rewrite all footnotes that present data from the statistical books. The data, with or without the footnotes, will not change the general statements from the graphs. However, the footnotes are available in the original publications.

In some cases I compared the capitalist data (years > 1989) to the data of the socialist year 1989, in spite of the fact that the 1989 data are, in some cases, lower than the data from 1988. This is because after November 17, 1989 until the end of 1989, some industrial, contractual and agricultural production decreased, because of a partial work stoppage. The main reason to compare the data from 1989 to the capitalist data is that the Statistical Yearbook presenting the 1989 data was compiled in 1990-1991 when the communists were not in power. Nobody can accuse me that communists fabricated the socialist data, as I sometimes hear from the propaganda even now.

1.1. Short history of Slovakia

Until 1918: Territory of Slovakia was part of Austria-Hungarian Empire.

1918-1938: After the First World War, Slovakia became a part of capitalist Czechoslovakia.

1938-1945: Slovak state was formed under the protection of Hitler's Germany.

1945-1948: Slovakia became part of the capitalist Czechoslovakia.

1948-1989: Slovakia is part of the socialist Czechoslovakia under Communist rule.

1989-1992: Slovakia is part of the capitalist Czechoslovakia under democratic-capitalistic rule.

1993 until now: independent capitalist Slovak republic was created (population 5.3 million, area 49000 km^2).

After 1989, the transformation of the socialist society to the capitalist one started with privatization of public property. Centrally planned economy was replaced by free market economy and communist rule was replaced by democratic rule. Before the transformation (<1990), nearly 100% of industry, agriculture, forestry, construction, transportation and trade were in public ownership. In 1989 the private sector included only 1% of employers, in 2002 it included 71%. In the beginning of 2004, the share of the private sector in the production of GDP in Slovakia was as follows: Agriculture 99%, forestry 49%, Industry 81%, construction 99%, transportation 64%, trade 99.7%.

1.2. Development of agriculture in Slovakia

The myths

During socialism the foreign propaganda was telling us that our agricultural cooperatives were primitive and not as effective as the private farms in the USA and Western Europe. They told us that socialism, the centrally planned economy and the collectivization of agriculture was responsible for our bad results during socialist agriculture. They said that we needed to get rid of socialism, the centrally planned economy, state farming and the co-operatives. We were advised that the best remedy for our agriculture was elimination of the state co-operative farms, their privatization and the substitution of centrally planned economy to the free market economy. That land in private hands is better than in collective hands. We were assured that democracy is a guarantee for our success in agriculture. During socialism, most people in Slovakia were convinced that the propaganda was right. After 1989 we followed this advice and, as it is shown below, the results are the opposite of what the propaganda persuaded us to do. In spite of the facts shown below, most people at home and abroad still believe the myth that socialist agriculture was very bad in comparison to capitalist. Why do most Slovaks believe this? They believe because, in hundreds of official or unofficial publications dealing with Slovak agriculture, nobody has compared the economic efficiency of capitalist and socialist agriculture.

The facts

During the capitalistic years up until 1948 nearly all agricultural production in Slovakia was in private hands. In 1948 communists came into power and started collectivization of the agriculture. In many cases, pressure was used to speed up the collectivization. Co-operative and state farming in 1957 used 54.4% and in 1960 more than 80% of the area was under cultivation. Later this share increased to nearly 100%. During socialism all agricultural policy was centrally planned. After coup d'État in 1989 in Slovakia, capitalism started with privatization and abandoned the socialist organization of agriculture. At the beginning of 2004, the private sector had a 99% share in agriculture production in Slovakia.

The total agricultural production in Slovakia from 1936 until 2002 at constant prices is shown in Figure 1. We can see in the figure an experiment that was performed when the country's agriculture was capitalist, socialist, and again capitalist (C-S-C). The production was low during capitalism before 1948. It increased during socialism and dramatically decreased after the transformation to capitalism after 1989. In spite of the "know how, advisors, foreign investment and democracy" from developed countries, those who came to help us, in 2004 agricultural production was only 60% of the production in 1989. The agricultural production in 2004 was similar to the production in Slovakia in 1955-65; i.e. the production was set back 40 years.

Total production of the cereals in Slovakia during the C-S-C is shown in the Figure 2. Again, the production of the cereals increased during socialism and decreased during capitalism after 1989.

The number of cattle in Slovakia during the C-S-C period is shown in the Figure 3. It increased during socialism and decreased dramatically, to 33%, during capitalism in 2004 with comparison to 1989. In 2004 it reached value, which is far below the number it was in 1936. Since I could not obtain the number of cattle in Slovakia before 1936, I do not know how many years it was set back.

The number of pigs in Slovakia during the C-S-C period is shown in the Figure 4. It was low during the period of capitalism from 1920-1948; it increased during socialism, and decreased after the transformation to capitalism after 1989. In 2004, it reached only 42% of 1989's numbers, which are similar to the ones in 1950. In this parameter the numbers are set back 56 years. It is astonishing to see how in the real experiment, democracy, free market economy, privatization of land, introduction of private farming with progressive agriculture methods decreased the numbers of cattle or pigs in Slovakia.

The production of eggs in Slovakia during the C-S-C period is shown in the Figure 5. It was low during capitalism until 1948; it increased during socialism, and decreased during capitalism after 1989. In 2004, it reached 57% of the value of 1989 and it is similar to the numbers in 1971. So, in this parameter, we are set back 33 years.

The total area of the vineyards in Slovakia during the C-S-C period is shown in Figure 6. It was low during capitalism until 1948; it increased during socialism, and decreased during capitalism after 1989. In 2004, it decreased to 51% of the 1989 value, what is similar to the one reached already in 1957, i.e. in the parameter of the total area of the vineyards Slovakia returned back 47 years. On Figure 6 the quota of the total area of the vineyards in Slovakia designated by European Union, which is only 72% in 1989, is also depicted.

The number of sheep in Slovakia during the C-S-C period is shown on the Figure 7. It was low during capitalism until 1948; it increased during socialism, and decreased during capitalism after 1989. In 2004, it decreased to 52% of the 1989 value, which is similar to the value in 1948 when the communists took power, and it is less than in 1936. It means that in the parameter of number of sheep, Slovakia returned back 56 years. On Figure 7 the quota of the number of sheep and goats in Slovakia by the European Union, which is only 49% of the 1989 number, is also depicted.

The production of milk in Slovakia during the C-S-C period is shown on Figure 8. It was low during capitalism until 1948; it increased during socialism, and decreased during capitalism after 1989. In 2004, it decreased to a value similar to the one which Slovakia already reached in 1965, 52% of the 1989 value. So, in this parameter, Slovakia is set back 49 years. One Figure 8 the quota of milk production in Slovakia designated by the European Union, which is only 52% of the production in 1989, is depicted also.

Production of meat in Slovakia increased gradually under socialism three times, and it has decreasing gradually after 1989. In 2004 the production was only 45% of the 1989 values; it was set back 50 years (Figure 9).

In May 2004 Slovakia joined the European Union. According to the Treaty of Accession to the European Union 2003, between Slovakia and the EU, Slovakia got quotas for the total area of vineyards, number of the sheep and goats, quota for milk production and so on. This kind of democratic standard will be discussed in the chapter "A crime of communism – colonization by Moscow".

The mysteries

I predict the argument from readers that I should compare development of agriculture of socialist Slovakia with developed capitalist countries. My answer is that it is very difficult to compare the development of agriculture in other developed capitalist countries since each country has different agricultural, demographic and historic conditions. The results I have showed are from the same agricultural, demographic and even cultural conditions.

The very telling figures, shown below, reveal the truth, which is exactly the opposite of the propaganda that has tutored us. It is seen from the figures that our agriculture was poor under capitalism (years < 1948), when Slovakia was politically and economically connected with the Western capitalist countries. It improved when it disconnected from Western countries, and declined again after 1989, when Slovakia was again politically and economically connected with Western capitalist countries. It is seen from the figures that in spite of the best capitalist theories and predictions, in the real experiment, the socialist system of agricultural production was better than the capitalist one. How is that possible? Why in some parameters does the capitalistic democracy destroy our agriculture to a greater extent than Hitler's army, the Red army and partisans combined during WWII.

The dramatic decrease in production after the transformation of socialist agriculture to capitalist was the result of the changing of the political and economic system of socialism to capitalism, which brought privatization, abandoned the centrally planned economy and opened Slovakia to liberal global democratic rules, where the stronger beats the weaker. During socialism we were self-sufficient, now we have to import food.

After 16 years of the transformation of socialist agriculture to capitalist agriculture, based on the presented facts, I understand that our socialist system with the planned economy was very good in comparison to capitalist free market economies. I realize that all myths from the capitalist countries were based, and had only the aim of economically and politically overcoming the former Eastern socialist countries. Basically, Slovakia was democratically-colonized after the coup in 1989 and it was the aim of the coup. As I will describe later, the main tool used for the democratic colonization were the rules of capitalistic democracies themselves. After 1989, democratically elected parliament adopted many laws which were disastrous for agriculture. Why did they do it? Because of democracy. After the introduction of capitalist democracy it was easy to manipulate public opinion in favor of anybody who has money. Anybody from home or abroad who wanted take state owned property into private hands used democracy to do it. Anybody with money could support political party, who will in turn pass a law convenient for donors.

The mystery of the Slovak agricultural development is that nobody in Slovakia or in the developed capitalist countries has mentioned the results of the real socialist-capitalist experiment during many discussions on TV or in other media sources. It still surprises me that nowadays, most of the respectful political and economic scholars from home and abroad are still repeating the myths about the inefficient and primitive socialist agriculture as the result of the socialist system. Maybe they do not know about it or are an integral part of demoserfdom, which we are currently living in.

How long will the myths about the failure of socialist agriculture and superiority of capitalist agriculture prevail? It seems to me for a long time, because the idea of socialist agriculture is very dangerous for the recent global liberal democracy, who are guarantying the good life for a few rich and the exploitation of many poor.

I wonder, who has the power to guard so that the truth cannot get through to our world, in spite of the free society we are living in, and the great quantities of free information running arounds. Who has the power and why he is doing this?

Another mystery. During socialism in Slovakia up until 1990, the communist party appointed all leaders dealing with agriculture, starting from the ministry of agriculture to the directors of agricultural cooperatives. There was no free election of any of these representatives. On the other hand, after 1989, democratically elected government started managing agriculture. As I look at the agricultural figures below, it strikes me that the managing of agriculture under communist rule was very good in comparison to how it is now managed under democratic rule. Results of Slovak agriculture prove that communists chose very good professionals to manage the agriculture. I cannot understand the mystery of why people, in free elections after 1989, have indirectly elected nonprofessionals to manage the agriculture.

How is the democratic system working as to not allow professionals to govern our agriculture? Why has democracy damaged our agriculture in spite of the generally accepted "law", that we are hearing everywhere, that democracy is a guarantee for success in anything including our agriculture? How do invisible forces of a totalitarian global capitalist democracy function in Slovak agriculture that they could not compete with the forces of the communist rules? What rules of the recent global democracy are responsible for the decline of our agriculture? Is it a totality of the recent liberal global capitalist democracy? Yes, I believe it is. I will discuss it later in the book. Is the system of the recent liberal global capitalist democracy a totalitarian system that one cannot escape from? Yes, I believe it is. Is the system of the recent liberal global capitalist democracy, a totalitarian system, which is the base of modern democratic serfdom? Yes, I believe it is. I will also discus these very basic questions later in the book.

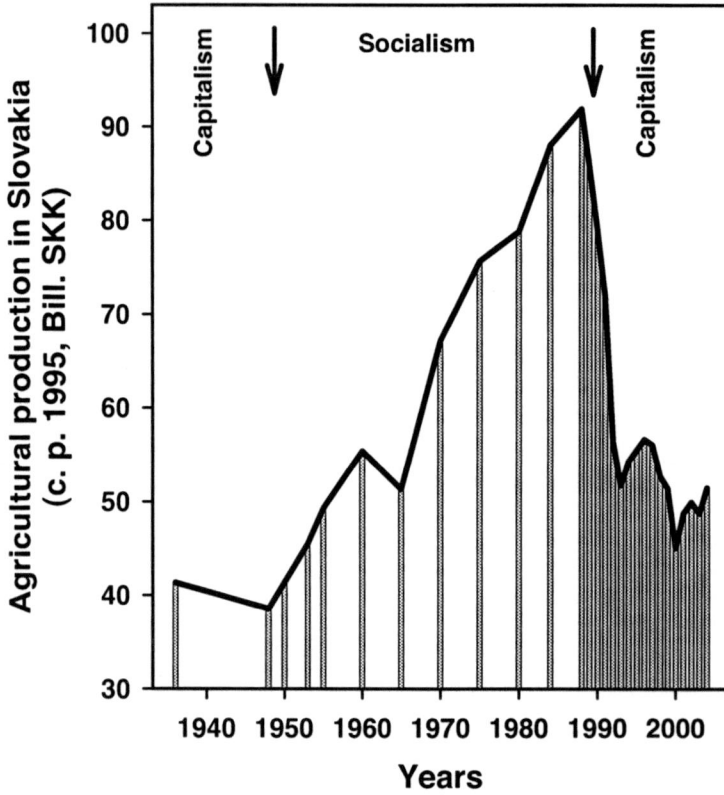

Statistical Yearbook 1991 of the Czech and Slovak federal Republic
Statistical Yearbook of the Slovak Republic 1999-2006

Figure 1

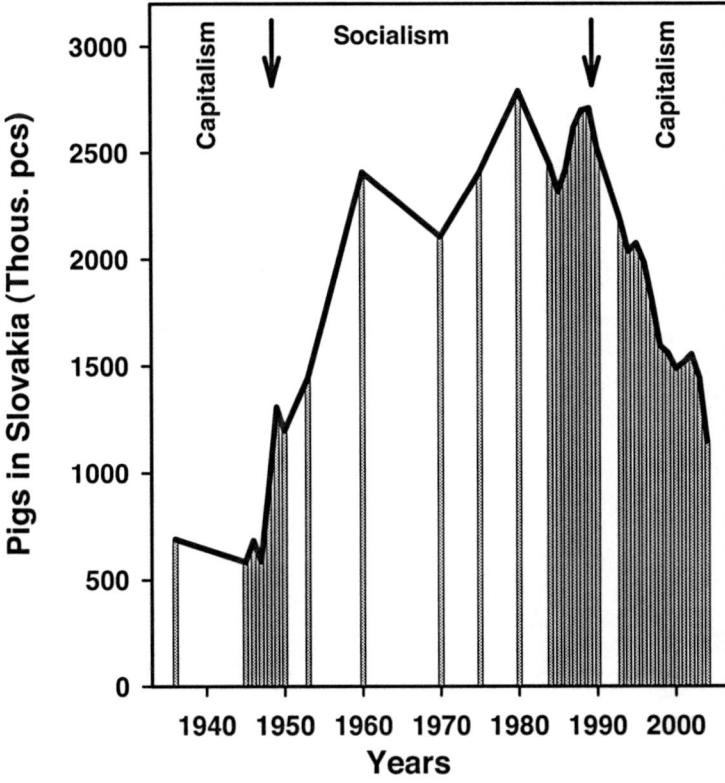

Historical Statistical Yearbook of the Czechoslovakia 1985
Statistical Yearbook of the Czech and Slovak Republic 1990, 1991
Statistical Yearbook of the Slovak Republic 1997-2006.

Figure 4

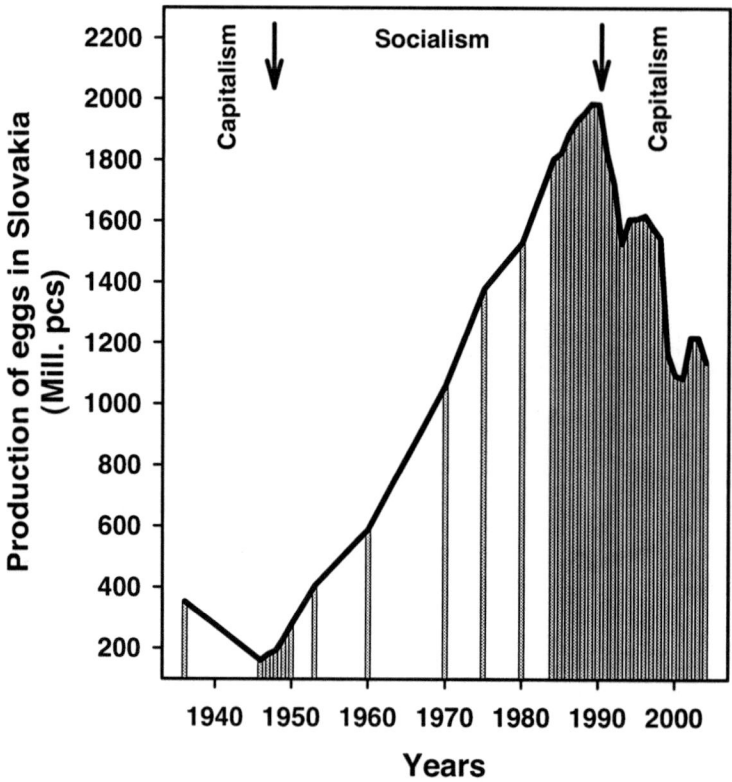

Historical Statistical Yearbook of the Czechoslovakia 1985
Statistical Yearbook of the Czech and Slovak Republic 1990, 1991
Statistical Yearbook of the Slovak Republic 1994-2006

Figure 5

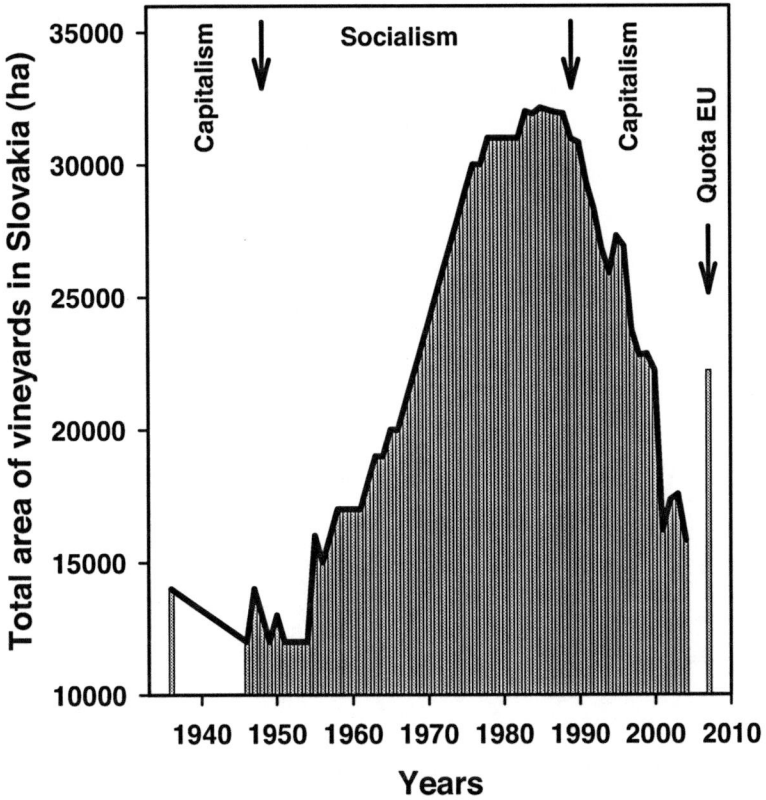

Historical Statistical Yearbook of the Czechoslovakia 1985
Statistical Yearbook of the Czech and Slovak Republic 1990, 1991
Statistical Yearbook of the Slovak Republic 1994-2006

Figure 6

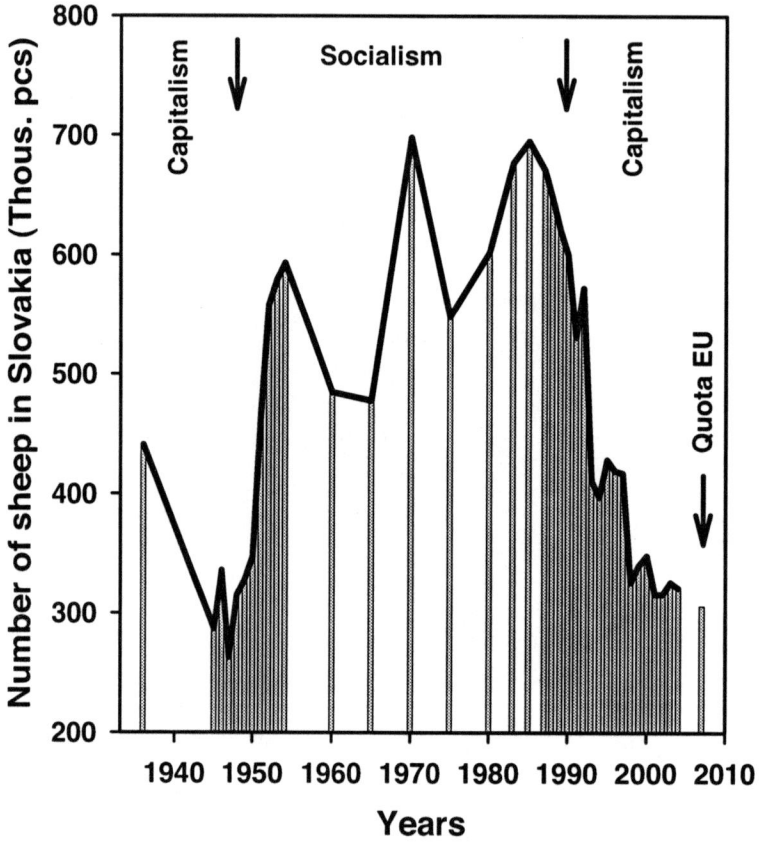

Historical Statistical Yearbook of the Czechoslovakia 1985
Statistical Yearbook of the Czech and Slovak Republic 1990, 1991
Statistical Yearbook of the Slovak Republic 1997-2006

Figure 7

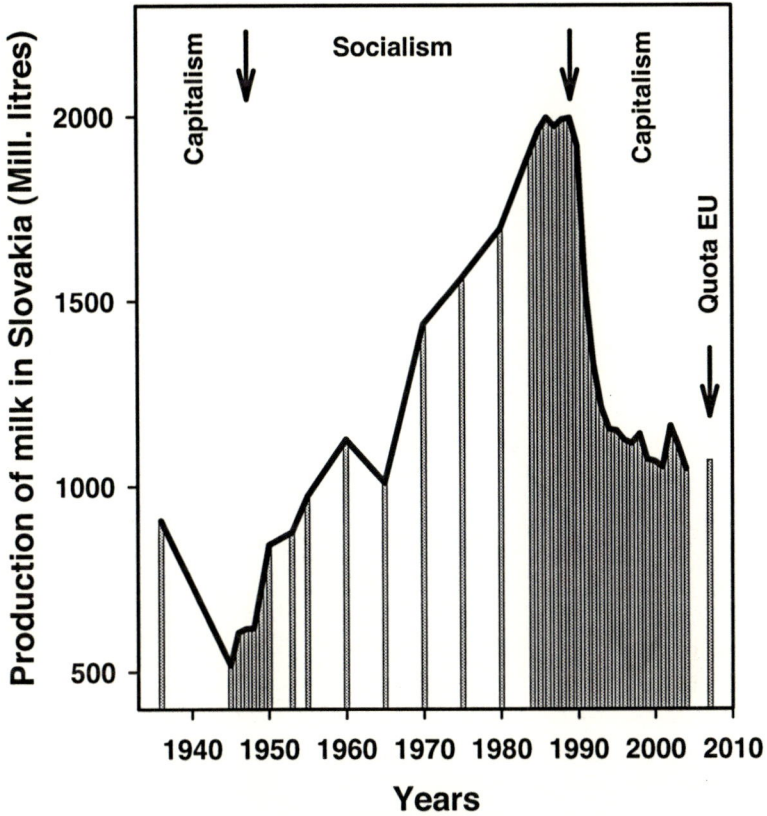

Historical Statistical Yearbook of the Czechoslovakia 1985
Statistical Yearbook of the Czech and Slovak Republic 1990, 1991
Statistical Yearbook of the Slovak Republic 1994-2006

Figure 8

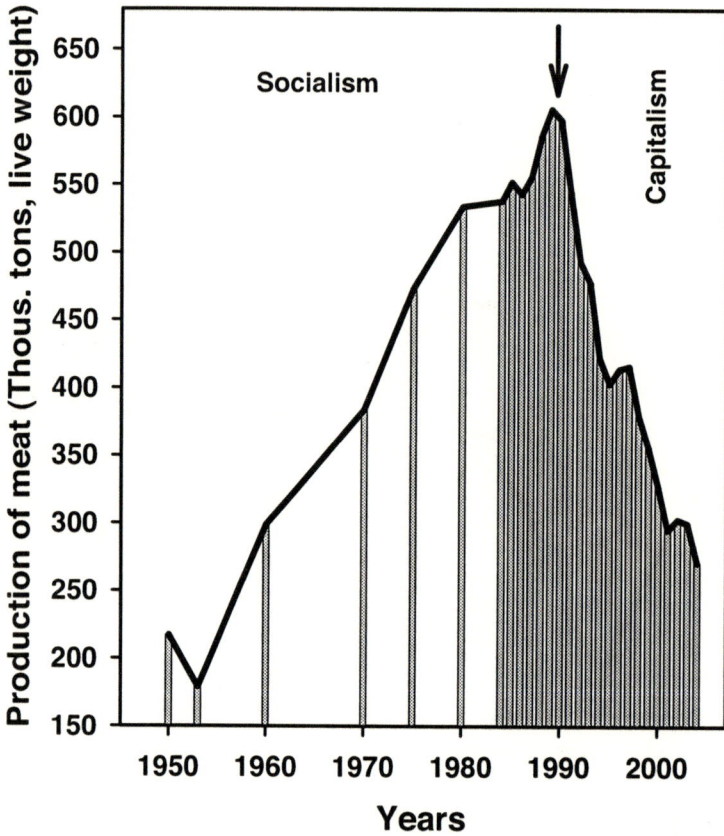

Historical Statistical Yearbook of the Czechoslovakia 1985
Statistical Yearbook of the Czech and Slovak Republic 1990, 1991
Statistical Yearbook of the Slovak Republic 1997-2006

Figure 9

1.3. Development of construction and industry in Slovakia

Capitalism means the complete separation of economy and state. Capitalism is the social system based upon private ownership of the means of production, which entails a completely uncontrolled and unregulated economy where all land is privately owned. But the separation of the state and the economy is not the primary goal, it is only an aspect of the premise that capitalism is based upon, which are individual rights. Capitalism is the only politico-economic system based on the doctrine of individual rights. This means that capitalism recognizes that each and every person is the owner of his own life, and has the right to live his life in any manner he chooses as long as he does not violate the rights of others.

This website is created to explain the Superiority of Capitalism over Socialism.

http://www.srsd.org/search/studentprojects/2001/communism/

The myths

Concerning the Slovak industrial and construction development during socialism, again propaganda from abroad during the last 40 years of socialism has persuaded us that our nationalized and centrally planned socialist economy has not been as effective as the private free marked economy in the developed capitalist countries. That socialism, nationalized property, collective ownership, centrally planned economy, socialist ideology and communism are responsible for our underdevelopment in industrial and contractual production. That in order to develop our construction and industry, we need to get rid of socialism, privatize industry and follow the free market economy. We believed the propaganda and followed the advice.

The facts

As I have mentioned before, until 1948, Slovakia was mostly an agricultural country and its industry was not well developed. The dividing of the shares of the national income in 1948 was 32.2% in agriculture, 39.9% in industry and 11.4% in construction. In 1947, 47.45% of Slovakia's inhabitants were working in agriculture. After forty years of socialism, Slovakia has become an industrialized country. The dividing of the shares of national income in 1989 was 10.1% in agriculture, 61.7% in industry and 11.6% in construction.

During the capitalistic years up until 1945 industrial and construction production in Slovakia was in private hands. In 1945 after the Second World War, banks, insurance companies, key industries (mines, smelters) and the factories with staff of 150-500, were nationalized. After the capitalist's nationalization, 57.7% of employees worked in state owned manufacturing plants and the value of the nationalized industry reached 69% [4]. In 1948 communists came to power, nationalized the rest of private property and started socialist centrally planned economy.

After the transition of socialism to capitalism, in 1989, privatization of industry started and the centrally planned economy was replaced by the capitalist free market economy. At the beginning of 2004, the share of the private sector in the production of GDP in industry was 81%.

Construction in Slovakia remained at constant prices from 1948 until 2002, as shown in Figure 10. Production before 1948 was low (data not shown), it increased during socialism to 2041% in 1948-1989, and dramatically decreased after the transformation to capitalism. Construction production in 2004 decreased to 41% of the 1989 value, and in 2004 it was similar to production in Slovakia in 1970, i. e. the production was set back 34 years.

It is seen in the figure that under the socialist system construction production was better than under the capitalist one. I will stress again that the dramatic decrease of construction production after 1989 was the result of the changing of the socialist system to the capitalist one, the privatization of socialist property, abandonment of the planned socialist economy and following the rules of the global liberal democracy of free market. The decrease in construction was the practical result of the laws passed by democratically elected parliaments and governments after 1989.

Now 17 years after the transformation of socialist construction production to capitalist, the results of the experiment show that our socialist system with planned economy was very good in comparison to the capitalist free market economy. Of course, as I said before, respected scholars dealing with socialist-capitalist issues do not remember to stress or even mention this fact. They are still repeating the myths about inability of socialist economies to advance in construction in comparison to capitalist economies.

One of the results of construction production is the number of dwellings completed in Slovakia. It is shown in Figure 11. The number of completed dwellings increased during socialism and decreased during capitalism after 1989. The number of dwellings completed per year in 2004 decreased to 38% of the level it was at in 1989. During socialism, this number was reached in 1950. It means that in this parameter we returned 54 years back. With the decreasing number of completed dwellings, price of flats and rentals increased several times.

The industrial production in Slovakia from 1936 until 2004 at constant prices is shown in the Figure 12. From the figure, one can see the C-S-C experiment again, when in the same country the industry was capitalist, socialist, and again capitalist. Production during capitalism until 1948 was very low, since Slovakia was mostly an agricultural country. Industrial production increased dramatically during socialism. From 1948 until 1989 it increased from 100% to 3286% and decreased after the transformation to capitalism after 1989 and later it increased again. Most of the industry was privatized and after that destroyed. The most profitable industry was privatized by foreign companies. In 2004 industrial production in the constant prices was about 3% higher with comparison to the value of 1989 (I remark that from 1998 a different system was used to calculate industrial production. Therefore, one may consider the data as approximate values. However it did not change the graph shape of production, or any general conclusions made from it). I remark that the recent published statistical data, e.g. the Statistical Yearbook of the Slovak Republic 2006 does not compare the 40 years of socialism with recent capitalism. It provides statistical information of primary economic indicators from 1991, but not before. The Statistical Yearbooks of the Slovak Republic published before 2006 provide limited economic and social information from before 1989.

According to respected scholars, and nearly everybody talking with the media, capitalism is the best system to carry on business and enterprise, which leads to increased production and satisfies demands. It may be valid in the theoretical world, but it was not valid in the real experiment in Slovakia. When I compared production of refrigerators and freezers in Slovakia during C-S-C period, I found that during capitalism, before 1948, Slovakia did not produce any of them. When capitalism was removed in 1948, production started and increased significantly during socialism, and the production decreased to zero when capitalism was introduced again after 1989 (Figure 13). Similar results were seen in the real experiment of tractor production (Figure 14). One can obtain similar results from the capitalist dependent production of many other goods. Paradoxically, the production of refrigerators, freezers or tractors in Slovakia during socialism is easy to obtain from the Statistical Yearbooks of Czechoslovakia, but the production of the goods is not given in the Statistical Yearbooks of the Slovak Republic after it was established in 1993. Probably the recent population, living in the free information society, does not need such information, which was easily obtainable during "totalitarian communism". Therefore in Figures 13 and 14, there is not detailed data after 1989.

One may argue that the quality of goods in socialist Slovakia was not competitive with the ones produced in the developed world. That may be true for some products, but when one is not producing anything, he does not have money to buy any imported products. It is better to improve the quality of goods produced, than to not produce them.

After 1989, production decreased in goods that were certainly competitive. For example, immediately after the coup in 1989 and the introduction of democracy, Slovakia was under pressure from democrats and humanists to decrease or abolish our arm production. Slovakia had to do it. It decreased arms production to 10% (Figure 15). Paradoxically, the democrats and the humanists did not decrease arms production in their own countries. Probably such behavior is old democratic tradition. Since a third of Slovakia's area is forest, we have (or had) a long wood manufacturing tradition. Even this production decreased to 50% after introducing free enterprises after 1989 (Figure 16).

Why was industrial production increased during socialism after capitalism was removed in Slovakia in 1948, when according to respected scholars, people were not free to do business and enterprise. Why was industrial production decreased after introducing capitalism in Slovakia after 1989, when anybody can participate in business and started a enterprise?

Of course, many foreign companies invested in Slovakia and started producing many goods there. Actually, we do not produce them; we are only giving our labor force to produce them. When foreign companies close factories in Slovakia, we can not continue production.

After 1989 most of the industry was privatized and many companies were purposely liquidated. The increase of the industry production after 1994 was mostly the result of increased foreign investment and the building of foreign industrial parks in Slovakia using our cheap labor. This reminds me of BBC TV news from ~May 2006: Automobile Firm Peguet decided to close its factory in England. The manager of Pegout explained that the cost of the Peguet automobile firm in Slovakia was only 10% of the cost to operate the English firm. A paradoxical relation of foreign investment and living standards in Slovakia is discussed in the next chapter.

Growth of GDP in Slovakia from 1948 until 2005, at constant prices, is shown in Figure 17. The GDP during capitalism until 1948 was very low. The GDP increased dramatically during socialism, and it decreased after the transformation to capitalism after 1989 and later increased again. In 2005 the GDP production at constant prices was 136% of the value in 1989, which was equal to 100%. The growth of GDP for the last several years was also a result of growing services, which reach about 60% of the share of the GDP (I remark that during the presented years calculation of GDP was changed. However that did not change the general view and the conclusions from the figure).

The share of the production of industry, construction and agriculture altogether in total GDP during socialism was high (68% in 1989), but it decreased to 33% after the transition to capitalism (Figure 18). On the other hand, many businesses and enterprises, which do not produce anything efficiently or produce something that decreased living standard, increased crimes and produced moral decay of society. These businesses started flourishing after 1989. Many of the enterprises produce services for riches.

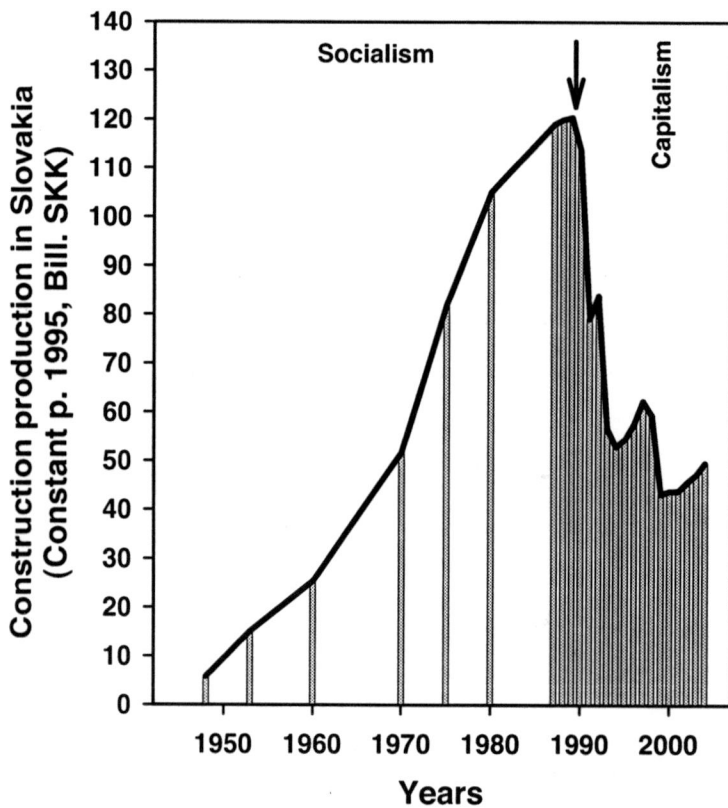

Historical Statistical Yearbook of the Czechoslovakia 1985
Statistical Yearbook of the Czech and Slovak Republic 1990, 1991
Statistical Yearbook of the Slovak Republic 1997-2006

Figure 10

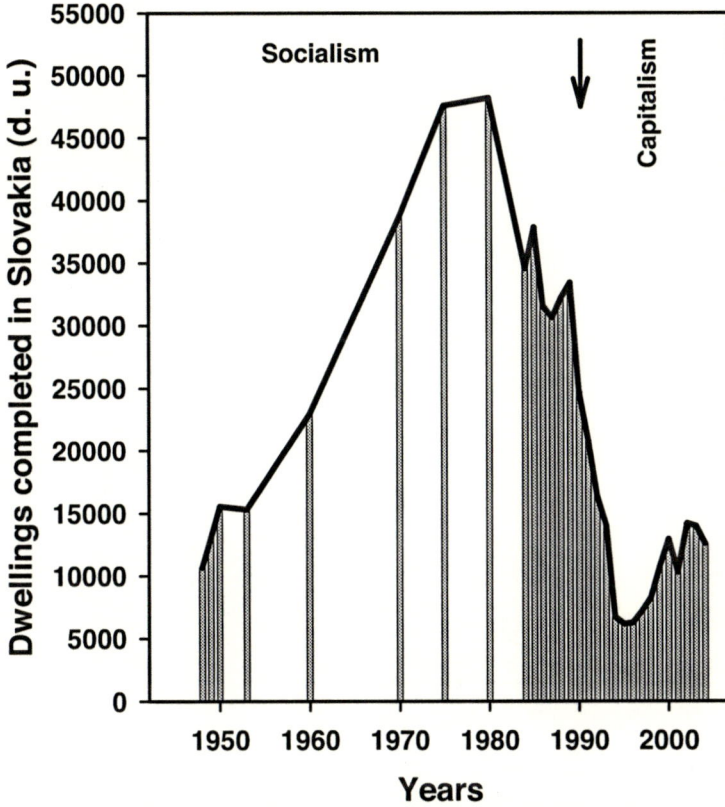

Historical Statistical Yearbook of the Czechoslovakia 1985
Statistical Yearbook of the Czech and Slovak Republic 1990, 1991
Statistical Yearbook of the Slovak Republic 1997-2006

Figure 11

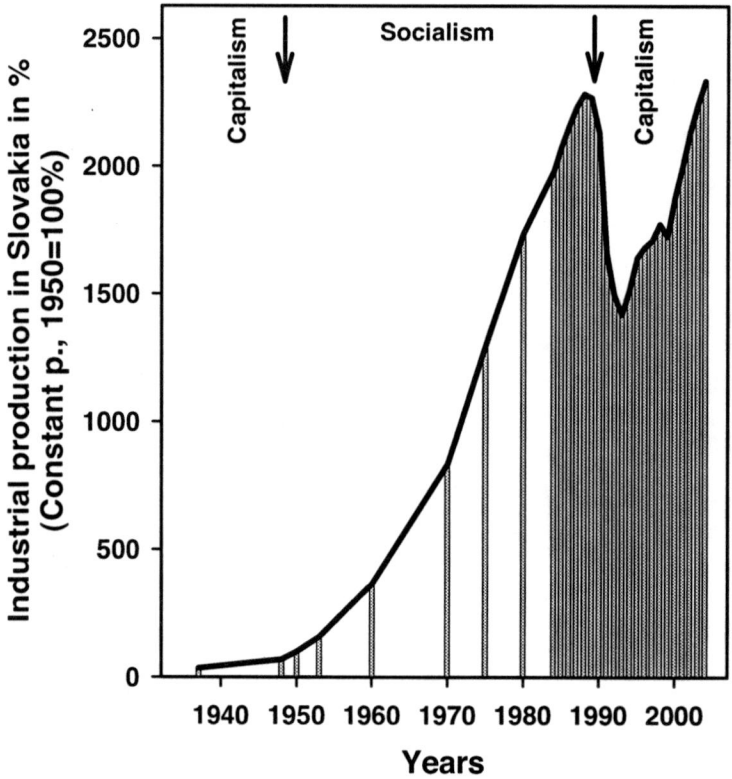

Historical Statistical Yearbook of the Czechoslovakia 1985
Statistical Yearbook of the Czech and Slovak Republic 1990, 1991
Statistical Yearbook of the Slovak Republic 1994-2006

Figure 12

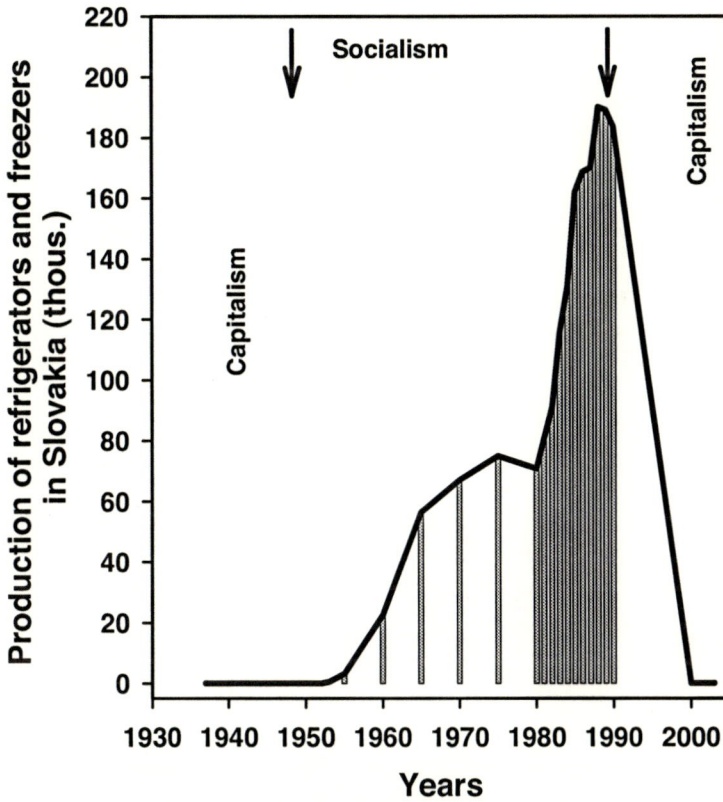

Historical Statistical Yearbook of the Czechoslovakia 1985
Statistical Yearbook of the Czech and Slovak Republic 1990, 1991

Figure 13

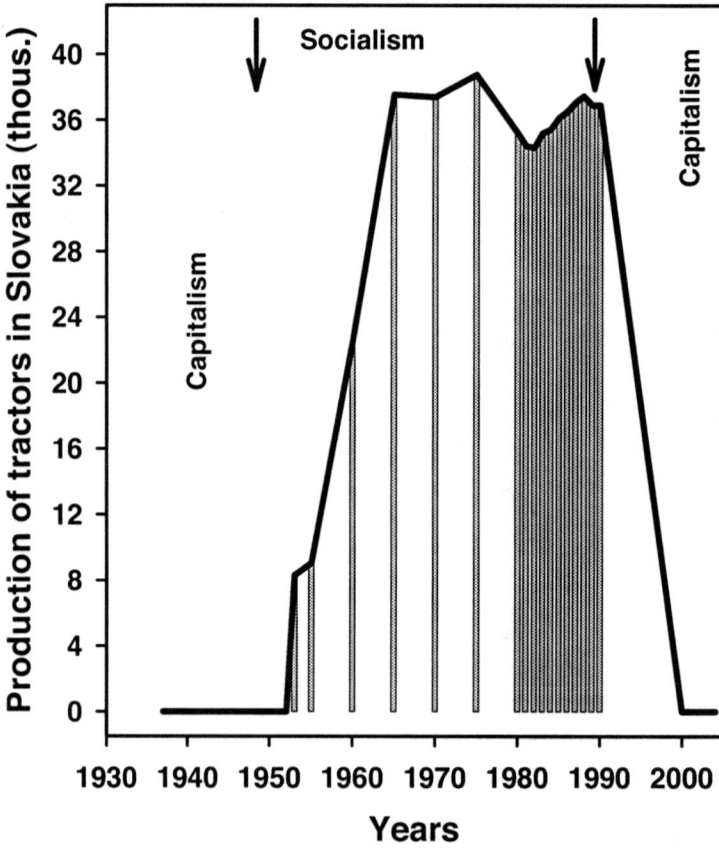

Historical Statistical Yearbook of the Czechoslovakia 1985
Statistical Yearbook of the Czech and Slovak Republic 1990, 1991

Figure 14

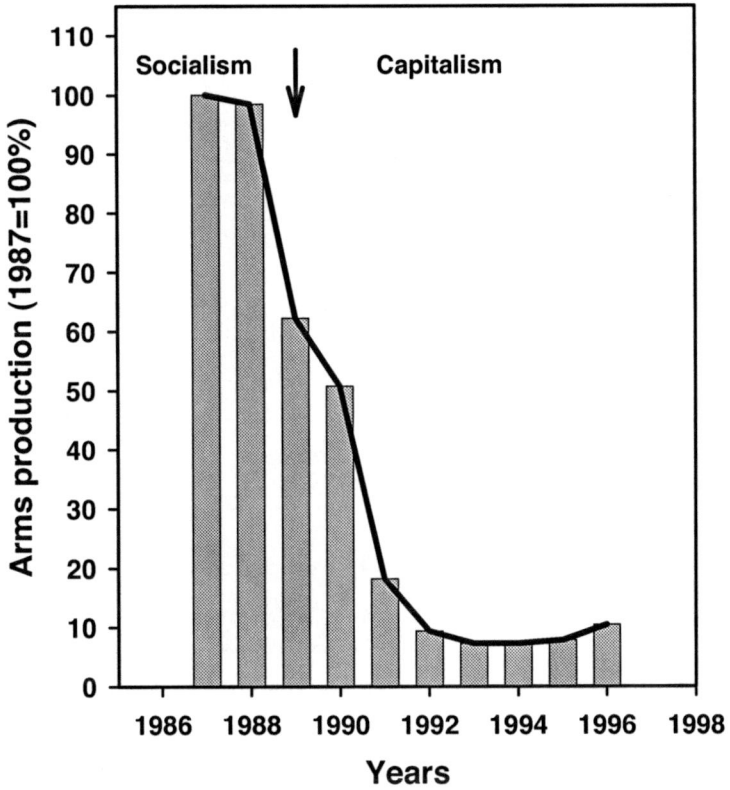

Figure 15

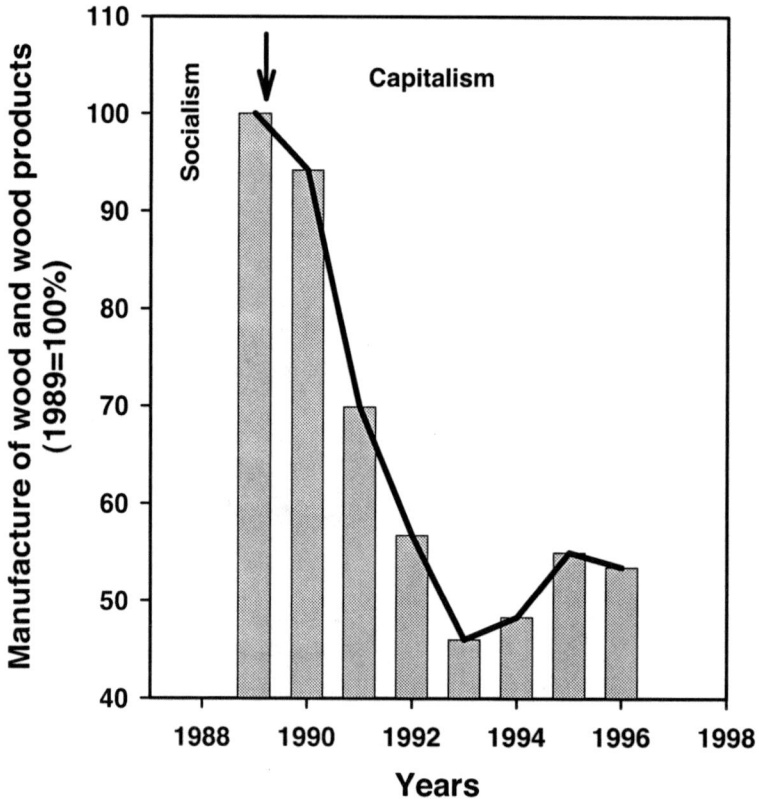

Statistical Yearbook of the Slovak Republic 1994-1997

Figure 16

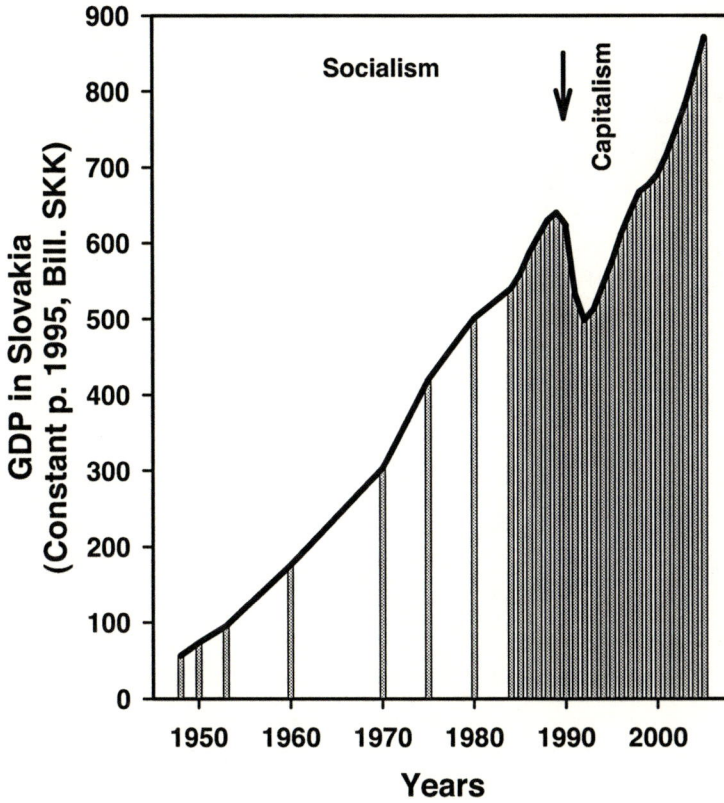

Historical Statistical Yearbook of the Czechoslovakia 1985
Statistical Yearbook of the Czech and Slovak Republic 1990, 1991
Statistical Yearbook of the Slovak Republic 1997-2006
Ekonomický informačný systém Slovensko

Figure 17

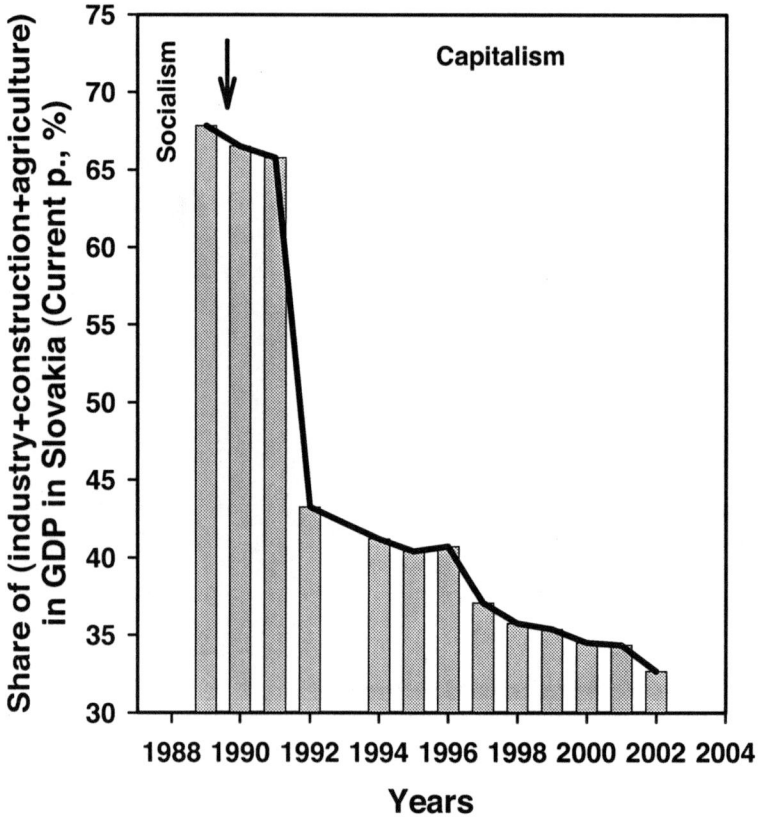

Statistical Yearbook of the Slovak Republic 1997-2003
Ekonomický informačný systém Slovensko 2004

Figure 18

1.4. Slovak's democratic colonization standard and the mysteries of liberation from communist totality

Also, capitalism around the world has undeniably contributed to America's New Economy boom. It has created millions of jobs from Malaysia to Mexico and a great variety of affordable goods for Western consumers. It has brought phone service to some 300 million households in developing nations and a transfer of nearly $2 trillion from rich countries to poor countries through equity, bond investments, and commercial loans. It has helped topple dictators by making information available in sheltered societies.

This website is created to explain the Superiority of Capitalism over Socialism.

http://www.srsd.org/search/studentprojects/2001/communism/

I would like to emphasize the mysteries that strike me concerning the growth of GDP (Figure 17) and the real life of the people during socialism and capitalism.

The real wage index in Slovakia from 1970-2005 is shown in the Figure 19. The real wages increased during socialism parallel to the increase of GDP (compare to the Figure 17). However, the real wages does not follow the shape of GDP after 1989, particularly after 1998, when national monopolies were privatized mostly into foreign hands. It is interesting to see that in spite of increasing the GDP to 136% after 1989, the real wages have not increased proportionally and were only 96% of 1989's values (Figure 20).

Similarly, the rate of increase of pension in Slovakia was higher than the increase of their living cost during socialism, parallel to the increase of GDP. But after the establishment of capitalism and the privatization of public property, the rate of increase of pensions was lower than the rate of increase of living (Figure 21). This is a result of free market economy versus planned economy.

The pension's security benefits paid during socialism and capitalism in Slovakia shows the same tendency (Figure 22). During socialism, the real benefits increased. On the other hand, after 1989 after Slovakia was liberated from "evil communism", it decreased significantly in spite of increased GDP.

From this data I will estimate a Slovak democratic colonization standard. In 2005 Slovakia GDP in real prices was 36% higher than in 1989 (nominal 1439 bill. SKK, SKK/USD ratio was about 30, Figure 17). On the other hand, real wages were only 96% of the level of 1989. This means that the

36% increase in production did not express itself into real wages. Similarly, real pension security benefits in 2003 were only 75% of the 1989 values, in spite of 22% real increase of the production in 2003 with comparison to 1989 (Figure 22). To calculate the Slovak democratic colonization standard, I will estimate that in 2005 real wages, pensions and real security benefits were equal to 1989. 36% of 2005s HDP was 518 bill. SKK, what was 200% of the state budgeted income in 2005. To conclude, in simple words, the democratic colonization standard of Slovakia in 2005 was 518 bill. SKK (≥36% of GDP, i.e. ≥200% of the state budget income in 2005), i.e. the amount of the GDP, which did not show up in living standard. I remark that using the above predictions, the Slovak democratic colonization standard is underestimated. There are two main reasons why 36% of GDP did not show up in wages, pensions or social benefits. A democratic free market economy produced 36% of something that is not useful for people, or 36% of the GDP was taken out of Slovakia. I think that both are partially true and form the Slovak democratic colonization standard. If I use crude estimation, the Slovak democratic colonization standard in 2005 was 3500 USD per capita. I do not know how many people in the world pay the colonization standard, but if they are paid as Slovaks are, it is 3500 Bill. USD per 1 billion people. The money should appear somewhere.

Somebody may argue that from the GDP in 2005 one had to invest some money. Yes, but it was the same as the GDP in 1989.

The result of the Slovak democratic colonization standard is described in nearly all data presented in the Figures in this book. For example, comparison of the distribution of real net income of households in Slovakia during socialism in 1988 and capitalism in 2002 show about a 20% shift to the lower income in 2002 (Figure 23), in spite of the increase GDP. The net income distribution is more asymmetric in 2002 than in 1988. When I obtained the results of the 'Microcensus 2002', I visited a statistical office in Slovakia and asked them, "what was the highest income in Slovakia, and how many people had higher incomes than 10 times the average?" They did not tell me, and explained me that the results of the highest income had big errors and the rich people might not tell the truth about their high incomes.

The paradox of real wages, pensions and security benefits is that the decline of real income, wages and social benefits after 1989 was in spite of the privatization of banks, insurance companies, industry, hotels, bars and nearly everything else to mostly foreign hands. Government received about 550 bill. Sk (18 bill. USD, which is about 200% of a year's income budget). During the period from 1990-2006, Slovakia's foreign debt increased from 2 bill. to 26 bill. USD (Figure 24). After a few years of democracy and free market economy, as a result of the foreign debt owed, we regularly pay a total debt service the same as 100 other countries do. As seen from the Figure 25, the introduction of free market economy in Slovakia effectively destroyed the people's savings. Paradoxically, the money from privatization and borrowing from abroad did not increase leaving standard, but increased unemployment (Figure 26), increased the number of people in poverty, increased crimes and number of mentally distorted people, increased the number of jobs one should to have in order to make ends meet (see Figures in the next chapter: 1.5 Development of the crimes of democracy in Slovakia).

How is it possible? How is it that in the real experiment in Slovakia, liberal democratic capitalism cannot compete with "totalitarian inefficient socialism"? Where does the money go from the increased GDP in Slovakia after the transition to capitalism after 1989? There are many possibilities. I will mention at least two. Firstly, after the transition of socialism to capitalism, all banks, insurance companies, most industries and services were privatized into foreign hands. This is a kind of democratic-colonization and we have made a 'democratically-colonized property' in Slovakia, which means that most profit goes out of Slovakia. Of course, this was one of the aims of the coup in Slovakia in 1989 and the aim of the "fight against evil communism". This is the real result of capitalist democracy in practice, based not on theory, but on the real experiment in Slovakia.

Secondly, the capitalist production of GDP is based partially on production, which in reality does not increase real wages, pension or other social benefits. Simply, the portion of production, which does not produce anything really valuable for people in capitalist countries, is higher than it was during socialism. For example, after the transition to capitalism, after 1989, the production of advertisements increased many times, as well as the security and consultation industry. It is very probable that the real capitalist production is more expensive than the socialist one.

Each day our democratic capitalist leaders emphasize that foreign investment and a free market economy will help increase our living standard. Paradoxically the number of people living in material distress increases with the increase of foreign investment (Figure 27). The mystery is, how during socialism could Slovakia build its own industry from its own sources? These sources have gradually increased living standard in spite of technological embargo, lack of foreign investment, and absence of foreign "know how". Why is it not possible now, when we have democracy, free market economy, foreign investment and "know how" from developed capitalist countries without embargo?

Development of Slovak agriculture, construction and industry during socialism was connected with development of education. Science and research facilities came after communists took power. Science and research started in Slovakia practically from zero in 1948. The number of research and development workers in Slovakia increased during socialism from 3218 in 1948 to 64944 in 1988 (a 20 fold increase). After transition to democratic liberal capitalism it decreased to 22294 in 2005 (34% of the number in 1988) (Figure 28). Similarly, the support of research and development in Slovakia decreased significantly after our liberation from "communist totality" (Figure 29).

How did the "totalitarian" communist system manage to increase the number of workers in science and development and support science? How did freedom and democracy effectively decreased it? How was freedom and democracy working in this case? How and who has democratically arranged that we lose a significant part of our research capabilities in spite of the everyday proclamations of our government and the highest representatives from EU that education, science and research development are priorities to be competitive and to have sustainable development? I can only say that it was reached by the uncompromising laws of democracy, which we have had to obey. The democratically elected representatives passed the laws, which effectively decreased our science and development capacity, decreased production of agriculture and construction and destroyed our industry. The democratically elected representatives passed laws that increased unemployment from zero to 20%, allowing foreign companies to profitably buy everything, including our cheap labor force.

The rules of democracy were the base for the decreased number of the research workers. It was that totality of democracy that arranged it, and any deviation from the totality of democracy was strongly criticized from the owners of the rules of democracy. The practical result of democracy: recent colonizers do not need researchers, they need cheap a labor force to work in their factories.

The practice of privatization of Slovak state property was done according to laws passed by democratically elected representatives in Slovak Parliament. In 1998 a new right wing coalition government was established as a result of the free democratic election in Slovakia. They scrutinized the practice of privatization of the previous government from 1994-1998. According to the official report of the government organization "Fond narodneho majetku" the state property (factories, banks, realities.…) were sold, on average, for 29% of their real values. This means that 71% of property was stolen. Paradoxically, the government, which found this discrepancy, did not do anything about it. The mutual involvement was probably high. How is democracy working when big thieves are safe?

I will repeat again that in spite of the best capitalist theories and predictions, in the real C-S-C experiment, the socialist system of construction and industry produced better output for people than the capitalist one. In spite of the real data, propaganda is still telling everybody that socialism, centrally planned economy and the collective ownership of industry were responsible for our underdeveloped construction and industry. Nowadays, Slovak media, politicians, advisors from abroad and respected scholars from everywhere are still repeating the clause: "how inefficient and primitive was the socialist construction and industry and how good the capitalist one is." It is possible that some construction and industry in Slovakia are better off now, but for whom? I remember prosperous industry of gold, platinum and chromium of the Republic of South Africa for hundreds of years, but for whom?

The mysteries of the governing of our construction and industry after 1989 are the same as the governing of agriculture. Why have people, in free elections after 1989, chosen nonprofessionals to manage construction and industry? How did "totalitarian" communists choose professionals to manage them? How do invisible forces of democracy function in destroying Slovaks construction and industry, and installing colonization and demoserfdom?

In this chapter I wanted to present more detailed data on industrial production in Slovakia during socialism in comparison to recent capitalism. I wanted to compare details of the state budget expenditure for science, education, health care and so on. As the member of the Slovak parliament, I went to the parliament library and asked for the approved state budgets for 1989 and 1988. I was surprised that the state budgets from the years before 1990 were not at the library. I remark that one could find many different books at the parliamentary library, including cookbooks. I asked librarians to find the state budgets for me. They could not find them. I was not able to find the detailed state budgets for the years before 1989 in Slovakia. I believe they must have been left somewhere left or hidden.

Finally, some data from the detailed budgets and other data from the years before 1989, I obtained from people who secretly sympathized with the Communist party of Slovakia and worked at high state institutions. The data were literally smuggled from the offices of high state institutions. I copied the data and returned it. The people that provided me with the data were afraid to lose their jobs if somebody found out about this procedure. Paradoxically, it was at the time when government proudly approved the law of free access to information as another pillar of democracy.

Similarly, I was looking for the data on production of goods during socialism in Slovakia, e.g. production of shoes, clothes, furniture, TV sets, and so on. I wanted to compare the data with the decline in production of the goods after 1989. To my surprise, I was not able to find any production data book after 1989. This is in spite of knowing that during socialism the data were published each year. I guess they must be somewhere and I am probably not clever enough to find them.

I am of the opinion that the destruction and colonization of the FSC was prepared in such detail that one point in a 'colonization protocol' might be able to destroy the detailed data of the state budgets before 1990 and any relevant information that would serve as a comparison between socialism in Slovakia with development after 1990. I suppose the totality of democracy, freedom of expression and right to have information combined with censorship is working very well. The capitalistic democracy thought of all the details.

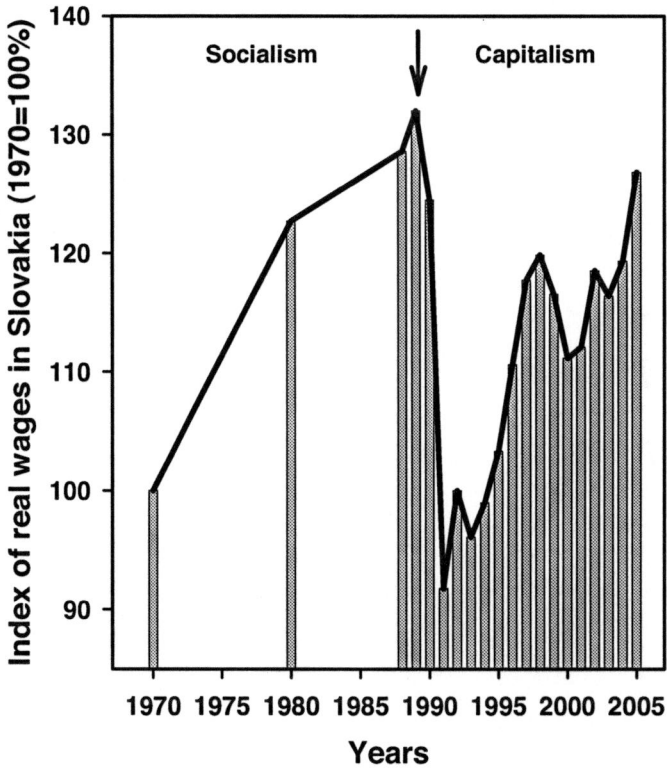

Statistical Yearbook of the Slovak Republic 1999-2006

Figure 19

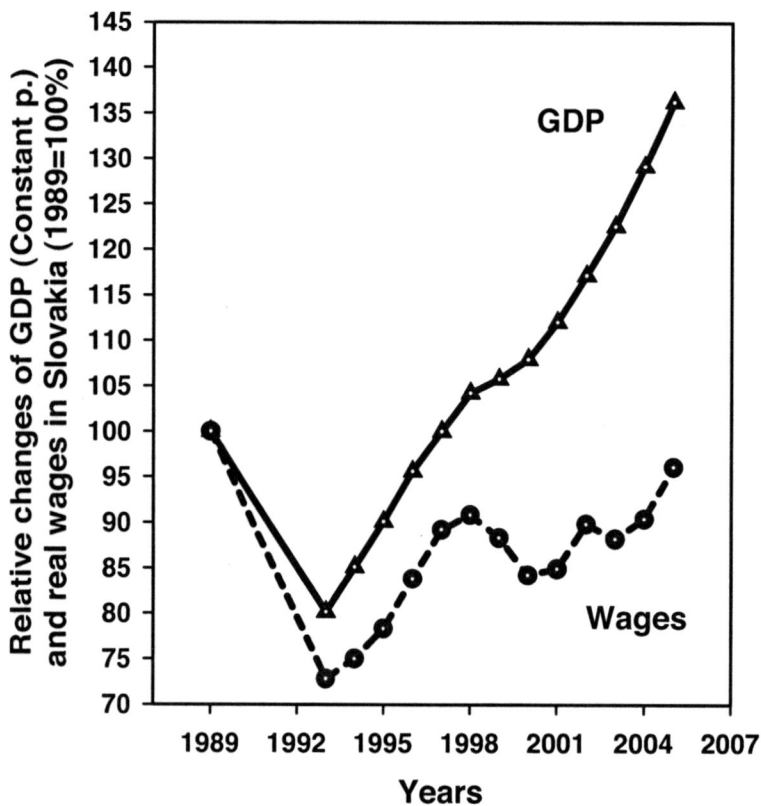

Statistical Yearbook of the Slovak Republic 1999-2006

Figure 20

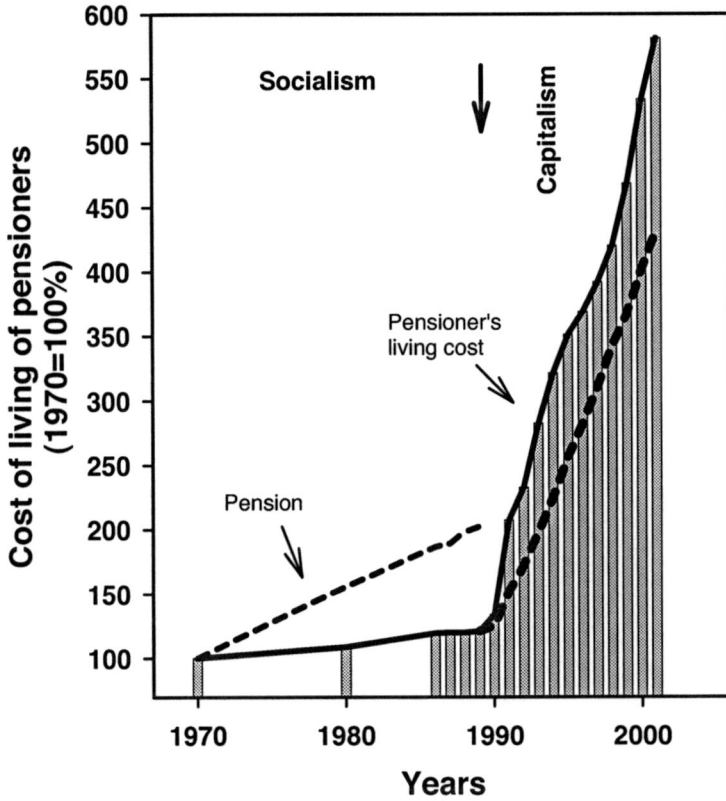

Statistical Yearbook of the Slovak Republic 1994-2002

Figure 21

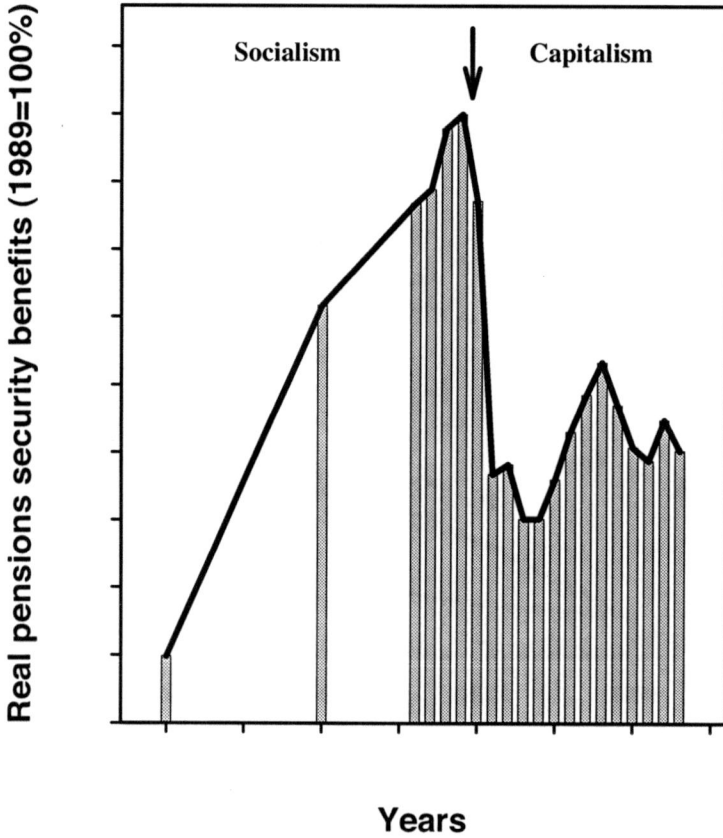

Statistical Yearbooks of the Czechoslovakia and the Slovak Republic 1991-2005

Figure 22

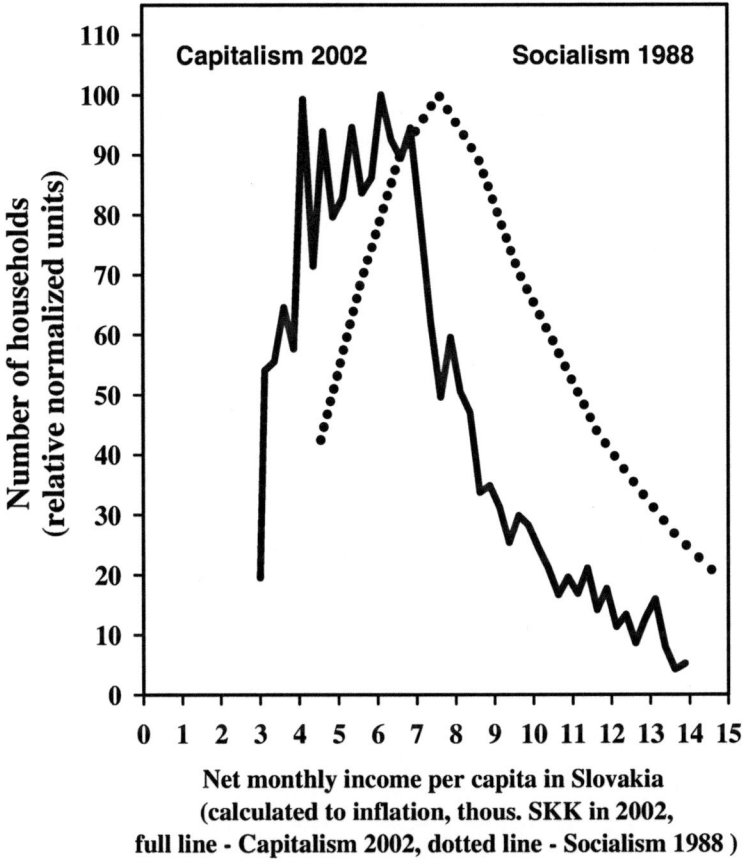

Net monthly income per capita in Slovakia
(calculated to inflation, thous. SKK in 2002,
full line - Capitalism 2002, dotted line - Socialism 1988)

Statistical Yearbook of the Slovak Republic 1999
Microcensus 2002

Figure 23

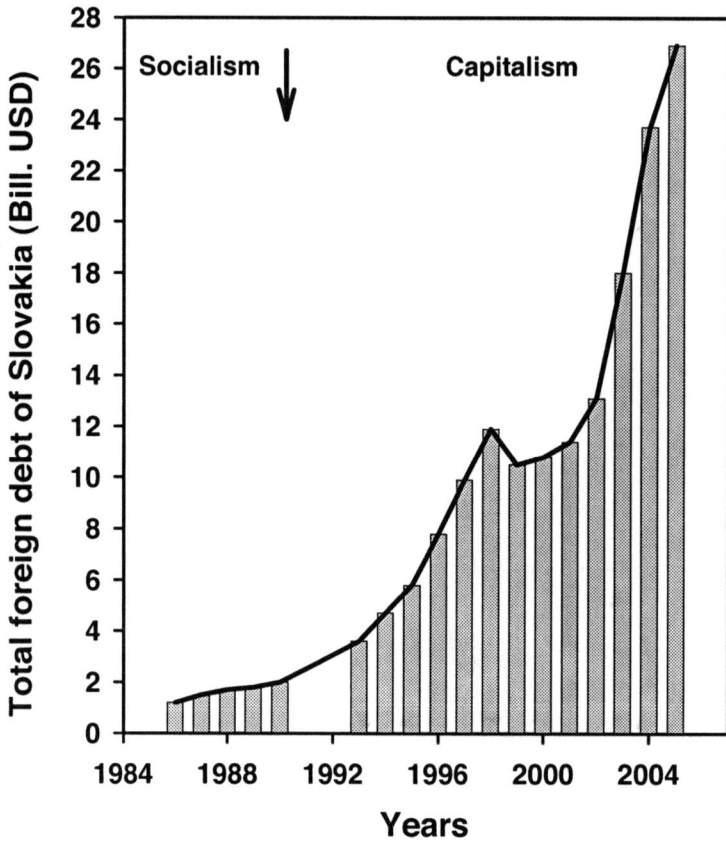

Figure 24

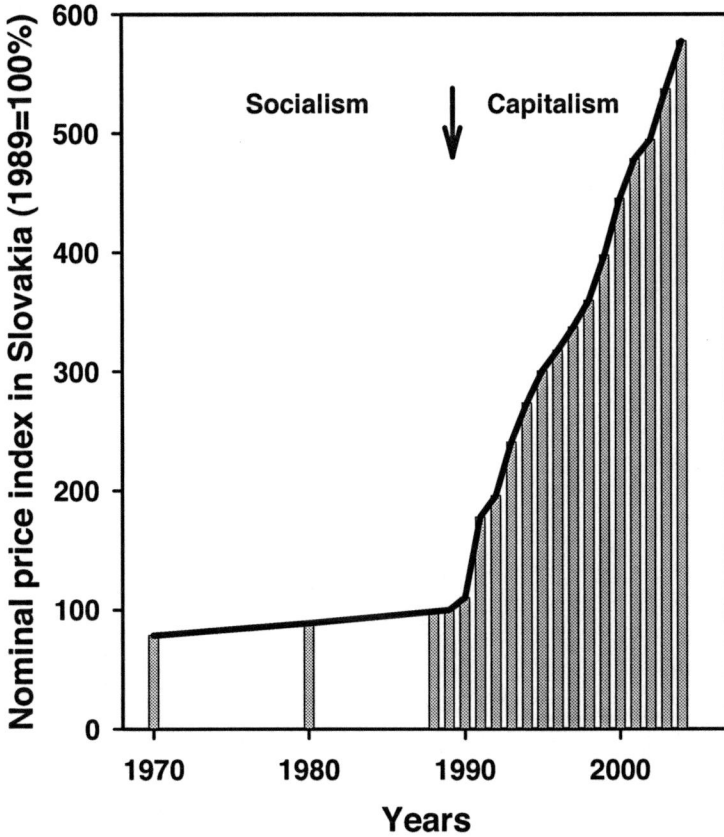

Statistical Yearbook of the Slovak Republic 1994-2006

Figure 25

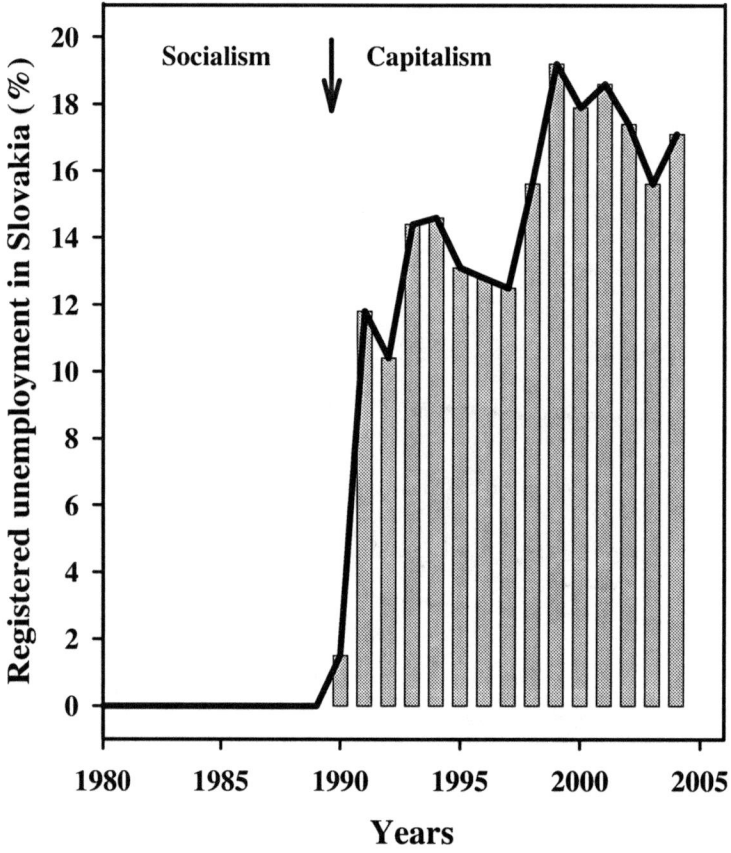

Statistical Yearbook of the Slovak Republic 1994-2005

Figure 26

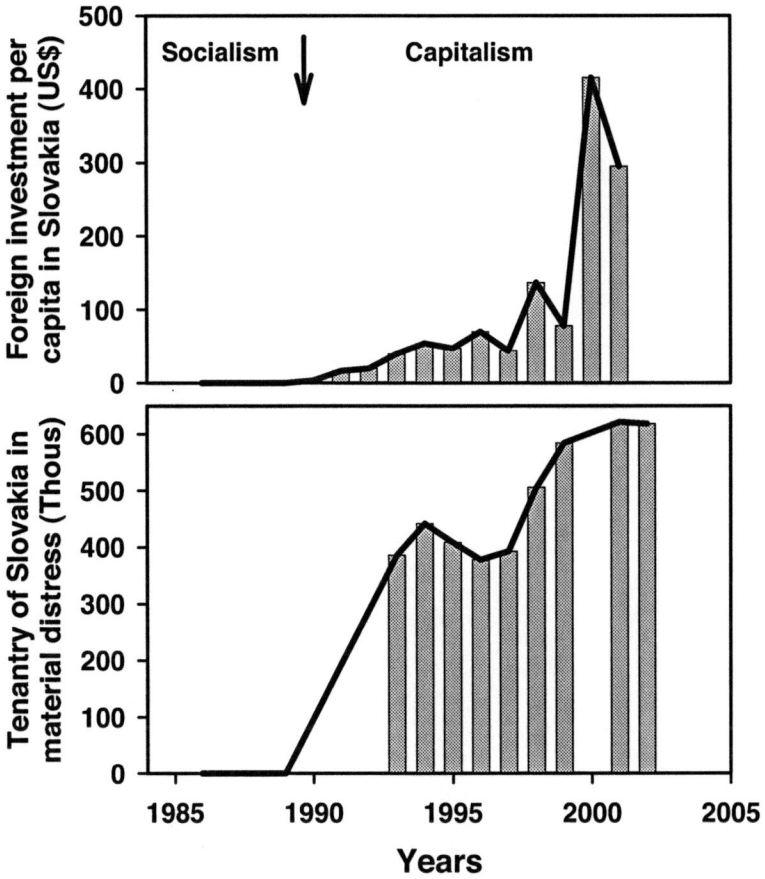

Report of World bank No. 22 351 SK, Aug 9, 2001

Figure 27

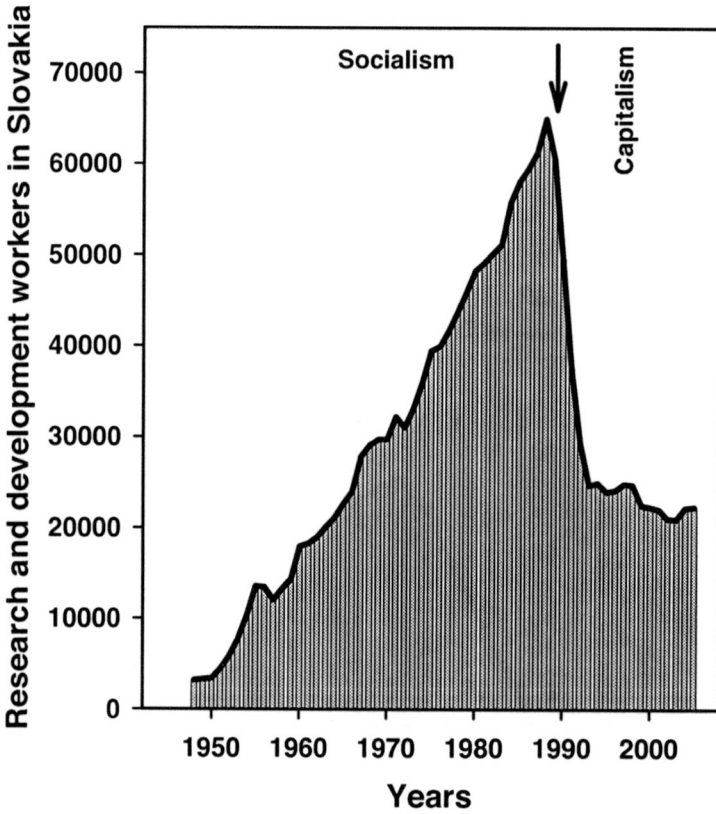

Historical Statistical Yearbook of the Czechoslovakia 1985
Statistical Yearbook of the Czech and Slovak Republic 1990, 1991
Statistical Yearbook of the Slovak Republic 1994-2006

Figure 28

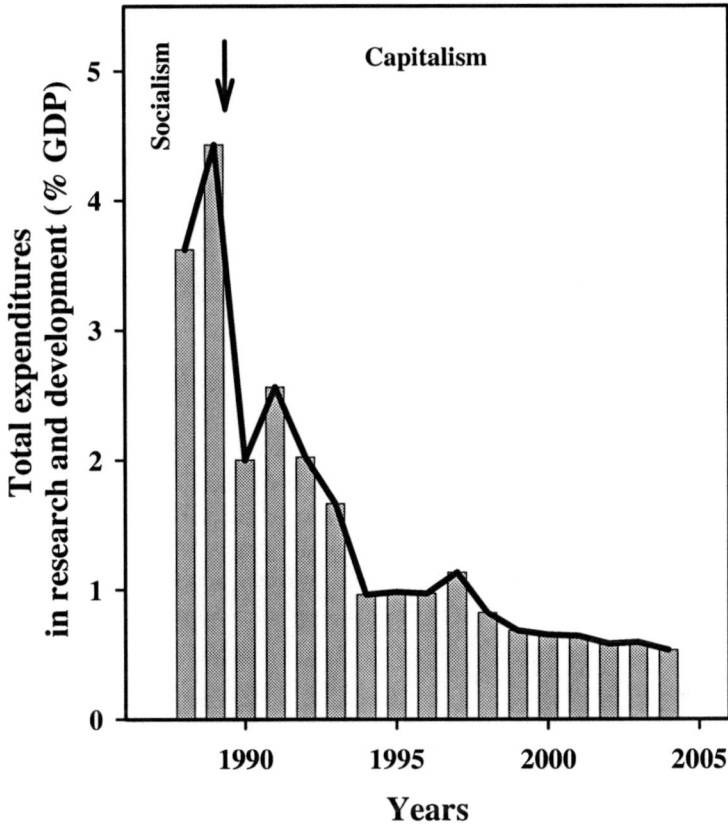

Historical statistical Yearbook of the Czechoslovakia 1985
Statistical Yearbook of the Czech and Slovak Republic 1990, 1991
Statistical Yearbook of the Slovak Republic 1997-2004
Badget of Slovak Republic 2003-2005

Figure 29

1.5. Development of the crimes of democracy in Slovakia

Capitalism has a main philosophical view. "Capitalism is implicitly based upon a world view which upholds that man's mind is competent in dealing with reality, that it is morally good for each person to strive for his own happiness, and that the only proper social arrangement for men to live under is one in which the initiation of physical force is banished".

This website is created to explain the Superiority of Capitalism over Socialism

http://www.srsd.org/search/studentprojects/2001/communism/

The myths

Concerning a social pathology, a generally accepted view about the Communistic system in the former socialist countries is well known: "Communists violated human rights, abused and imprisoned its citizens, killed many of them and violated their privacy. There was not freedom." During socialism our "friends" from abroad insured us that the capitalist system is democratic, respects human rights, freedom, rights of law, where citizens are not subjected to violence and crimes. We need to get rid of socialism to be civilized society.

The facts:

The clear proof of the decline of the Slovak society (and societies in the FSC) and the crimes of democracy after the transition from the socialist system to the capitalist one are provided by the data of a social pathology. A social pathology, in common words, means illness of a society. It also provides clear evidence that the capitalist society after 1989 deteriorated with comparison to the socialist one. In other words, the crimes of democracy were significantly more pronounced in comparison to the crimes of communism.

The security of the people in Slovakia deteriorated significantly after the transition of socialism to capitalism after 1989. The number of recorded criminal offences in Slovakia more or less stabilized during socialism at the level of 50,000 offences per year. It doubled after the transition to capitalism to about 100,000 offences per year (Figure 30). In 2005 it was 266% of the 1989's level. In 1991, 22.9% of the total population was victimized by crimes [5]. In 1996, in the Slovak capital Bratislava, 36% of the population was victimized[6].

Not only did the number of criminal offences increase, but also the number of offences that were cleared up decreased significantly (Figure 31) from 90% during socialism to the nearly democratic 48.6% after the transition to capitalism. This indicates that the capitalist society is not so efficiently protected against criminals, and that capitalistic democracy guarantees more freedom for criminals than "communist totality".

The number of recorded criminal offences per 1,000 inhabitants in 2002 in other post-socialist countries are even higher than in Slovakia (20.2) such as: Czech Republic (36.3), Poland (36.4) and Hungary (41.4). The criminal offences cleared in these countries were similar to Slovakia: 40.7%, 54.9%, 51.2%, and 51.5% respectively [7]. So criminality increased and the clearing of crimes also decreased in other post-socialist countries similarly to Slovakia. We reached the level of old developed democratic countries.

The number of homicides in Slovakia during socialism was more or less stabilized at the level of 60-70 homicides per year. But it nearly doubled after the transition to capitalism (Figure 32). The number of the homicides cleared slightly decreased after the transition to democracy (Figure 33).

As seen from the Figure 34, the homicide rate in Slovakia reaches levels comparable to the other former socialist and developed capitalist countries. In other words, Slovakia and other former socialist counties have reached the high capitalist standard of criminality. However, the homicides cleared vary between counties. Only Germany has cleared up the homicide rate to the level Slovakia had during socialism (Figure 35). I compared homicide in Slovakia with murder and non-negligent manslaughter in the USA: According to the FBI 'Number of the crimes in USA in 2005', total murders and non-negligent manslaughters in 2005 were 15,495, or 5.9 per 100,000 citizens [8]. This number is three times higher in comparison to the homicides in Slovakia in 2005. It is 4.5 times higher in comparison to the homicides in Slovakia in 1989.

The loss of social security, increased unemployment, poverty and corruption caused by capitalistic democracy resulted in the dramatic increase in crimes of violence and number of outpatient psychiatry care examinations. The crimes of violence in Slovakia were stabilized at low levels during socialism, about 7,000 per year. After the transition to capitalism crimes kept raising steadily until 2002, reaching 206% in 2005 when compared to 1989's levels (Figure 36). We have become a violent capitalistic society, as most capitalist counties are. To compare Slovakia with the USA: according to the FBI's 'Number of crimes in USA in 2005', the violent crime total in 2005 was 1,287,981, and per 100,000 it was 490.5 [9]. This number is two times higher in comparison to the number of violent crimes in Slovakia in 2005. It is 4 times higher in comparison to the violent crimes in Slovakia in 1989.

The psychological deterioration of democratic society, expressed as a number of examinations of outpatient psychiatry care, are shown in Figure

37. The number was low under socialism (my estimation is 100,000-300,000) and increased to 1.4 million examinations in 2002 out of 5.4 million people living in Slovakia.

After 1989 our capitalist society has given emphasis to the protection of private property. Paradoxically, property crimes rapidly increased after 1989. According to the Report of Police 2004, property crimes comprised 58.7% of all crimes in 2004. The number of economic crimes increased (Figure 38). Similarly, the number of burglaries in Slovakia increased dramatically after the transition from socialism to capitalism. As is seen from Figure 39, we had about 5,000-6,000 burglaries per year during socialism. It increased about four times after the transformation to capitalism. Burglaries increased 335% in 2005 in comparison to 1989 levels. It proves again that the capitalist society has deteriorated in comparison to the socialist one. As in previous cases, the number of burglaries cleared decreased very significantly after the transition to capitalism (Figure 40). In 2005 it was 25% in comparison to 68% in 1989.

More proof of the criminalization of the Slovak society after the transformation to capitalism is seen also in Figure 41. The figure shows the damages caused by criminality in Slovakia. The damages were very low during socialism and started to rapidly increase, even 10-times in real prices, after the transformation to capitalism. The damages caused by criminality in Slovakia, costing 40-60 bill. SKK, are comparable to the Slovak education budget for 2004 (41 bill. SKK) and are 2-3 times higher than the health budget. The deterioration of society after the introduction of capitalistic democracy in Slovakia is also characterized by the rapid and very pronounced increase of drug addiction. During socialism it was nearly zero. After 1989 it increased 1,000 or 10,000 times to the West European democratic standard. According to official estimate, drug users in Slovakia spent 4 bill SKK (133 mil USD) to buy drugs in 2005. That is about 10% of the total Slovak education budget for 2004. Damage caused by crimes of drug addiction was estimated to be 4 bill. SKK, which was 2.6 times higher than the state budget for the Slovak Academy of Sciences. I remark that during socialism the drug business and the damage caused by drug crimes were close to zero or zero.

The flourishing of poverty and criminality has caused an increase in the number of dead people found in the street or in junkyards in Slovakia (Figure 42). It also accounts for the increase of people lost in Slovakia (Figure 43). The number of lost people increased more than 4-times and is still rising.

Another indication of the decline of our capitalist society, in comparison to the socialist one, is the appearance of new inhuman crimes, previously known in Slovakia only from western movies. Many violent crimes, e.g.

killing of mother or father for money or the ordering of a murder, were unknown or very rare in socialist Slovakia. Other unknown crimes during socialism in Slovakia such as organized crime, drug trafficking, people trafficking, drug addiction, prostitution, mafia, and blackmail started flourished after the transition to capitalism based on democracy. Figure 44 shows the appearance of people trafficking after the capitalist system was established in Slovakia. Similarly, drugs (Figure 45), drug trafficking or drug users were rare or unknown in Slovakia during socialism. Capitalism has brought the increase of private and state corruption into our daily life. The result is an appearance of a few millionaires and many poor.

Our crime situation was well-termed in the official report of the National Report of Human Development - Slovakia 1998: "while society was not interested in crime until 1989, now 84% of inhabitants are afraid for their security. Until 1989 most of the crimes were caused only by negligence and violent disposition, after 1990 the crimes of theft and burglary increased and started to become a style of living (for poor people)".

The number of people who lost their lives as a result of crime and poverty during the last 15 years of capitalism in Slovakia is about 3,500 higher than the average over 15 years of socialism. The crimes of democracy for 15 years is more than 10 times higher than the number of all the real and made up crimes of communism put together for 40 years in Slovakia.

The mysteries

Why has society deteriorated after the rules of democracy came into effect? Why has democracy and not the "evil" communist regime brought criminality into our daily life? Why has democracy and freedom forced more people to seek psychiatric treatment? Why, after we have adopted rules observing human rights, has criminality significantly increased? More people are killed, robbed, and subjected to violent crimes. Why has democracy brought the freedom to kill, steal, burgle, traffic people and drugs, racket, prostitute children, and kidnap? Why did the "evil" communist regime bring the freedom to live nearly without crimes and distress? Why, in the real experiment, are the crimes of democracy higher than the crimes of communism? Why have people, in free elections after 1989 up until now, elected nonprofessionals to deal with criminality? How do the invisible forces of democracy and capitalism function in our society when criminality and corruption are flourishing? What are these forces? Is it the totality of recent global democracy, based on capitalistic rules? My answer is simple. Yes it is. It is the results of the real experiment in Slovakia. It is global, liberal, democratic capitalism or simple capitalistic democracy.

Since the deterioration of society after the transition from socialism to capitalism occurred in all post-socialist counties, I consider it as evidence that the significant increase of criminality is based on the capitalist system of democracy and capitalist policy. On the other hand, low levels of criminality before 1989 were the result of the rules of socialism.

The results clearly show that capitalism, based on the capitalistic democracy, is a very good matrix for flourishing criminality. Practical results from other developed capitalist countries prove that it is practically impossible to get rid of the high level of extreme crimes, which was unknown in socialist Slovakia. It means that the capitalistic matrix of democracy is very strong and many powerful democratic institutions could not do anything about it.

What strikes me even more, is why most respected scholars, writing books about "evil communism" do not discuss the mental deterioration of society after the transition from socialism to capitalism? Do not they know it? Do not they respect it? Do not they believe the official data of social pathology? Paradoxically, the basic rules of recent capitalistic democracy such as freedom of speech, freedom of expression, and the right to have information are forbidden to function in practice by the recent capitalistic democracy. Is this a democratic Catch-22? Why is it so? I assume because it is an integral part of demoserfdom.

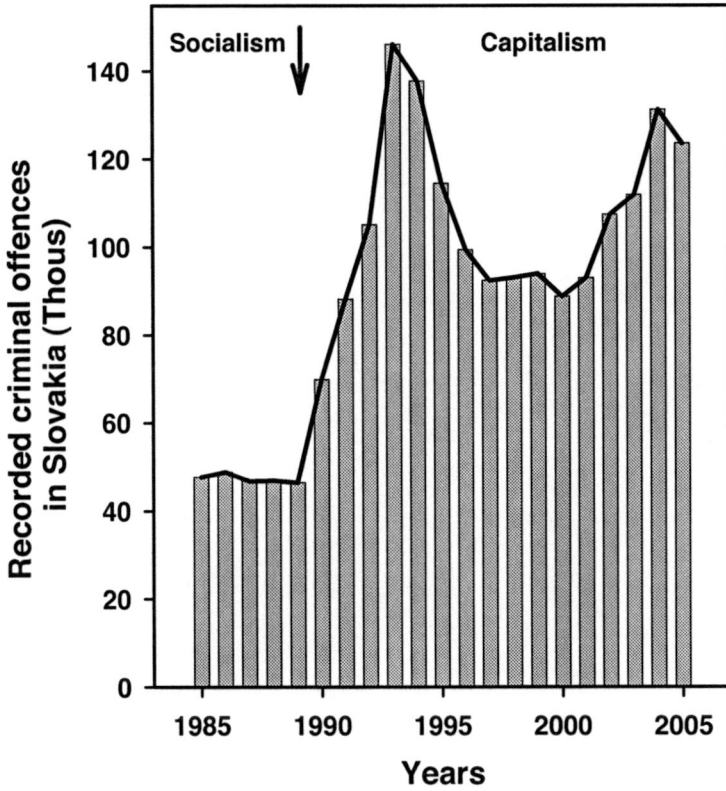

Report of the Ministry of Interior of the Slovak Republic

Figure 30

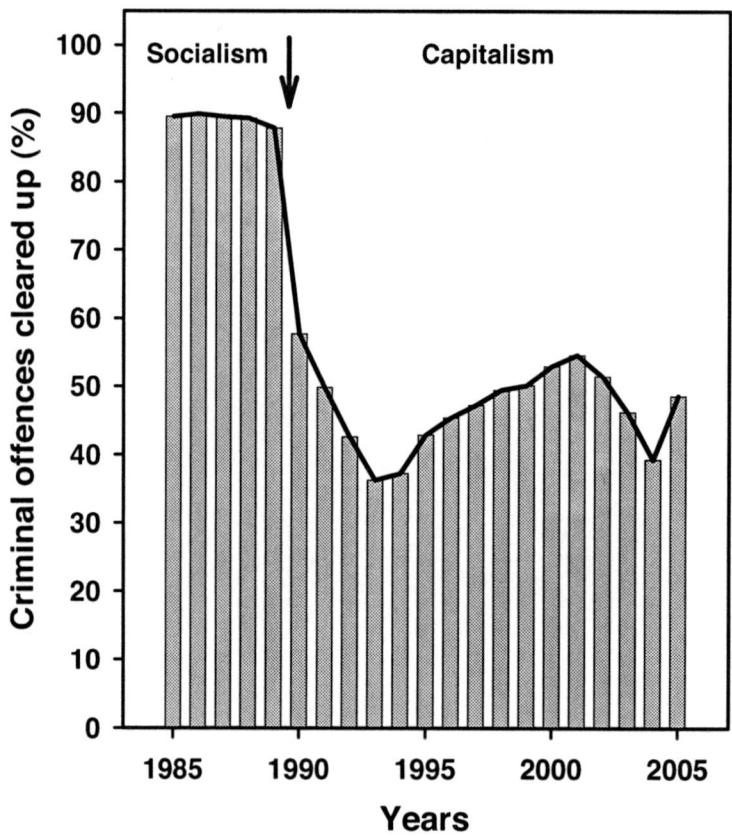

Report of the Ministry of Interior of the Slovak Republic

Figure 31

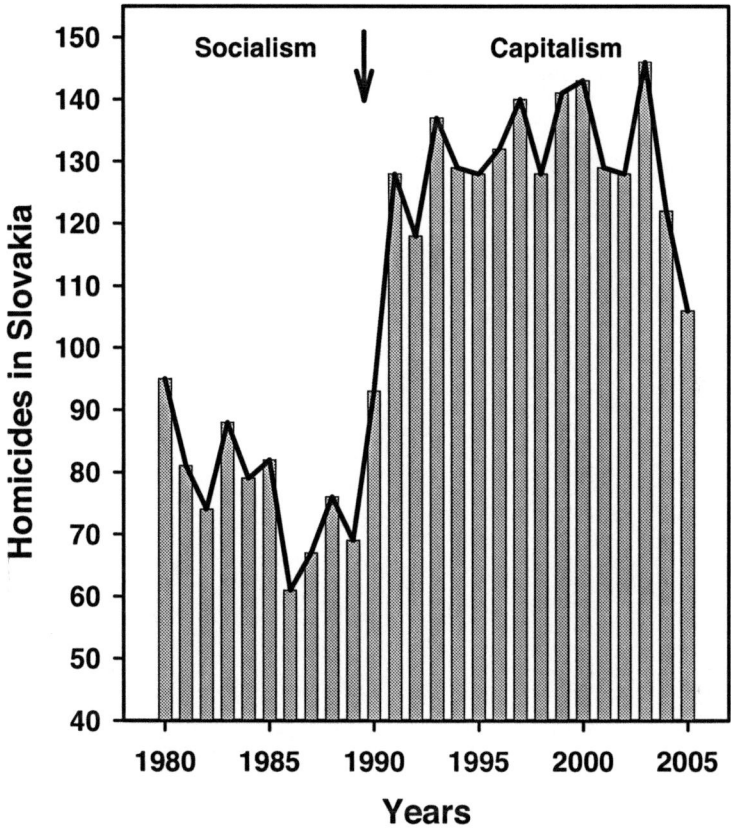

Report of the Ministry of Interior of the Slovak Republic

Figure 32

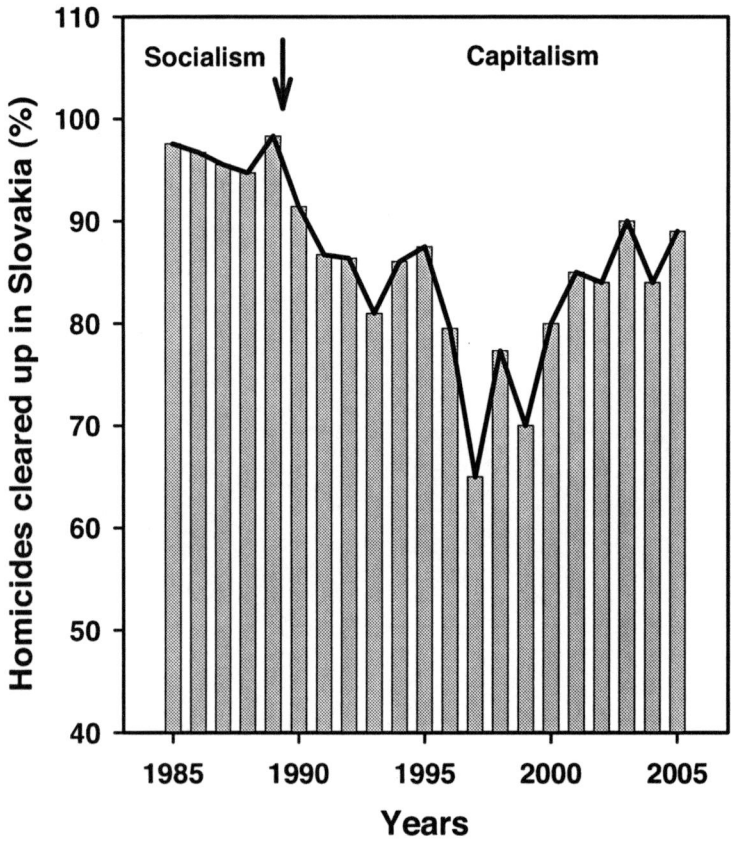

Report of the Ministry of Interior of the Slovak Republic

Figure 33

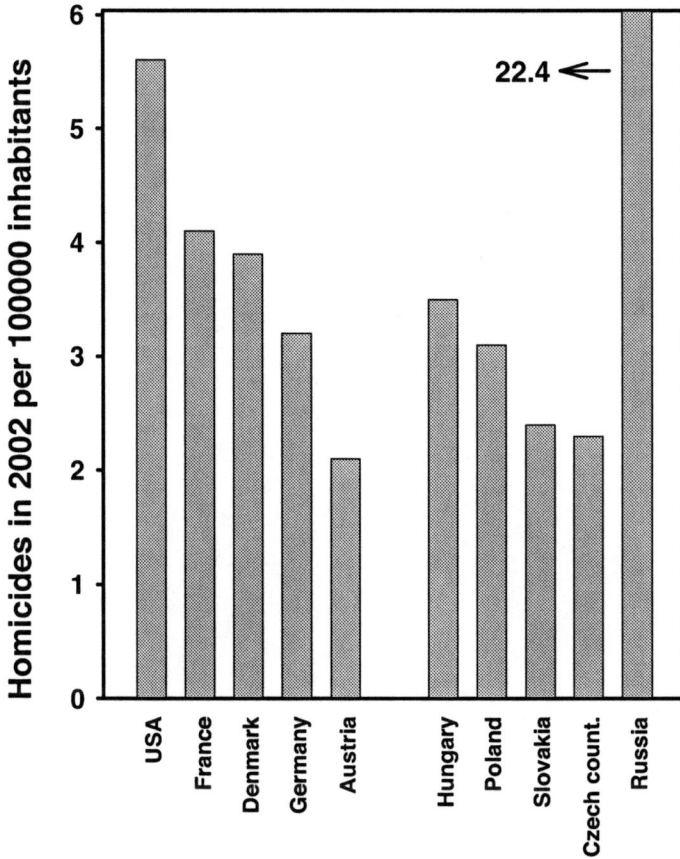

Miroslav Kollar a Grigorij Mesežnikov (Eds.):
Slovensko 2003 Súhrnná správa o stave spoločnosti.

Figure 34

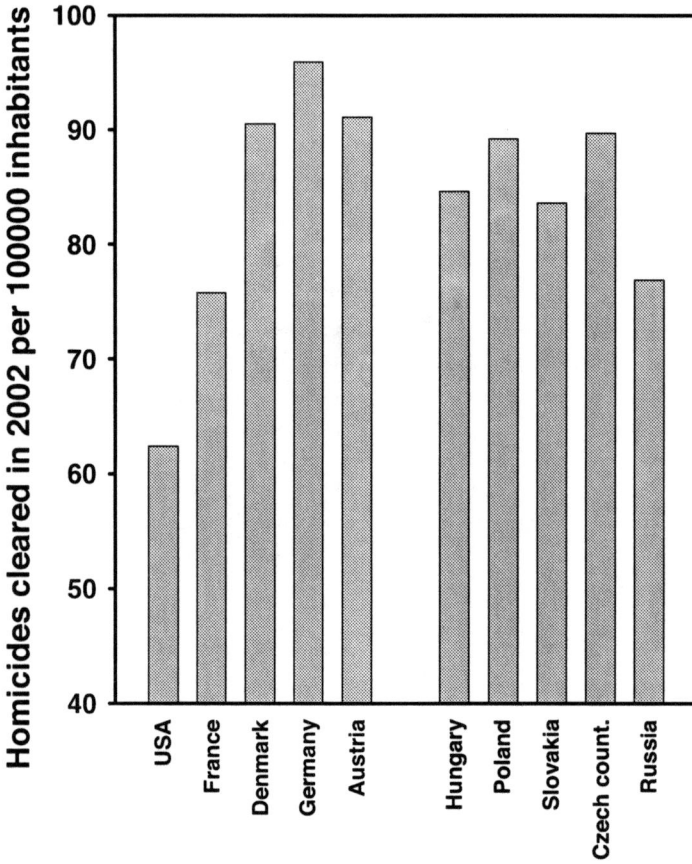

Figure 35

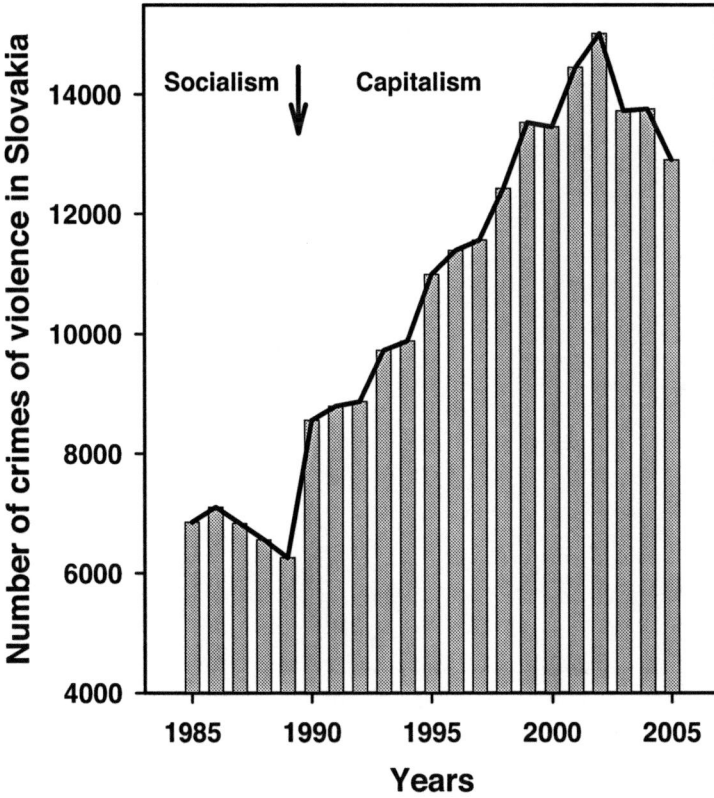

Report of the Ministry of Interior of the Slovak Republic

Figure 36

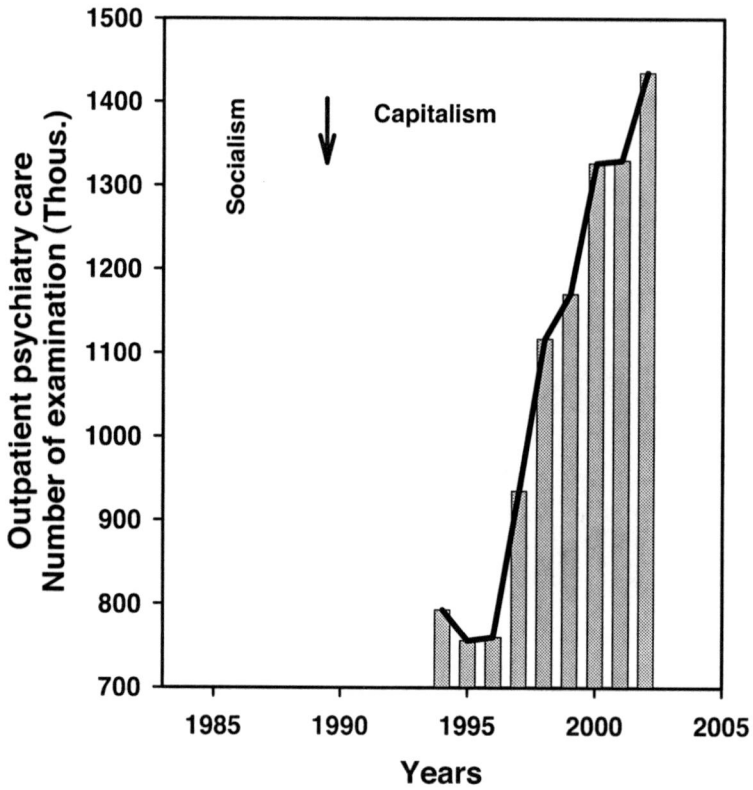

Health Statistics Yearbook of SR 1997-2002

Figure 37

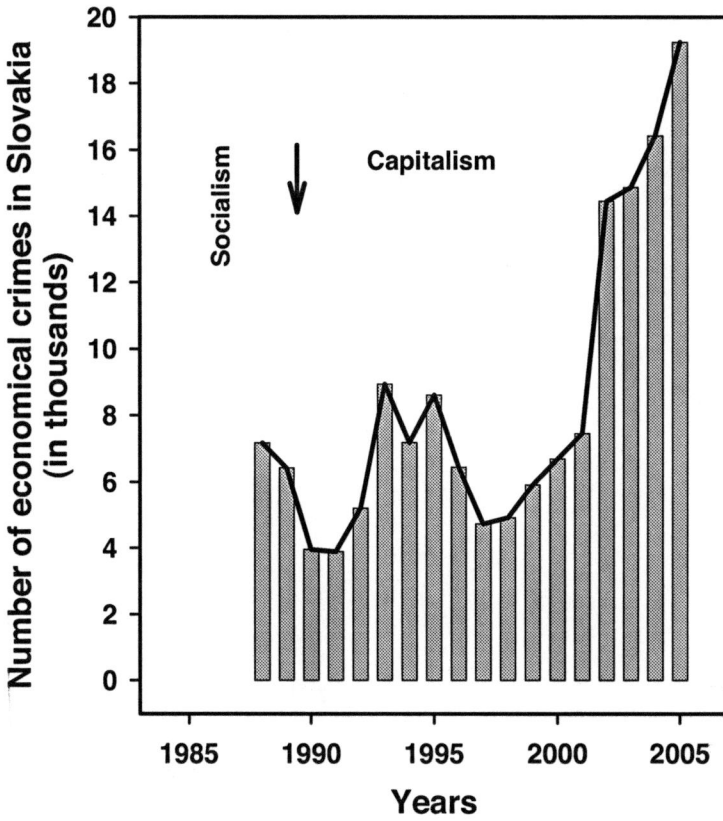

Report of the Ministry of Interior of the Slovak Republic

Figure 38

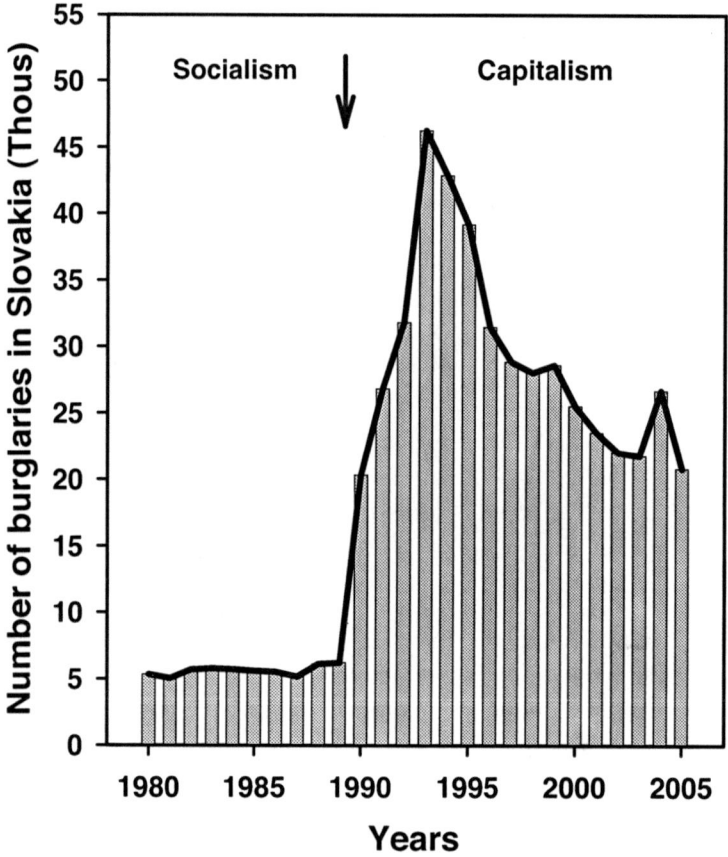

Report of the Ministry of Interior of the Slovak Republic

Figure 39

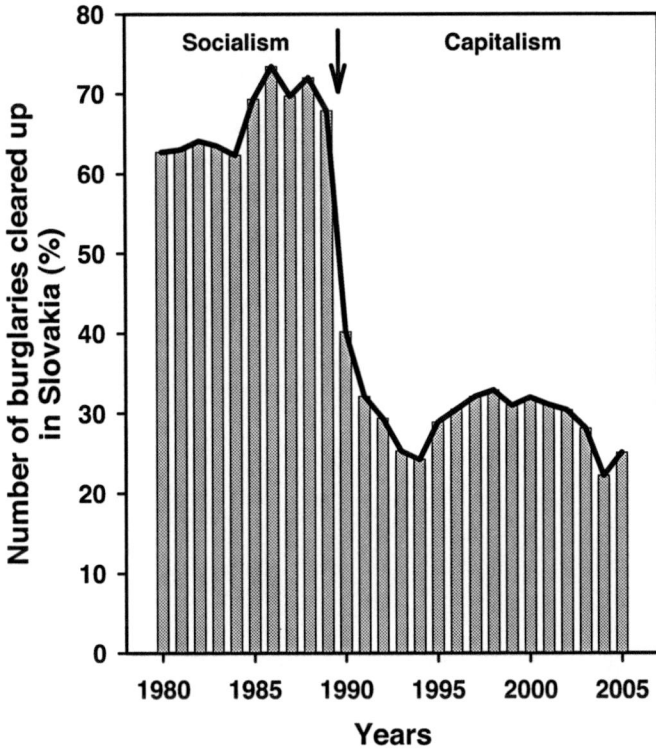

Report of the Ministry of Interior of the Slovak Republic

Figure 40

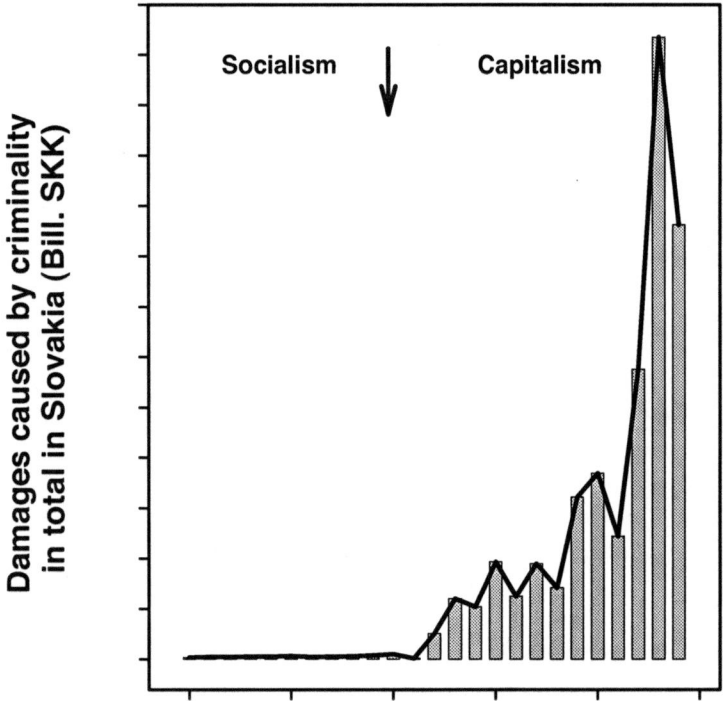

Report of the Ministry of Interior of the Slovak Republic

Figure 41

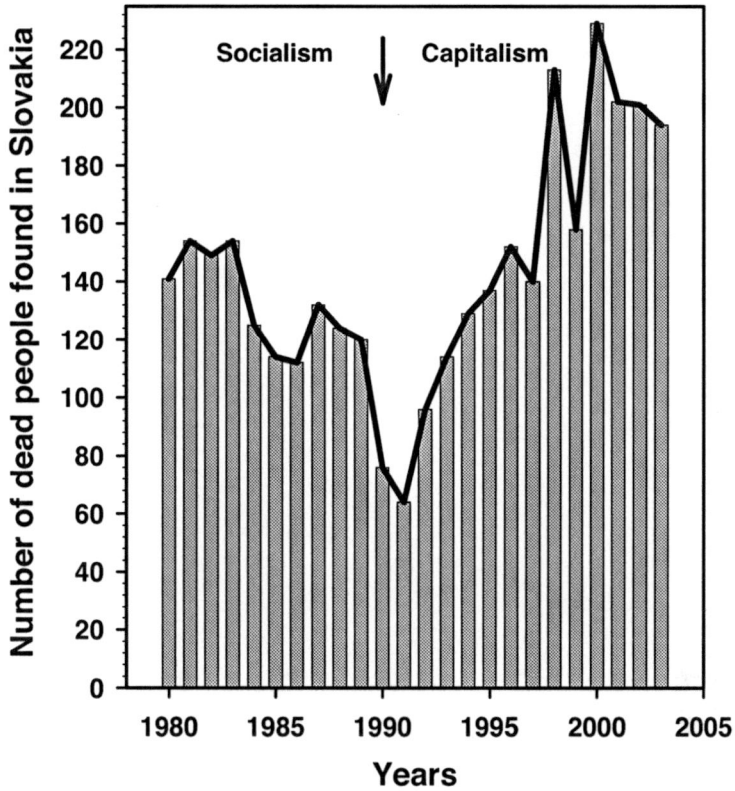

Report of the Ministry of Interior of the Slovak Republic

Figure 42

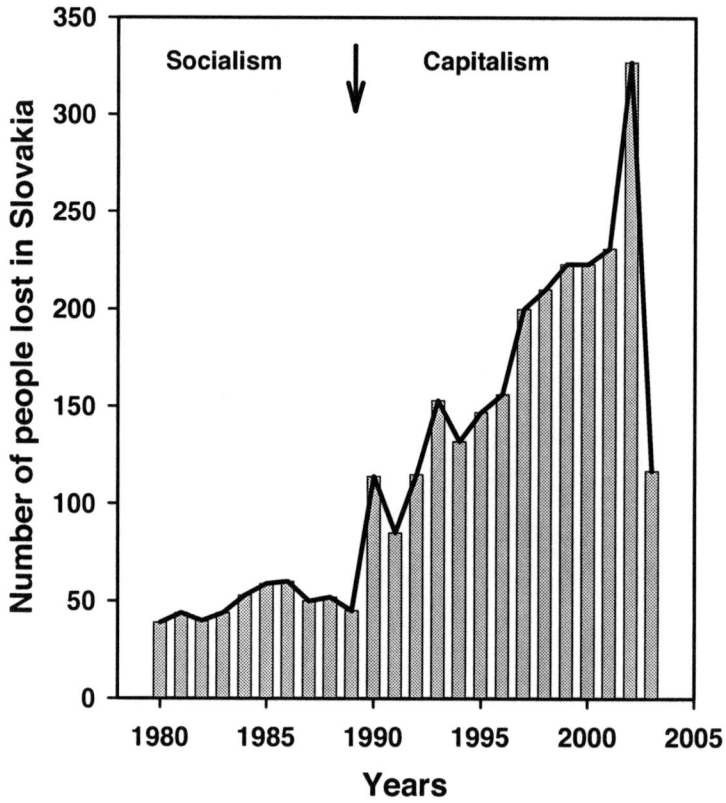

Report of the Ministry of Interior of the Slovak Republic

Figure 43

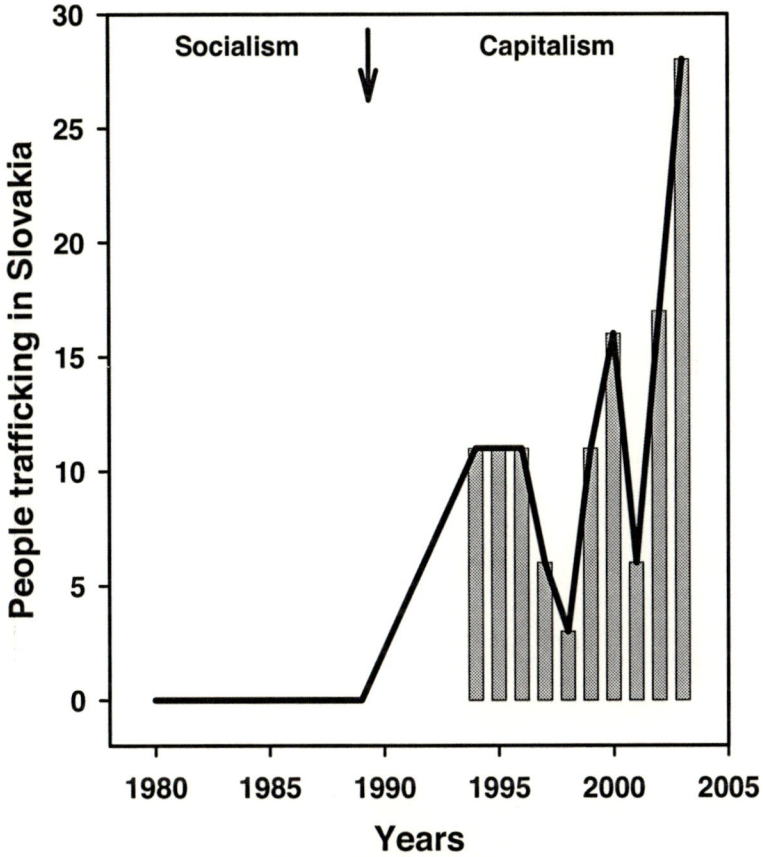

Report of the Ministry of Interior of the Slovak Republic

Figure 44

[78] Karol Ondrias

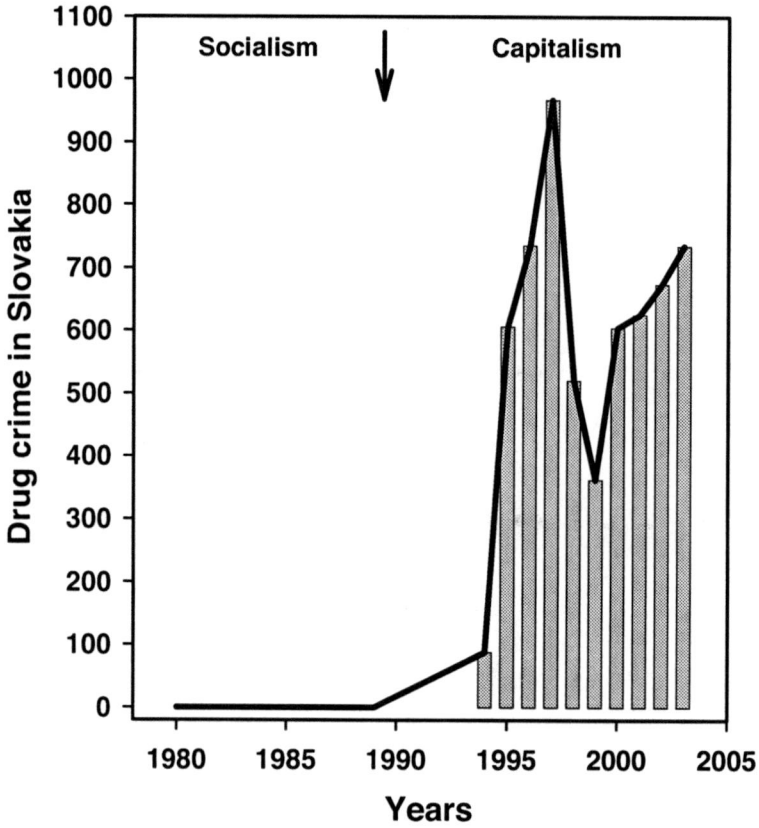

Report of the Ministry of Interior of the Slovak Republic

Figure 45

2. Other well-known myths and secret facts of the "crimes of communism" (socialism) in Slovakia

The data presented in this book clearly indicate that socialism in former socialist countries was, in some or many ways, better for society than recent capitalism. It implies that socialism may be an alternative to capitalism. This kind of thinking is dangerous for recent aristocracy based on the capitalist democratic system and is generally forbidden. Therefore, recent oligarchs, in order to sustain their privileges, speak, via their media instead of telling the truth, about socialism persistently use the expression "crimes of communism". This is in spite of the fact that there was never communism in any of the former socialist countries. I assume that the results of socialism in Slovakia, in comparison to recent capitalism, are so dangerous for the capitalists that they have established an official institution in Slovakia named the Institute of Memory of the Nation, which repeatedly condemns communism and emphasizes its crimes.

Therefore, I will present some more examples of well-known myths and secret facts of "crimes of communism".

2.1. A crime of communism - shortage of food

The myths

Everybody knows about the shortage of food during socialism in Slovakia. How people queued for meat or bananas. How groceries were nearly gone. We are reminded of this very bad aspect of socialism regularly by respected scholars, our politicians, media and representatives of many nongovernmental, non-profit organizations established in Slovakia from abroad who came to help us build a democracy. I remember watching the TV news in 1988, in the USA, about the shortage of food in Czechoslovakia. To support the opinion, they showed 20-meter queues of people on the street buying food. I recognized the place where the people were queued as main Wenceslas Street in Prague. The shop was not a grocery but a quick food stand, selling hot dog for tourist on the street.

The facts

Consumption of meat in Slovakia is shown in Figure 46. The consumption was low in 1936. It gradually increased under socialism and then gradually decreased under capitalism after 1989. In 2003, due to decreased living standard, consumption was only 72% of 1989 values. This means we returned to 1970, 33 years back.

Similar results are observed in the consumption of milk and diary products, as shown in Figure 47. Consumption increased under socialism and decreased under capitalism. In 2004, it decreased to 61% of the 1989 value, which is similar to what Slovakia reached already in 1964 and is less than consumption in 1936.

Consumption of sugar, vegetables, and fruits increased more or less under socialism and deceased under capitalism (Figures 48-50). One exception is fat consumption, which did not decrease under capitalism (Figures 51).

The mysteries

Looking at the figures, I ask myself, how is the brainwashing machine effectively working so that the gradual increase in food consumption during socialism is interpreted as a shortage of food? Additionally, how is the gradual decrease in food consumption interpreted as resolution of the problem of food shortages? Even worse, as the figure shows, people now eat less vegetables and fruits than during socialism. Only the consumption of fat did not decrease. Why do respected scholars and others repeat the lie about the difficulties people had with food during socialism and glorify the resolution of the problem by capitalism? Reality is that due to less real income, common people stint on food. Of course, the real data about food consumption are kept secret. They are hidden by all media operating under the rules of capitalistic democracy.

To summarize the mystery: why, when people do not have enough money to buy adequate amounts of food, do respected scholars not call this the crime of capitalism, or the crime of democracy,? Why is it so? I assume because it is an integral part of demoserfdom.

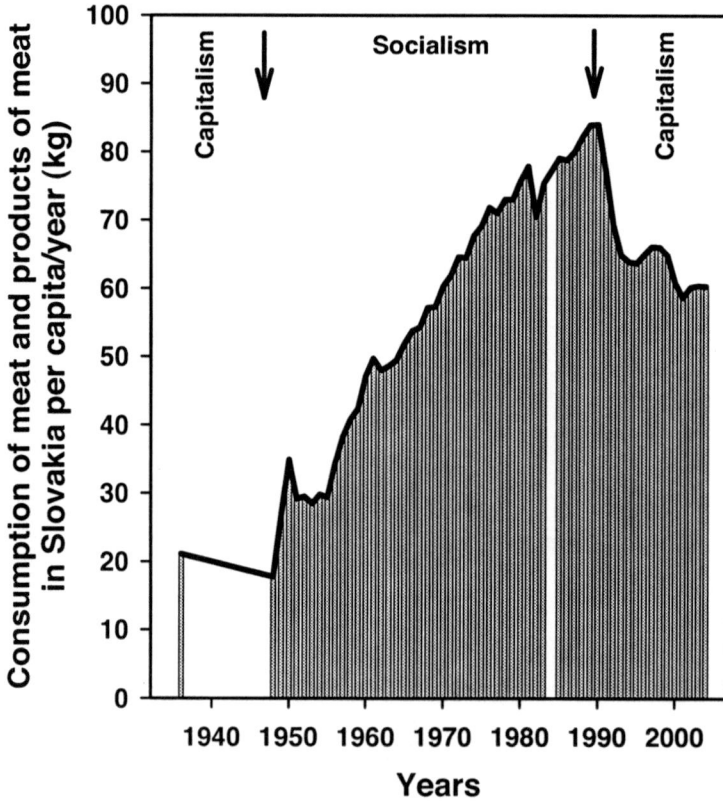

Historical Statistical Yearbook of the Czechoslovakia 1985
Statistical Yearbook of the Czech and Slovak Republic 1990, 1991
Statistical Yearbook of the Slovak Republic 1997-2006

Figure 46

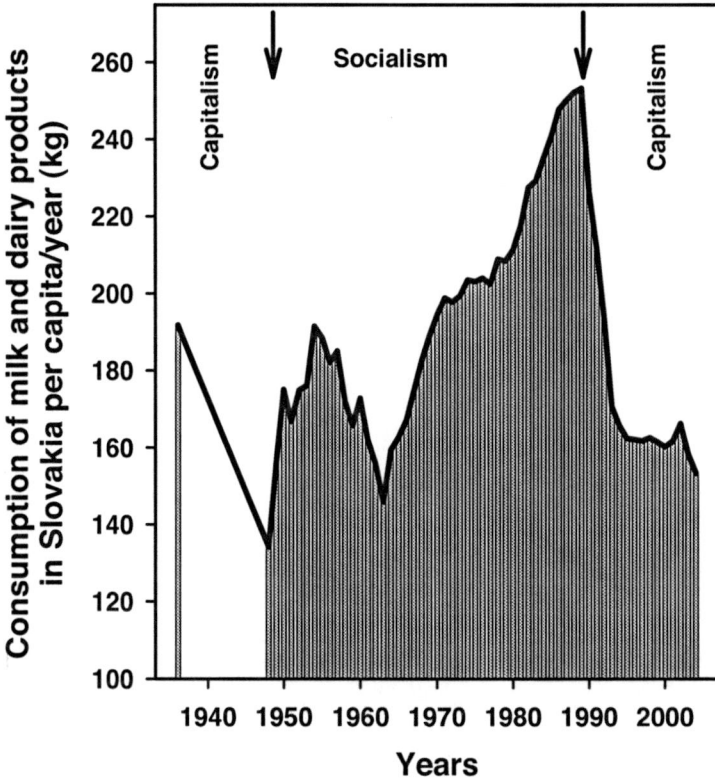

Historical Statistical Yearbook of the Czechoslovakia 1985
Statistical Yearbook of the Czech and Slovak Republic 1990, 1991
Statistical Yearbook of the Slovak Republic 1997-2003
System of Economical information of Slovakia

Figure 47

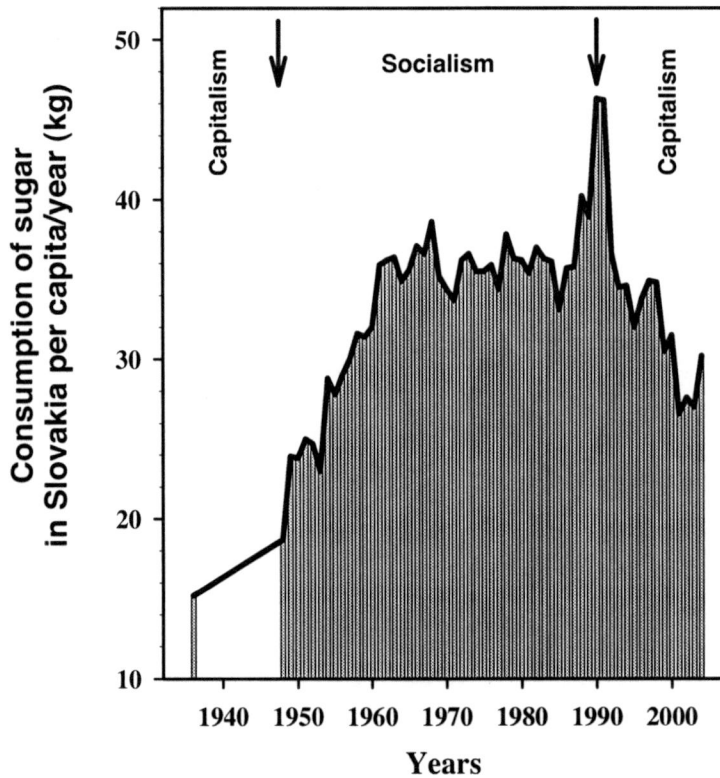

System of Economic Information of Slovakia

Figure 48

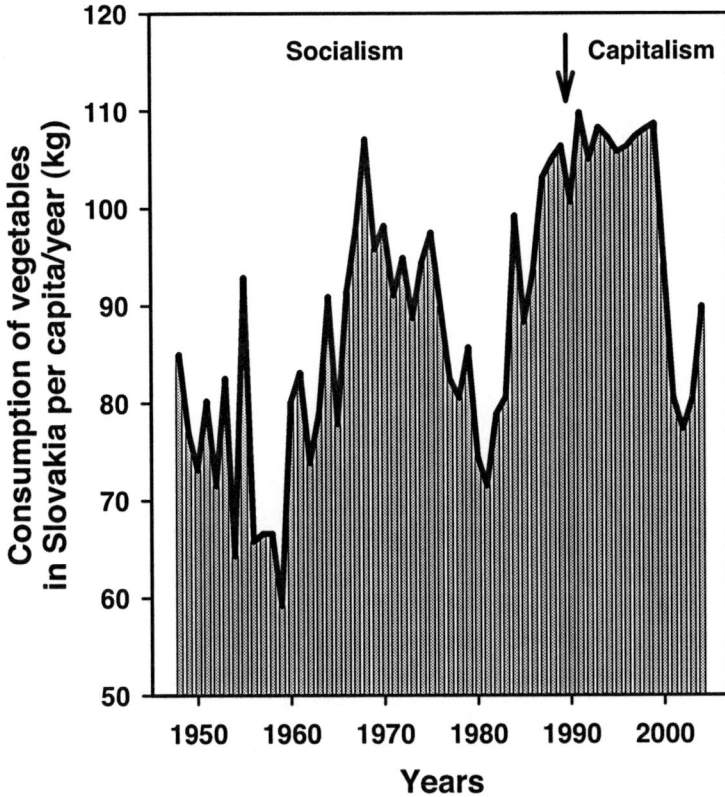

Historical Statistical Yearbook of the Czechoslovakia 1985
Statistical Yearbook of the Czech and Slovak Republic 1990, 1991
Statistical Yearbook of the Slovak Republic 1997-2003
System of Economic Information of Slovakia

Figure 49

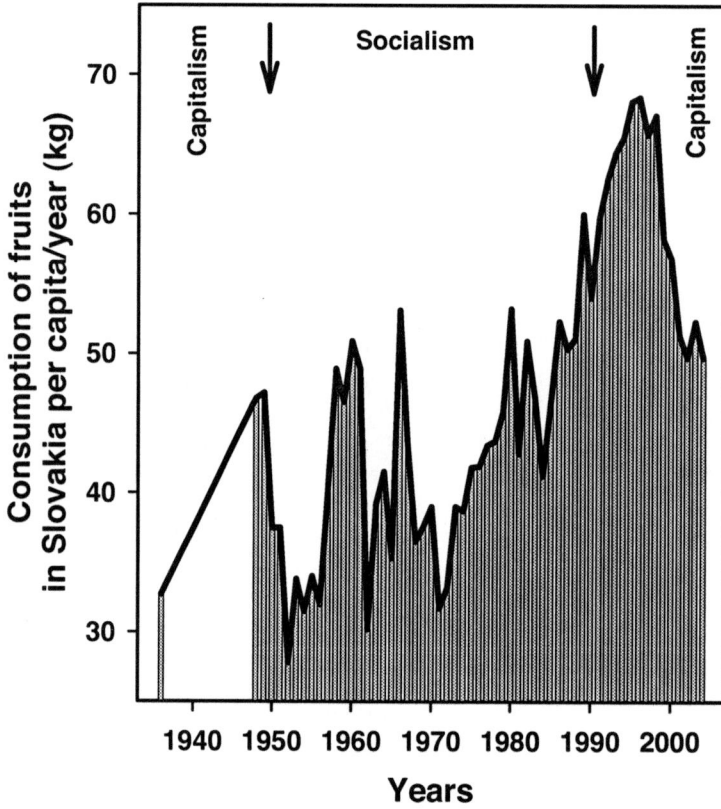

Historical Statistical Yearbook of the Czechoslovakia 1985
Statistical Yearbook of the Czech and Slovak Republic 1990, 1991
Statistical Yearbook of the Slovak Republic 1997-2003
Ststem of Economical Information of Slovakia

Figure 50

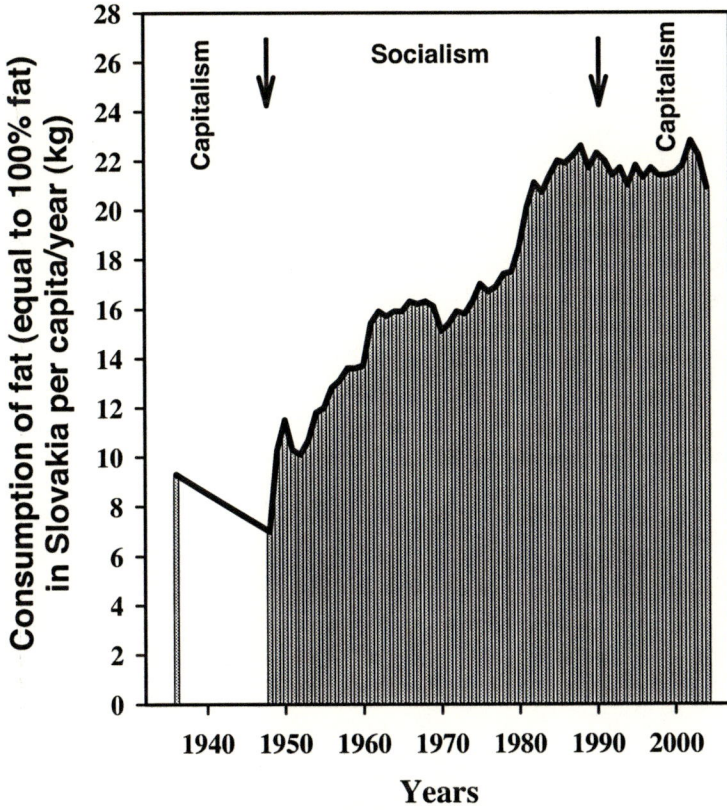

System of Economic Information of Slovakia

Figure 51

2.2. A crime of communism – its reality for 40 years

The myths

Recently, as well as for 40 years during socialism in Slovakia, we have been subjected to foreign propaganda. The foreign propaganda during socialism compared political, economic, cultural and social life in Slovakia (or Czechoslovakia) with developed capitalist countries such as the USA, Germany, England, France, etc. It persuaded us that Slovakia had fallen behind the developed capitalist countries during the years of socialism (1948-1989), and that socialism was responsible for our underdevelopment. The myth was based on the lie that during 1918-1938 development of the capitalist Slovakia was more or less similar to other developed capitalist countries. The fact that capitalist Slovakia was behind developed Western European countries during 1918-1938 is still hidden today. However, the propaganda was, and is still effective, the myths are generally accepted as valid and periodically repeated by nearly all the members of our capitalist governments, recent "Slovak intellectuals", main media and by many respected scholars from abroad.

The facts

The data about the development of capitalist Slovakia during 1918-1938 are shown below. Capitalist Slovakia, during 1918-1938, was a poor, economically, educationally and culturally underdeveloped country in comparison to developed capitalist counties. An estimated gross domestic product (GDP) per capita in purchasing power parity (PPP) in Slovakia during 1925-1934 was 2-5 times lower than in developed counties (Figure 52). The difference between Slovakia and the developed countries were gradually reduced during socialism, and in 2001 the deference was reduced even more, as seen in the Figure 53.

Industry production in Slovakia per capita in 1938 was around 15-20% of Germany, Great Britain or France (data calculated from [4]). The illiteracy rate was 15-20% in 1921 [10]. Living standard and industrial development of Slovakia during 1918-1938, estimated as consumption of electric energy per capita, was behind developed countries (Figure 54). The electric consumption per capita in 1935 in Slovakia was only 42% of Czech, 22% of Austria, 21% of UK and 19% of Germany (Figure 55). The difference of electric energy consumption between these countries significantly decreased during socialism as shown in Figure 56, for 1980, when Slovakia reached 87% of the electric consumption of Austria.

Poor economic conditions during capitalism before 1939 led to poor health conditions and increased mortality. The infant mortality rate in 1937, in Slovakia and other eastern European backward capitalist countries was high in comparison to the developed countries (Figure 57). It was 151 infant (under 1 year of age) deaths per 1,000 live births in Slovakia versus 40-80 in Western European countries. Results of the poor living conditions in Slovakia (3-3.5 mil. population) was the emigration of 204,000 people to the USA and Western Europe between 1918-1938. The differences between many socialist countries, including Slovakia, and developed countries decreased during socialism indicating health improvements in socialist countries (Figure 58). Poor health conditions are also documented by the comparison of the number of deaths per capita in Slovakia, caused by tuberculosis and pneumonia. In the years1921-1925, deaths were about 2-times higher than in Western European countries (Figures 59-60). During socialism numbers of deaths due to infectious and parasitic diseases and number of people per 1 physician decreased significantly (Figure 61-62). However, the positive development in Slovakia after the transformation to capitalism is the increase in life expectancy, which did not increased during socialism from 1960-1989 (Figure 63).

The decreased quality of life after the transformation of Slovakia to capitalism indicates also the time dependency of HDI values (Figure 64). The HDI shows that Czechoslovakia was 27th from 1988-1990. The HDI of Slovakia decreased to about 40th after the transformation to capitalism. For comparison, the HDI index did not changed significantly during that period for Austria and the USA.

The mysteries

Data clearly show that capitalist Slovakia lagged behind developed capitalist countries and the difference decreased during socialism. Paradoxically, the lag increased again after establishing capitalism in Slovakia. This may also be the reason that communism must be presented as criminal society. Why are these data hidden for the public?

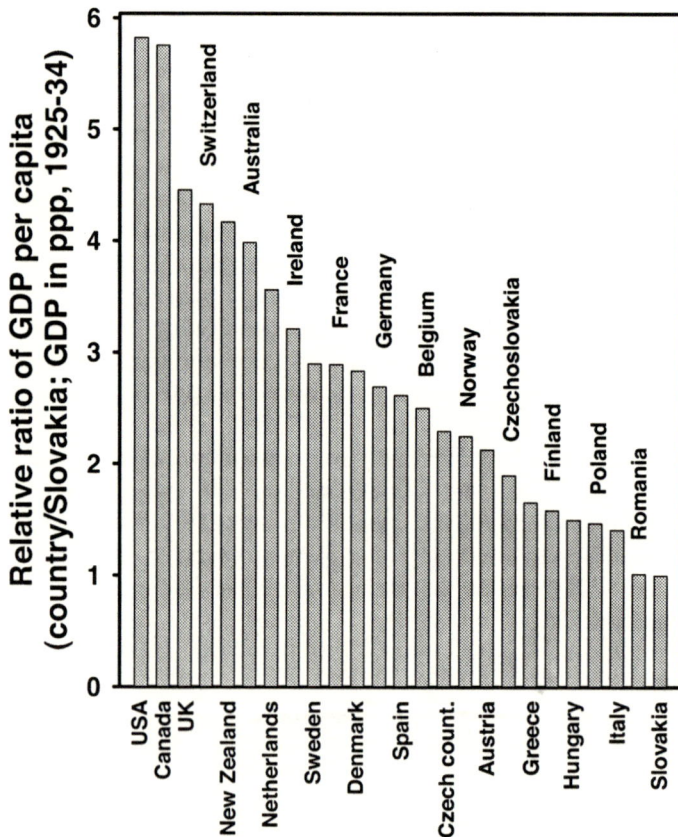

Figure 52

Clark, C.: Internationaler Vergleich der Volkseinkommem,
Weltwirtschftliches Arch. 1938, No: 1.
Kubu, E - Pátek, J.: c.d., s. 45-53,289.
Mészáros, H.: Národný dôchodok Slovenska. Bratislava 1934, s. 47-49.
Krajčovič, V.: Národný dôchodok Slovenska 1944, 166-171

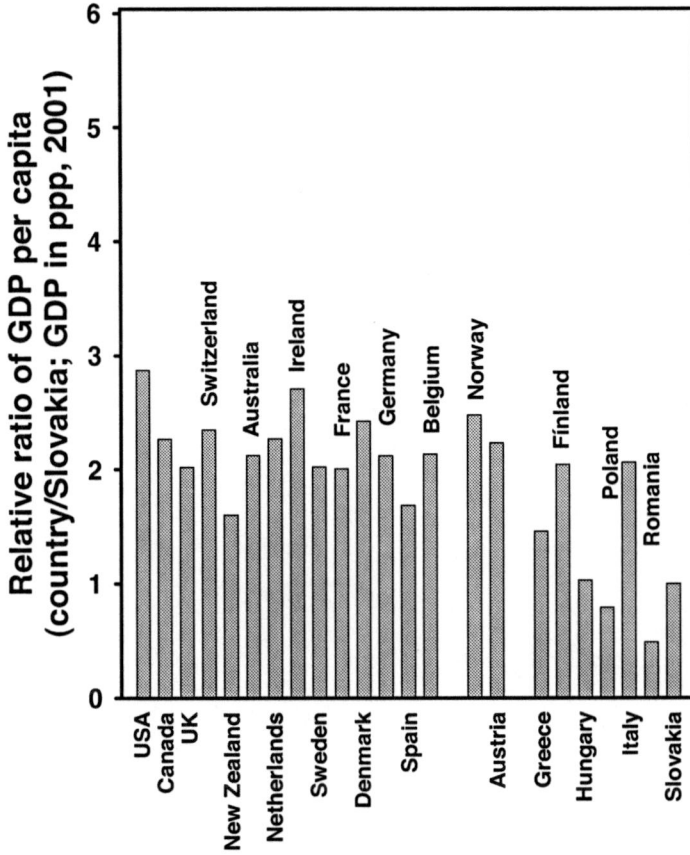

Human Development Report 2003

Figure 53

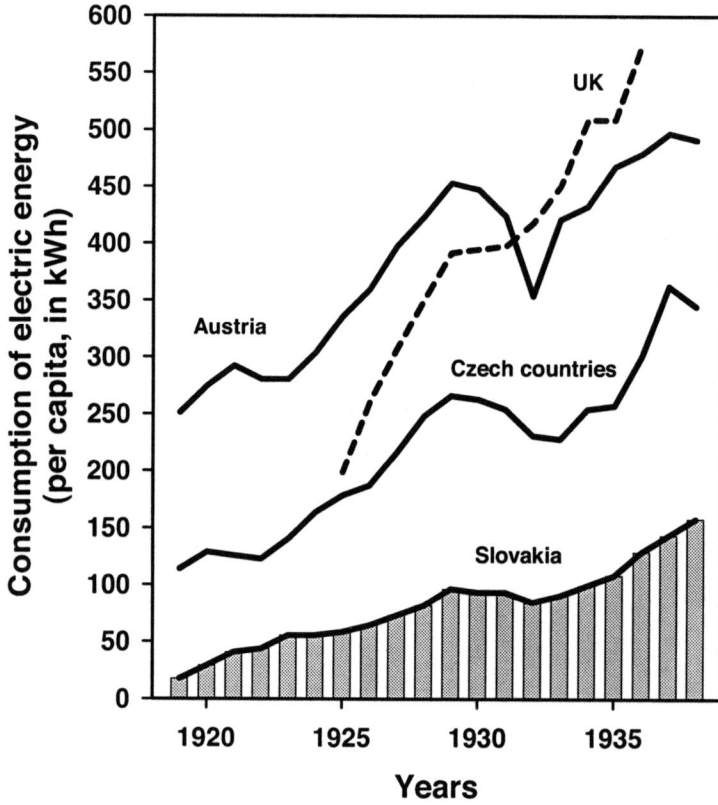

L'. Hallon: Industrializácia Slovenska 1918-1937
(Rozvoj alebo úpadok?). VEDA 1995

Figure 54

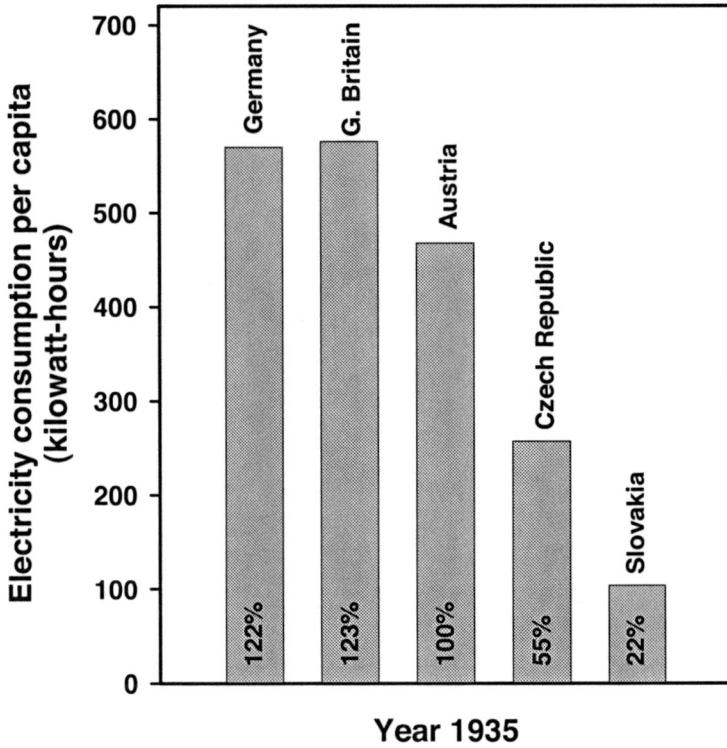

Year 1935

**L. Hallon: Industrializacia Slovenska 1918-1938
(Rozvoj alebo upadok?). VEDA 1995**

Figure 55

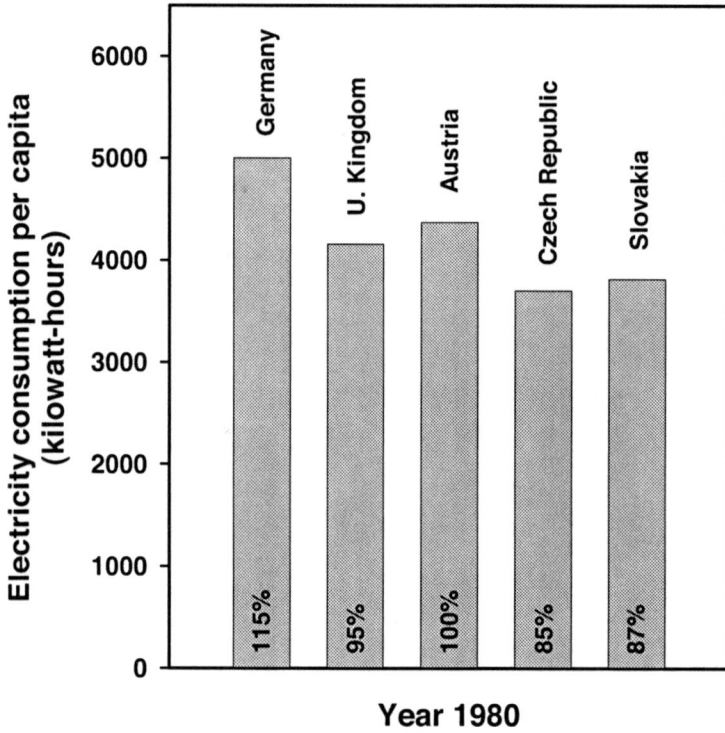

Year 1980

Human Development Report 2001

Figure 56

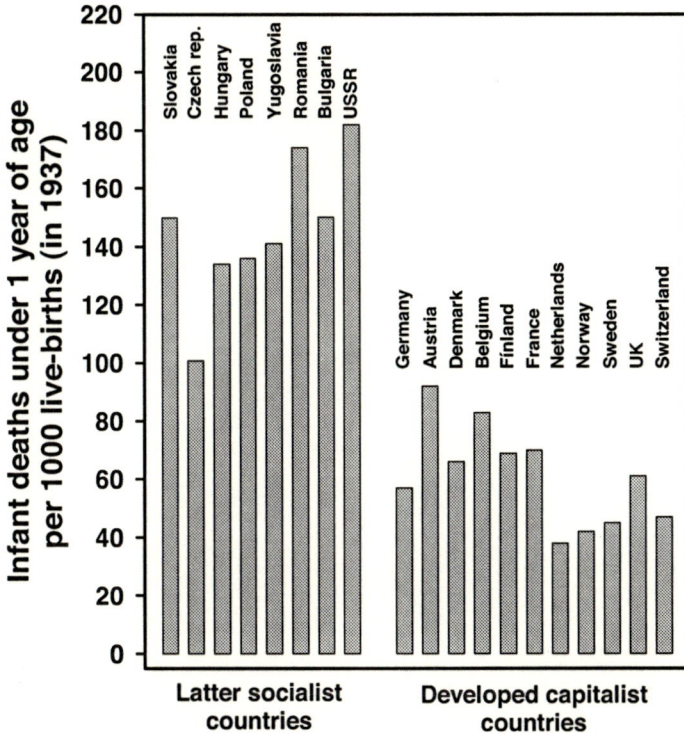

Statistical Yearbook of the Czech and Slovak Republic 1991

Figure 57

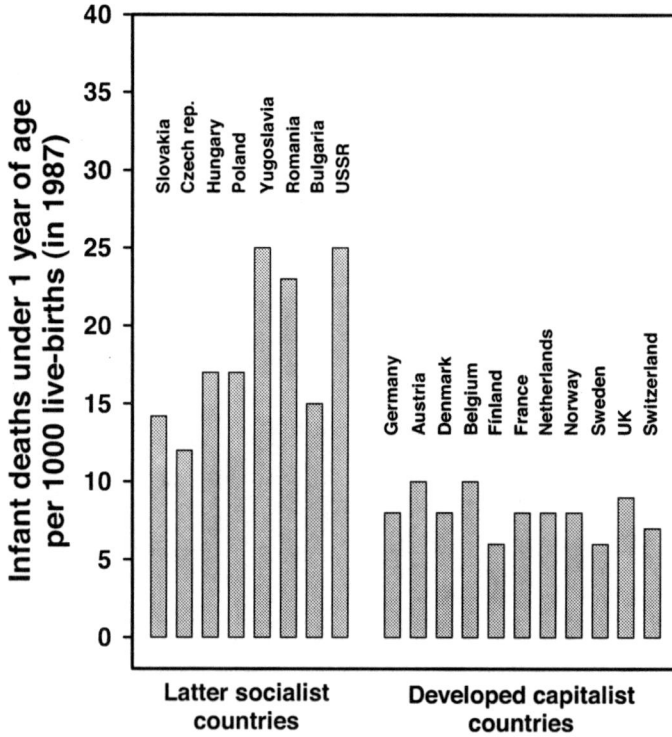

Statistical Yearbook of the Czech and Slovak Republic 1991

Figure 58

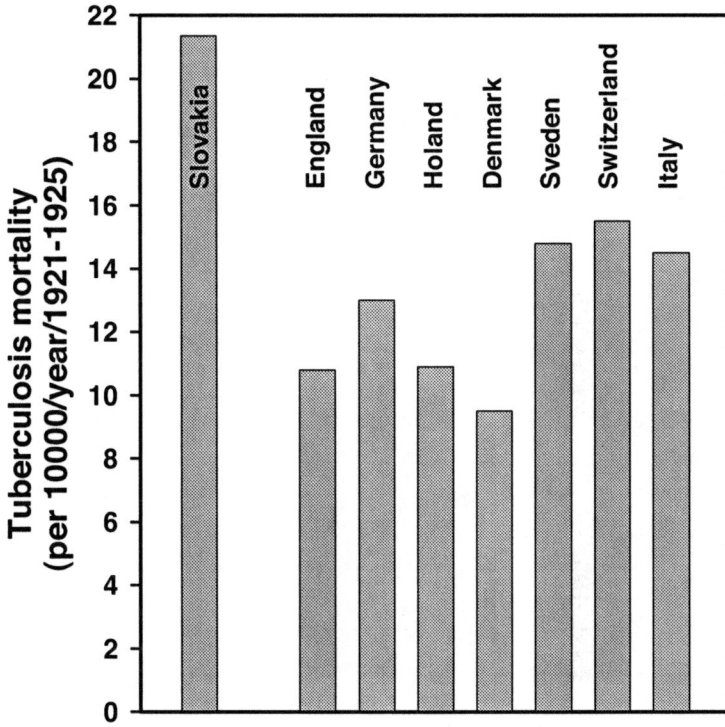

A. Falisová: Zdravotníctvo na Slovensku
v medzivojnovom období.
VEDA 1999, Bratislava

Figure 59

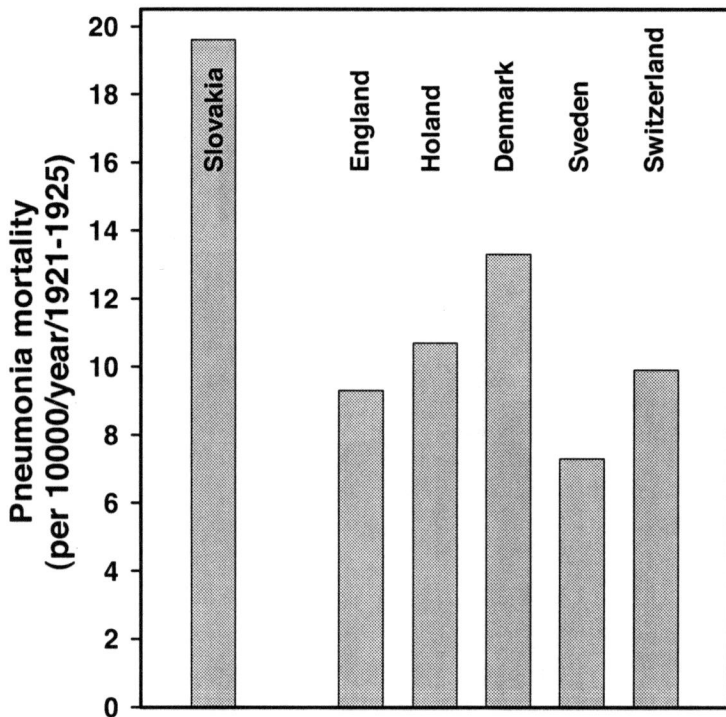

A. Falisová: Zdravotníctvo na Slovensku
v medzivojnovom období.
VEDA 1999, Bratislava

Figure 60

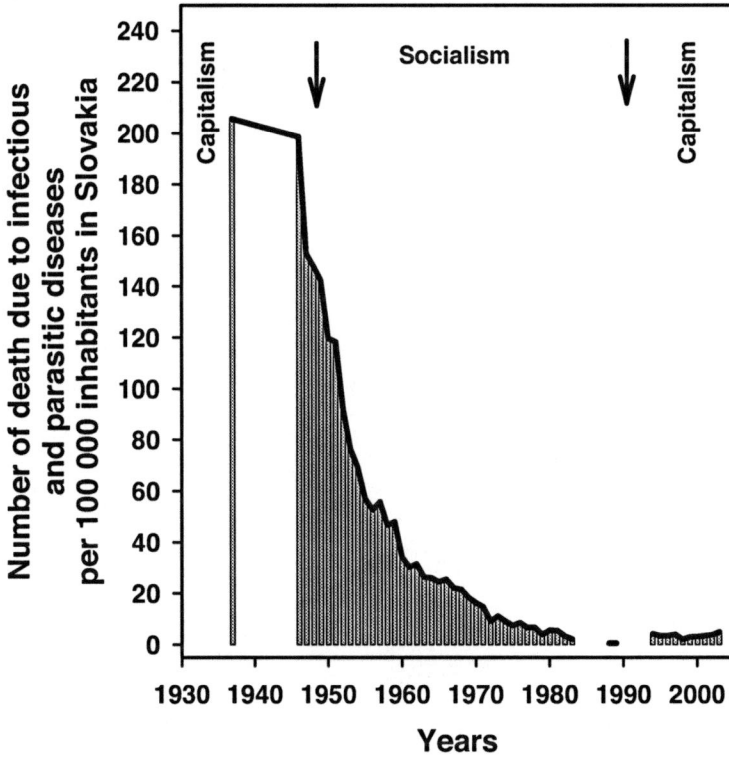

Historical Statistical Yearbook of the Czechoslovakia 1985
Statistical Yearbook of the Czech and Slovak Republic 1990, 1991
Statistical Yearbook of the Slovak Republic 1997-2004.

Figure 61

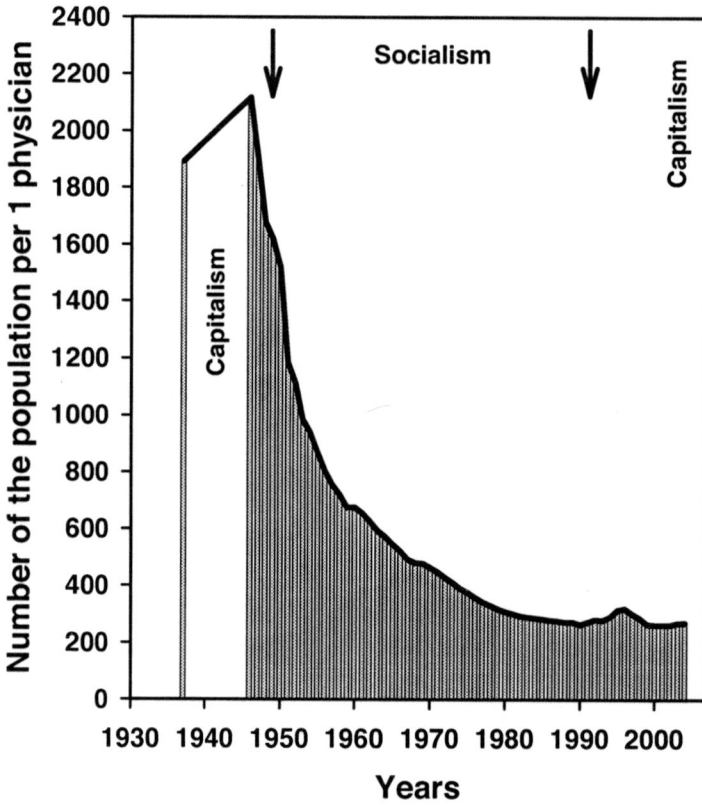

Historical statistical Yearbook of the Czechoslovakia 1985
Statistical Yearbook of the Czech and Slovak Republic 1990, 1991
Statistical Yearbook of the Slovak Republic 1997-2006

Figure 62

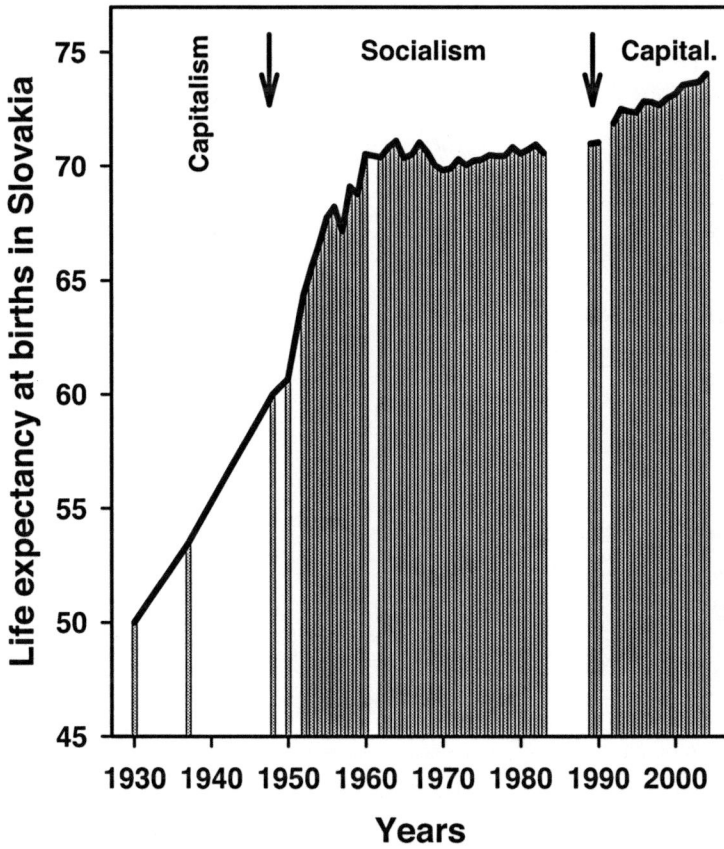

Historical statistical Yearbook of the Czechoslovakia 1985
Statistical Yearbook of the Czech and Slovak Republic 1990, 1991
Statistical Yearbook of the Slovak Republic 1997-2002.

Figure 63

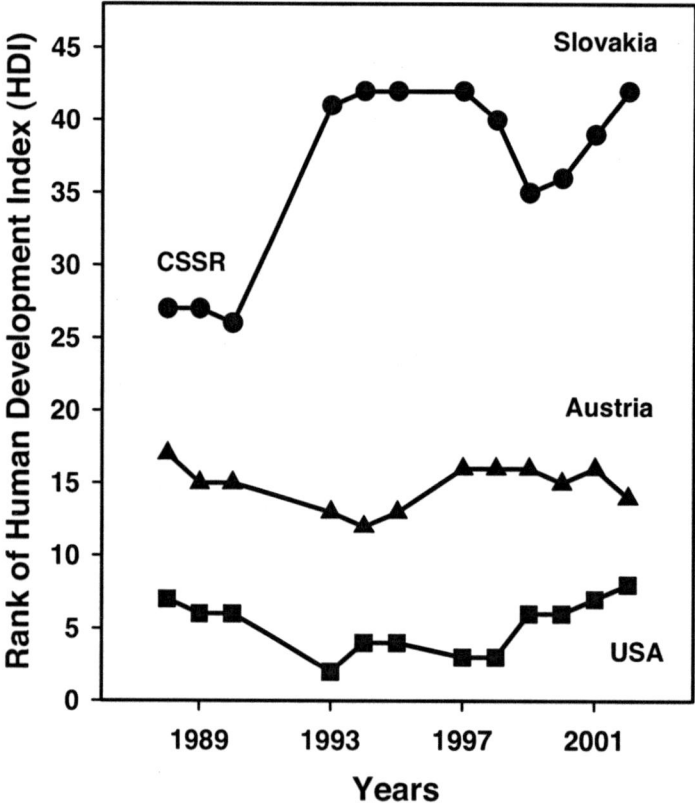

Human Development Report 1991-2003

Figure 64

2.3. A crime of communism – many innocent dead in Slovakia

The myths

"Crimes of communism" is well known phrase we are subjected to hear repeatedly. They form basic proof that communism was and is a criminal society comparable to fascism. When I asked my 14-year-old son, "how many people in Slovakia were killed by communists?", his estimation was 30,000. This was the result of recent primary education and media propaganda in Slovakia. According to the statement presented to the Slovak National Assembly on June 30, 2005 by Jan Langos, director of the Institute of Memory of the Nation, "In concentration camps and prisons (during communism in Slovakia) guards tortured to death about 44,000 innocent people".

The facts

In this chapter, I do not want apologize for any crimes or injustices committed by the communist regime. I am looking for the truth.

Yes, there were victims of communism in Slovakia, mostly in 1948-1955. The communists rehabilitated most of them in the 1960's. Concerning the innocent dead, yes, there were several judicial murders. How many? It is difficult to say, since present propaganda is doing everything it can to show that socialism was generally a criminal society. Unfortunately, it has not given enough important details about it. In the last 10 years I have been looking for professional books describing the victims of socialism in Slovakia during the socialist period from 1948-1989. I was looking for books describing not only the crimes and number of the victims, but also the reasons why they were persecuted and sentenced to death. So far there is not such book in Slovakia, in spite of many books, which generally condemn the crimes of communism. This kind of information could not be given to me by the Ministry of Justice, or by many other official organizations dealing with the crimes of communism in Slovakia. Fortunately, the scientific institution in the Czech Republic (Institute for Contemporary History, Academy of sciences of Czech Republic) published a book [11] that had described under what conditions the victims of communism were imprisoned, but it did not described the charges under which they were sentenced to death. Interestingly, there was only one copy of the book in Slovakian libraries. In this book, unknown to the public, most of the victims were imprisoned under parameters common in all democratic countries. According to the book, 30 people in Slovakia were sentenced to death and executed for political reasons during 1948-1989 (during 1960-1989 the number was 6, Figure 65). It was not 44,000 innocent people tortured to death by guards as was reported in the National Council in Slovakia in 2005, and it was not 30,000 deaths as estimated by a14-year-old student, who was using information learned in school and in the media. However, there was no information in the book, what was the reason to sentence them to death? What offences did these 30 victims of communism commit against people? Were these crimes against the communists or against the state? Why is there no detailed information about these 30 people, who were executed in Slovakia during 1948-1989 by the communists?

In 2001, a new book was published in Slovakia (Crimes of Communism in Slovakia 1948-1989, two volumes, [12]). The two volumes are very huge having 743 and 575 pages of A4 format type and weighing 2.6 kg. Even though the reason to publish the books was to emphasize the crimes of communism, I found it very important to understand the crimes of communism in Slovakia and compare them with the crimes of democracy in Slovakia after 1989. Even in this book, there is not a reason given for the execution of people by communists.

To have better view of the victims of communism in Slovakia, I compared innocent victims of the last four different regimes in Slovakia:
- Clergy-fascist regime (1939-1945) 72,000 Jews and 24,000 Romany people sent to death in Hitler's concentration camps.
- Capitalistic regime (1945-1948) killed several thousand Germans in Czechoslovakia (Germany claims 300,000 victims).
- "Totalitarian" communist regime 1948-1989 in Slovakia killed 30 (?), or even 500 (?) innocent people.
- Democratic capitalistic regime during 1989-2006 has produced ~4000 extra victims with comparison to socialism.

Conclusion from the comparison: The "totalitarian" communist regime was relatively the best in protecting the lives of the people.

The mysteries

The innocent dead from the communist regime were the result of the socialist system in practice for 40 years in Slovakia. After 1989 we have the innocent dead of democracy, as a result of the capitalist system in practice. The number of the innocent people, as a product of democracy, that were murdered, found dead, froze to death, died from drug overdose and were lost in Slovakia during the last 17 years of capitalism, is about 4,000 higher than average during last 16 years of socialism. As I said, this number is more than 10 times higher than all real and made up victims of 40 years of socialism. Why are the crimes of recent democracy 10 times higher than the crimes of communism in Slovakia? Why has nobody noticed that? I assume, because it is an integral part of our demoserfdom.

Victims of the democracy in Slovakia including the number of people who are unemployed, homeless or beggars increased more than 10,000 times compared to socialism (actually no one was unemployed, homeless or beggars during socialism). The number of people who were murdered, robbed or subjected to violent crimes increased several times under democracy in comparison to the crimes of communism.

If I write a book about the victims of the democracy in Slovakia after 1989 in the same style as the book "Crimes of Communism in Slovakia 1948-1989" [12] was written, the book would weigh more than one ton. The mystery is why nobody has written such a book. The answer is simple; the one ton book would be so huge that it would not fit on any shelf in the library or at home.

Why are children, students, honored people and nearly all media entertainers in Slovakia talking about ten's of thousands of innocent victims of communism in Slovakia in spite of the fact that anticommunists from all over the world have not been able to give evidence that even the 30 people sentenced to death and executed in Slovakia were the real innocent victims of communism? Why is there no detailed information about 30 people that were executed in Slovakia during 1948-1989 by communists? In my opinion, it is forbidden to publicize the reasons for the death sentences, because everybody might realize that some of, or even the most of, the victims were criminals or terrorists, according to recent definition. I suppose it is likely that the sentences given during socialism were more severe than in Western European countries at that time.

I do not remember anybody freezing to death during socialism in Slovakia. There was no homelessness at that time in Slovakia. On the other hand, in the winter of 2005/2006 18 homeless people froze to death in Bratislava. I do not know how many of them had been in Slovakia. I do not know how many of them died during 16 capitalist winters. Maybe 100 or 500. How come nobody cares about this?

Imagine that communists during socialism in Slovakia sentenced 100 or 500 innocent people to freeze to death outside because they have no home. It would be a very inhuman act committed by the communists. It would be real crime of communists. But what is the case when capitalists did it indirectly by passing new democratic laws, a result of which was 18 deaths by freezing in one winter in Bratislava only. Is it not considered as crime? According to the general capitalist view, their death by freezing is not a crime of capitalism, but is a matter of individual freedom and responsibility. It is simply a product of democracy.

Imagine that communists during socialism in Slovakia sentenced 10,000 innocent people to be homeless or to be fed on garbage. It would be a very inhuman act committed by the communists. It would be real crime of the communists. Similarly I can describe people, after 1989, who died from a drug overdose, from a bad social situation, who were murdered or trafficked abroad. Who will count these people and ask why nobody is punished for these crimes of capitalism, for these crimes of democracy? Is anybody, who does not understand these crimes of capitalism with comparison to communism morally ill? Or it is part of democracy, to be morally ill? Practice shows that it is.

The main mystery concerning the crimes of communism in Slovakia is that nobody who was indicted of crimes of communism, or crimes of the communists against humanity, was sentenced to prison or punished (at least I could not find any cases). Nobody was found guilty. Some people were tried for crimes of communism in the Czech Republic. Paradoxically enough, they were sentenced to prison for contravene of socialist law, but not for a crimes of communism. They were sentenced to prison after 1989, because they were not good communists. Judges in Slovakia have not sentenced anybody for crimes of communism so far in spite of the daily talk about the crimes. Why?

Finally, the establishment of an international court to judge communist leaders for crimes against humanity has never occurred. Why? It is likely that anticommunists are afraid that the court will give a judgment of no communist crimes. After such a judgment, it would not be easy for anticommunists to persuade everybody about totalitarian, nonhuman and criminal acts of communism. Since nobody was convicted, De Jure: the communists committed no crimes.

A philosophical statement: after the transformation of Slovakia from "communist totality" to capitalistic democracy, after 1989, growth of the population significantly decreased and in some years was even negative (Figure 66). This is the result of democracy which brought new opportunities and freedom, including the freedom to be fired from work, the freedom to be killed, the freedom to abuse drugs, the freedom to be unemployed or homeless, the freedom to beg and the freedom to not have enough money to bear and raise children in dignified conditions. In 2005, there were 26,000 less children born (30% decrease) than in 1989. It means that democracy might have caused 300,000 less children to be born over the last 15 years. Is it a crime? Or is it freedom or democracy? When should one decide between the two alternatives in Slovakia, when one choice is 300,000 children not being born? If somebody decides to kill 300,000 children in Slovakia, it would really be a crime. But, if somebody established conditions where we do not give birth to 300,000 children, what is it? Is it enough to say that its democracy?

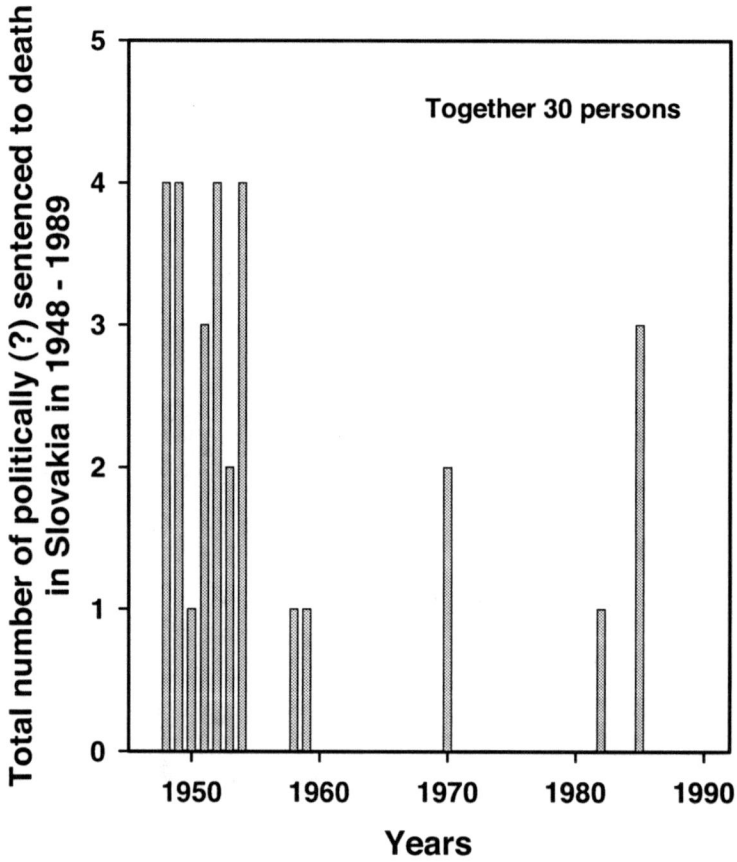

Gebauer *et al.*:
Soudní perzekuce politické povahy v Československu 1948-1989
(Ústav pro soudobé dejiny AV ČR, Praha, 1993, str. 223)

Figure 65

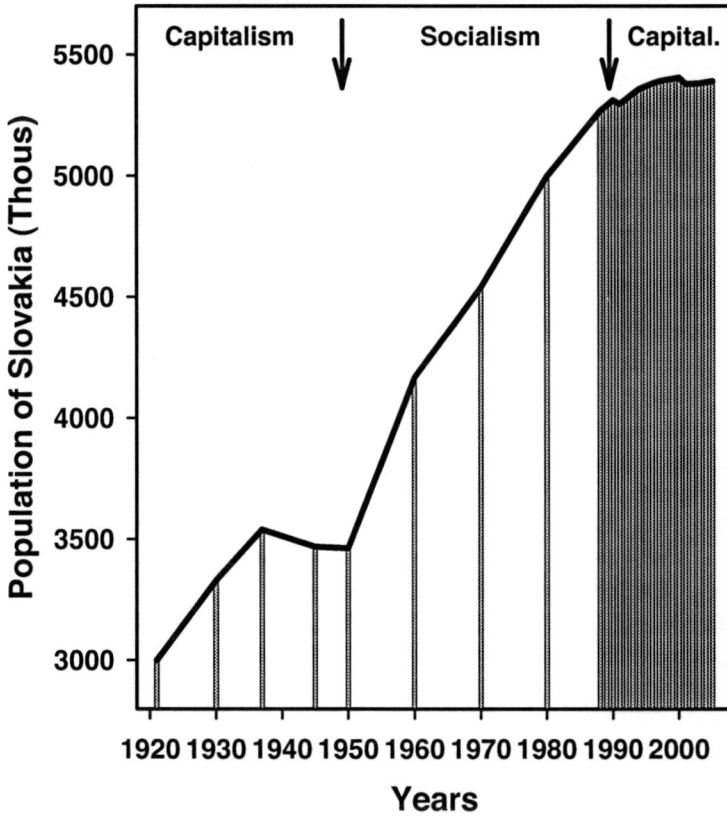

Historical statistical Yearbook of the Czechoslovakia 1985
Statistical Yearbook of the Czech and Slovak Republic 1990, 1991
Statistical Yearbook of the Slovak Republic 1997-2004.
Statistical Office of the Slovak Republic

Figure 66

2.4. A crimes of communism – suppression of freedom of expression

The myths

As everybody knows, the communists suppressed freedom of expression. Citizens in communist countries were brainwashed. Everything was controlled and censored.

The facts

Yes, there was a suppression of the freedom of expression. However, it is difficult to determine to what extent. The communist government tried to manipulate public opinion and the results of that manipulation can be seen in the previous chapters on economic, social and cultural development of Slovakia, living standard and crime during socialism. It can be explained partially by conditions of the cold war.

Now we have the capitalist freedom of expression. This means that most of the media belongs to foreigners, who manipulate public opinion according to the will of somebody abroad who we do not know. The results of this manipulation, one can see in the previous chapters on economic, social and cultural development of Slovakia, increased crime and decreased living standard after 1989.

There are few contrasts to be made between the freedom of expression during socialism and now capitalism. During socialism in Slovakia, we were subjected to communist propaganda, but most people could listen to broadcasts of the Voice of America, Radio Free Europe, watch Austrian or German TV broadcast or read smuggled magazines or books from abroad. Nearly anybody who was interested could find information from the capitalist counties about capitalism abroad and about the socialism we were living under. In my personal experience, when I visited the USA in 1988, I did not find anything new about the USA or world. I did not feel that in communist Slovakia, due to lack of information, my knowledge was restricted. What I did find in the USA was that most of the communist propaganda in Slovakia, which I considered to be pure propaganda, was right. Most of the capitalist propaganda I had received in Slovakia from abroad and considered as true was pure propaganda – a democratic lie.

On the other hand, the recent capitalist propaganda that we are subjected to does not have a counterpart. We do not have radio or TV broadcast from abroad, which would give us information from the other side. The same or ideologically similar groups of people who own foreign media own the main Slovak domestic media.

After the coup in 1989 many non-governmental organizations appeared in Slovakia. Many of them have been specifically created and financed from abroad in order to democratically colonize Slovakia. They have received money from foreign governmental or private sources such as: the US Agency for International Development, the National Endowment for Democracy, the International Republican Institute, the National Democratic Institute, Democratic Institute Freedom House, the Open Society Institute, the Trust for Civil Society in Central and Eastern Europe and many others. What is worse, these organizations have easier access to private and public media than Slovak intellectuals. They have successfully manipulated everything what they wanted, including "democratic opinion" during elections. The results of this are that all banks, insurance companies, most of the industry, and services are in foreign hands. The result of the freedom of expression is that we have democratically colonized property and pay colonization tax as described in the Chapter: 1.4. Slovak democratic colonization standard and the mysteries of liberation from communist totality. The GDP increase in Slovakia is real, but there has not been an adequate increase in wages, pensions or social securities.

The recent "democratic" freedom of expression means freedom to mentally colonize a population by anybody who has the money to do so. Foreign democratic organizations and owners of our media effectively decreased the level of education, culture, morality and living standard of our population.

According to experts, about 80% of the population can be manipulated by media. Therefore, the freedom of expression was the main power in colonizing the FSC. It is also the main democratic power in keeping demoserfdom. Recently freedom of expression has included anybody who owns one to ten TV channels, one to ten radio channels, and one to ten newspapers. We can be mentally colonized by racists, terrorists, the mafia, Semitists, anti-Semites, Slovaks, or anti-Slovaks if one has the money to arrange it. Nearly everyday we hear in the media a professional opinion or important issue given by an expert. I find it interesting that the professional expert sometimes was not Slovak, or he or she was not living in Slovakia before, and he or she was a member of nongovernmental organization supported from abroad. These experts have advised us on how to manage agriculture, industry, construction, banks, referendums or elections, how to privatize, and how to reform our media or health care. The results of this advice are shown in this book.

Now democratic freedom of expression is so powerful that it assigns how we should dress, cut out hair, and behave. It dictates what one should buy, who is a good or bad guy, a good or bad politician, who are good or bad terrorists or evil countries. It tells us how privatization and foreign investment saved our economy, how criminal communists were, and so on. The freedom of expression in the recent democracy secured that many of those lovely discussions have never crossed the border set by the rulers over democracy.

The plan for the democratic treatment of the FSC by the democratic USA was presented in 1946 by the late director of the CIA Allen Welsh Dulles. They planned to fight communism by democratic means to decrease the level of culture, introduce and cultivate a cult of sex, violence, sadism, greed, impertinence, alcoholism, drug addiction, animal fear of each other, treason, and animosity between nations. They have used democracy to achieve their goals; they have used the freedom of expression. After 1989 each former communist country has gotten at least one foreign TV station, radio station, and printed media, which have introduced and cultivated the mental disorder. The results of the mental colonization based on democratic freedom of expression can be seen everyday. After 1989, it was enough to switch on the TV for 5 minutes or open a popular magazine.

Peoplemeters were established in Slovakia a few years ago. They measure the ratio of the population who watch various TV programs. This means that if there is a thriller film on one TV channel and a primitive show on another, an educational program on next one and so on, the peoplemeters collect data on how many people watch each channel. According to the data from the peoplemeters one can sort the population by mental level, by education level, obedience, and so on. One can even find how many people are interested in basic animal needs only such as eating, drinking, pooping, pissing and having sex. According to the data from the peoplemeters one can easily manipulate the population to buy, vote, celebrate, colonize, fight, kill, and so on. When I, as a member of the Slovak Parliament, asked the Minister of culture whether we could obtain the peoplemeter data the answer was no. This was because a private company managed the peoplemeters and the data was for private use only. This is a typical example of the freedom of expression in capitalism. I have the freedom of expression to ask the ministry, and the ministry has the freedom of expression to answer me. This is the professional totality of the freedom of expression based on the rules of democracy.

I will mention at least three more examples of the democratic freedom of expression. Before Slovakia joined the EU in 2004, there was discussion in the Slovak parliament and in the public about how we could influence and control our representatives in the administrative body of the EU. We were aware that EU policy would have a big influence on Slovak development. After long discussion, to achieve this, Slovak Constitution was changed and new laws were enacted. So now we can influence and control our representatives in the EU. After that we asked a question to the Parliament, since we were also going to join NATO: how could we influence and control our representatives in the administrative body of NATO? We argued that it was necessary, because NATO policy would have a similarly big influence on Slovak development as the EU policy had. The answer to our questions was simple. There was neither discussion in Slovak Parliament, nor in the TV or printed media on the issue. The discussion, how to influence or control our representatives in NATO was not even asked in the media. It was behind the limit set by the rulers over democracy.

The second example was the issue of the referendum to join NATO. We had a referendum to join the EU, but not to join NATO. As some politicians put it, to join NATO is so important a decision that the public would not understand it.

The third example is about democratic education by TV. A few years ago I found a new cable TV channel 'soft porno - Blue Hustler' on TV at my home. I called the cable company and told them that by mistake we had the Blue Hustler TV channel and that I would like to cancel the channel. The answer was simple. The Blue Hustler cable channel is free; it is part of the TV channel package, and they could not cancel it for me. Simply put, if I want to watch the cable channels Euronews, BBS, Russian news and CNN, the 'Blue Hustler' channel is obligatory. I assume that the obligatory commitment to have the 'Blue Hustler' channel is part of the education of demoserfs.

In 1988 when I arrived in the USA, it was the first time in my life to visit a western capitalist country. I was surprised about the relatively low cultural level of many radio and TV broadcasts in comparison to the "totalitarian" ones in Slovakia. Many of the radio or TV shows were primitive to me. Many of the topics were about eating, drinking, dressing, sleeping, having sex and consuming. Since I was not accustomed to this cultural quality in "totalitarian" communist TV programs in Slovakia, I could not find it interesting. I had the feeling that the freedom of expression did not allow talk about serious issues. Recently, we have the same freedom of expression in TV or radio and the cultural quality of the programming decreased. The audience gradually becomes accustomed to it, likes it, and in a few years nobody will remember the high cultural quality of "totalitarian communist" freedom of expression in TV or radio.

The mystery

As I will describe in the Chapter: 4.3. The capitalistic totalitarian democracy as a base for demoserfdom, the democratic rule of the freedom of expression is mainly based off the totalitarian democratic system we are living in. It is the base for recent demoserfdom. Slovakia and the FSC are a textbook example of how freedom of expression was used to democratically colonize the country.

Communists tried for 40 years to manipulated public opinion but were unsuccessful. Recently, our population has been successfully manipulated by the owners of media, who are mostly unknown foreigners. The mystery is why the recent manipulation based on "democratic" free expression is more efficient that the "totalitarian" manipulation of "totalitarian" communism. Is it because "democratic" free expression is telling the truth, and the "totalitarian" communist manipulation was a lie? I have no relevant data to support this.

2.5. A crime of communism - suppression of human rights

The myths

Generally, as everybody knows, communism is a "evil society" that suppresses human rights and so on...

The Facts

Yes, communists in Slovakia violated human rights. Most of their crimes were in 1948-1955. The violations were juristically in murders, suppression of the freedom of expression and the freedom to travel, non-democratic elections and so on. It is written about in many books.

However, not many people know what human rights are about. According to the Universal Declaration of Human Rights (Adopted and proclaimed by General Assembly resolution 217 A (III) of 10 December 1948), the first three articles read:

- Article 1: All human beings are born free and equal in dignity and rights...
- Article 2: Everyone is entitled to all the rights and freedoms set forth in this Declaration, without distinction of any kind, such as race, color, sex, language, religion, political or other opinion, national or social origin, property, birth or other status.
- Article 3: Everyone has the right to life, liberty and security of person.

Other articles talk about the right to have a job, education, health care, accommodation and so on. Results of the violation of the human rights in the communist and the capitalist Slovakia (see Chapter: 1.5. Development of crimes of democracy in Slovakia), and in FSC (see Chapter: 3.1. Transition from socialism to capitalism in the former socialist countries - mysteries of the magical world 'democracy') indicate that the introduction of democracy in Slovakia and in the FSC, after 1989, increased the violations of human rights, (e.g. increased the number of deaths, poverty, or deprived people, increased inequality under practice of neo-liberal capitalism in violation of Article 1. of the Declaration. The mystery is: why is the increase of violations of the Declaration of Human Rights in FSC after the abandonment of socialism not generally noticed?

Many democrats and humanists have underlined that communists were totalitarian and therefore had to control the entire population. I do not know how they controlled it, but I can mention how recent democratic states control their own and foreign populations. In democratic Great Britain 4.2 million cameras control the behavior of free people. One camera per 14 people is watching what people are doing on the street and probably everywhere else. I do not know how many more cameras the secret police have in Great Britain. I do not know whether the ratio of camera/citizen is higher or lower than it was in 1984 as described by George Orwell.

On February 26, 2003, a car bomb was detonated in an underground parking garage below Tower One of the World Trade Center in New York City. I was watching a TV broadcast from the scene on-line at the time. A few minutes or hours after the detonation, the chief of the New York City police said that, unfortunately, they did not have cameras monitoring the entrance to the underground parking garage because it was a public garage. A few minutes or hours later, the New York state police said the same, they did not have cameras around or in the garage. In spite of this, a few hours or days later, the FBI said that they had camera records of cars entering the underground parking garage on February 26, 2003. Using the camera records they solved the case. I was surprised watching on-line TV that even state police do not know where the secret cameras are.

How many secret cameras or satellites are taking pictures of my smiling face each day? How many of our phone calls, mail and faxes need to be recorded in order to secure the freedom of a neo-liberal capitalistic democracy? Is it really true that the computers of some security agencies can read this book on-line as I am writing it on my personal computer connected to the internet? According to internet reports, special access codes prepared by the US National Security Agency have been secretly built into Windows. Version of ADVAPI.DLL shipping with Windows 2000 contains not two, but three keys [13].

Why does a neo-liberal capitalistic democracy need to know what I am writing about?

2.6. A crime of communism – suppression of culture

The myths

The generally accepted view of the development of culture during socialism in former socialist countries is well known: the communist totalitarian regime did not permit the development of culture. Everything was censored. Artists could only produce art that was in accordance with accepted communist ideology. Many actors were on the black list and could not participate in artistic projects. Many writers could not write books, many filmmakers could not produce movies, many stage players could not perform and so on.

The facts

The socialist government controlled culture during socialism to a great extent. There was censorship of many cultured products. More or less, artists could produce only art that was in accordance with accepted socialist ideology. Some actors were on the black list and could not participate in artistic projects. Some writers could not write some books, some filmmakers could not produce some movies, some stage players could not perform and so on. What I do not know is the percentage of artists that could not produce the art they wanted, what percent of writers could not write the books they wanted, the percentage of filmmakers who could not produce the movies they wanted, how many stage players could not perform and so on. My estimation is that it could be between 2-20%.

After 1989, we finally had democracy and freedom of culture. Film directors can produce the movies they want, but, as one can see from the Figure 67, only a few can do it. Most of them cannot do as they could under "totality". Production of full-length films decreased rapidly after 1989. Why?

During socialism Slovak TV and Slovak radio produced many television and radio plays, most of them being very high quality. Now they produce mostly programs that have low cultural quality. They produce mostly TV soap operas and primitive TV shows. Many of these shows deal with animal instinct only, as I mentioned before. The same primitive topics are discussed in nearly all magazines produced by the culture of the free market democracy.

Where are the films that were on index during socialism? They are probably showed somewhere. How many of them? I do not know. How many people are interested in those movies? I do not know.

Where are the new TV-movies, which were not allowed to be produced during socialism? They are probably produced somewhere. How many of them? I do not know. How many people are interested in those movies? I do not know.

Where are the books that were on index during socialism? They are probably published somewhere. How many of them? I do not know. How many people are interested in those books? I do not know.

How many people going to finally see the cultural B-films? I know, many of them. How many people watch the cultural trash on TV? I know, many, nearly all. How many people read the cultural crap in magazines? I know, many, nearly all.

It is difficult for me to address the extent of the involvement of government in culture control during socialism in Slovakia. It is not easy to obtain relevant data (at least for me), to evaluate culture, but I will present at least two examples of statistical data. The official number of people employed in the cultural business during 40 years of socialism increased from 3,000 to 32,000. The budget for culture in 1989 was, in real prices, 2.6 times higher than that of 2005. Of course, we still produce high quality cultural programming, but for how many people? Most of the culture that is a product of capitalistic democracy has a very low value. It is probably in accordance with the cultural level of the people produced by a capitalistic democracy. In my opinion, the development of public culture for 40 years during socialism in Slovakia was very positive in comparison to the low public cultural level of recent capitalism.

The mysteries

Why has our public culture deteriorated after the introduction of democracy and freedom of culture? I have the feeling that everything in mainstream media that is not connected with animal instincts is not welcomed by the free market democracy.

Since most of the mainstream media belongs to foreigners it means that Slovakia is mentally colonized. As I mention before, we have peoplemeters, which measure what we watch on TV. Somebody analyzes the data from the peoplemeters and knows the level of our cultural interest. Unfortunately, the public does not know the results of the analyses. Why? I assume that this information is censored by the free market democracy, similarly to our freedom of culture.

Sex is one animal instinct; maybe it was propagated after the establishment of capitalistic democracy in Slovakia. More sex on TV, radio, and in magazines was noticed as more democracy came to Slovakia. Maybe it is an integral part of the democratic mental colonization.

Is sex used to promote colonization similarly as opium was used to promote colonization of China by Britain? Britain had to fight two opium wars with China, one between 1839-1842 and the other during 1856-1860, to sell opium there. China lost the wars and had to relinquish Hong Kong to Britain and open several ports to ships importing opium. The result was that more than one million opium-smoking restaurants were functioning in China, which effectively disturbed society.

Many girls in the U.S. are entering puberty much earlier than normal, according to a study reported in the journal PEDIATRICS [14]. The study found that the average age for onset of puberty was just under 9 for African-Americans and was 10 to 10 1/2 for whites. Current medical texts say puberty begins between the ages of 11 and 12, on average. There is some evidence that exposure to environmental chemicals may be contributing to the phenomenon. Common wisdom - but no data - suggest that the increasingly overt sexuality of popular media may stimulate earlier sexual development. The social implications of early-onset puberty are obvious. Young children with mature bodies must cope with feelings, urges and differences from their peers that most children are not well equipped to handle. For many children, early pubescence may be a significant burden to bear. Early sexual initiation was also associated with a number of behavioral problems. Ignoring the age of the partners, the earlier a girl was when she first had intercourse, the greater her risk of suicide attempts, alcohol use, drug abuse, truancy and pregnancy [15].

Is sex used to promote and secure our democratic colonization? Is it possible that early sex and sexual maturation before brain maturation is a disadvantage for development of individuals and society? I assume so, but I must accept that colonization by sex is healthier than colonization by opium.

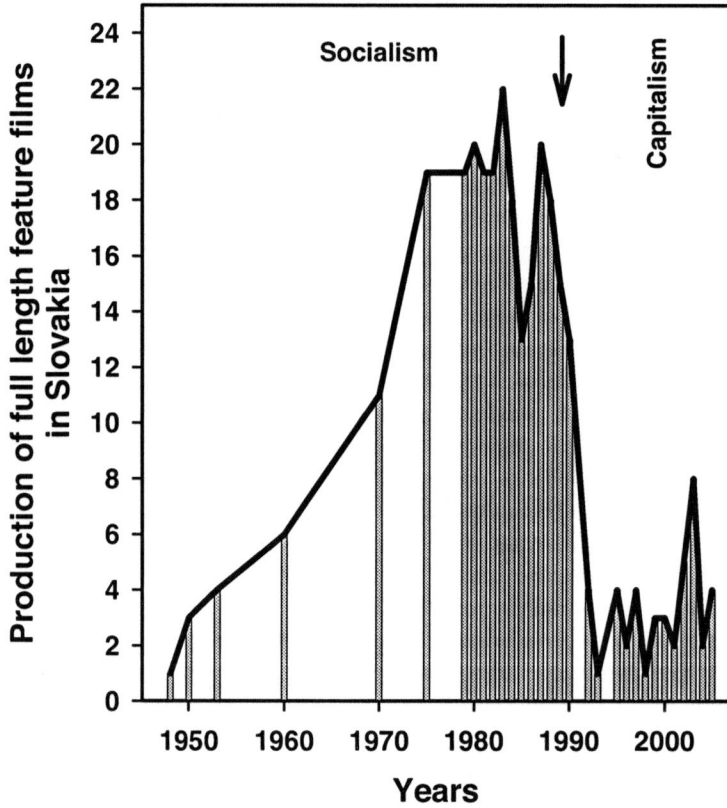

Historical Statistical Yearbook of the Czechoslovakia 1985
Statistical Yearbook of the Czech and Slovak Republic 1990, 1991
Statistical Yearbook of the Slovak Republic 1997-2006

Figure 67

2.7. A crime of communism – suppression of religion

The myths

Everybody knows that one of the many crimes of Communism in former socialist countries was suppression of religion. The communist regime in Slovakia did not allow freedom of religion and persecuted those people who professed religion. Communists destroyed churches. Respected scholars repeated this everywhere; it is written in all respected academic books and presented by media anytime and everywhere. Our good friends and advisors from abroad during socialism ensured us that we needed to get rid of socialism. Democracy will guarantee freedom of religion, freedom of ideology and their evolution.

The facts

Slovakia was, and still is, a religious country. According to the Housing and population census in 2001, 84% of the population reported themselves as being religious (69% Roman Catholic), and only 13% were without religion.

Yes, it is true that after the communists were democratically elected to govern in 1948, they tried to suppress religion. They said that religion is the opium of the people and that many conflicts, wars and intolerance are based on religion. I agree with them. They committed several undemocratic acts to reduce the power of religion and the power of the Church. They tried to build an atheistic society. Most of the Holy orders, cloisters and monastery buildings were closed and nationalized. Monks and nuns (numbering about 5,000) were forced to stop practicing professional religion and they were forced to make a living by working in industry, agriculture or service. The state provided jobs for them. Many protesting religious people (about 1,000-10,000) were accused of activities against the state and sentenced to prison. Some of them died as a consequence of the injustices. It is not yet known exactly, which of the cases were real and which were not. How many of the persecuted persons practiced activities, which nowadays would be determined as terrorism against the state.

During socialism, the church was under the control of the communist government. Paradoxically, priests were paid by the state and divine services were practiced more or less freely. In public primary schools, children could learn religion for free in optional classes. The local priests, paid by state, taught them. In 1953-54, 66% of students attended the religion classes; in 1962-1963 it dropped to 35%. Students could study theology for free at three theological facilities in universities in Slovakia. The theological facilities were fully supported by the state. In 1989, the number of the students at the facilities was 461.

After 1989, Christian democratic parties have governed in Slovakia in coalition. They have introduced many democratic laws. According to the laws, the churches received back their property and state support of the churches increased significantly.

Next, for simplicity, I will describe data for the Roman Catholic Church only since it is the main religion in Slovakia. The number of Roman Catholic priests with and without catechizers in Slovakia increased in 2005 in comparison to 1989, 173% (Figure 68) and 339% (Figure 69), respectively. On the other hand the number of churches during 1989-1998 increased by only 7% (Figure 70, in ≥1999 chapels were included) and the number of divine services increased during 1989-2002 only to 125% (Figure 71).

The mysteries

The absolute number of ecclesiastically baptized children in Slovakia decreased after 1989 (Figure 72). This was mainly caused by the decreased birth rate after 1989. However, in 2005 still only 69% of babies were baptized in total. Relative to the decrease of the birth rate in Slovakia after 1989, this number is similar to that in 1989. In other words, there was no significant increase in the ecclesiastically baptized children in Slovakia after 1989. It is a mystery to me, why the number of the ecclesiastically baptized children did not increase after 1989. How is it possible that the number of the ecclesiastically baptized children during socialism when "the professing of religion was not free and religious people were persecuted", was the same as the number after 1989, when the Christian democratic parties are in power and religion is supported by the state? My answer from these data, and the data described below, is simple. There was no practical restriction to baptizing children in Slovakia for common people during socialism in 1989. Of course, to practice Christian religion was more or less restricted for higher officials of the Communist Party of Slovakia and their families. This is similar to as today it would be unacceptable if children of higher officials of the Catholic church were members of the Communist Party of Slovakia, and if they propagated Marxism and attended communist meetings.

The absolute number of ecclesiastical marriages in Slovakia decreased after 1989 (Figure 73). It decreased also in relative values. In 2005, there were only 59% of the ecclesiastical marriages in comparison to 1989. In other words, there was an absolute and relative decrease in the ecclesiastical marriages in Slovakia after 1989. This again indicates that there was neither significant restriction to profess religion or persecution of religious people during socialism in 1989. This is confirmed also by data of the absolute and relative numbers of ecclesiastical funerals in Slovakia, which did not change significantly after 1989 (Figure 74). During 1989- 2005 about 69% of funerals were ecclesiastical.

The rate of religious broadcasting on public radio is also significant. In 2005 religious broadcasting was higher than educational and cultural and it was similar to advertising (Figure 75). On TV in 2005, religious, educational, and advertising broadcasting was 260, 58, 95, 417 hours, respectively. Even the Christian religion is highly supported by state and media. Two facts strike me. First, the observation of the Ten Commandments, which are the base of the Christian religion, was significantly more observed during socialism, under the rule of the atheistic communist party, then now, under the rule of Christian democrats. This is proven by the results described in Chapter: 1.5. Development of crimes of democracy in Slovakia, of the increase in homicides, thefts, violence, adulteries, and so on, after the freedom of religion was guarantied after 1989. Even the First Commandment was better observed by communists during socialism than now. Recently, there are other religions besides Christianity practiced in Slovakia, e.g. Hindu, Buddhism or Satanists, which were not practiced during socialism. I wonder why all Christians and clergy do not vote for the Communist Party of Slovakia in parliamentary elections, in order to better observe the rules of the Holy Ten Commandments. Especially now since it is clear from the real experiment that communists better practiced the Holy Ten Commandments, than Christian democrats do now. This may be one of the main reasons for the fight of Christian churches against communism.

After 40 years of the suppression of religion by communists, 73% and 83% of the population reported themselves as Christians in 1991 and 2001, respectively. These numbers are higher than in most Western Europe capitalistic countries in which freedom of religion has been guaranteed. Why was the practice of Christian religions better preserved in the communist regimes than in Christian democrat regimes in Western Europe? Why is the mystery of the better preservation of the Holy Ten Commandments by communists in comparison to Christian democrats not generally recognized by recent democrats, humanists and Clergy in the Vatican? Why were the "crimes of socialism–suppression of religion" in practice better for the observation of the Holy Ten Commandments, than the "democracy of capitalism–freedom of ideology"?

Christian democrats have had significant power in the coalition governments in Slovakia after 1989 when we started to follow democratic rules. During their governance, nearly all the property of the Communist party was taken out. All schools, teaching centers, nearly all facilities of universities teaching Marxism-Leninism or communist ideology were abolished and teachers were suspended unless they changed ideology. Today all religions are supported by the state, besides nonreligious – atheistic organizations. Religion or ethics are optional study in primary school. The students choose mostly religion. There is no option to study atheism, Marxism or communism.

The atheist ideology is not supported by the state in spite of fact that it is the second most popular ideological group, accounting for 13% of the population. Now it is impossible for anyone to go into a public school and teach Marxism or atheism in voluntary classes, as it was normal for Christian priests to teach catechism at the public communist schools. Why is the suppression of Marxist and communist ideologies seen nowadays in accordance with the rules of democracy, and suppression of religion by Communists was a crime and sign of totality? Why is the recent totalitarian religious democracy democratically accepted?

Imagine that Communists suppressed religion during socialism to the same extent as the recent government is suppressing Marxist and Communist ideology. Imagine if Communists would not financially support the Church and instead nationalized all churches and used them for other purposes, as recent governments did with communist property. What would recent respected scholars call such communist rules?

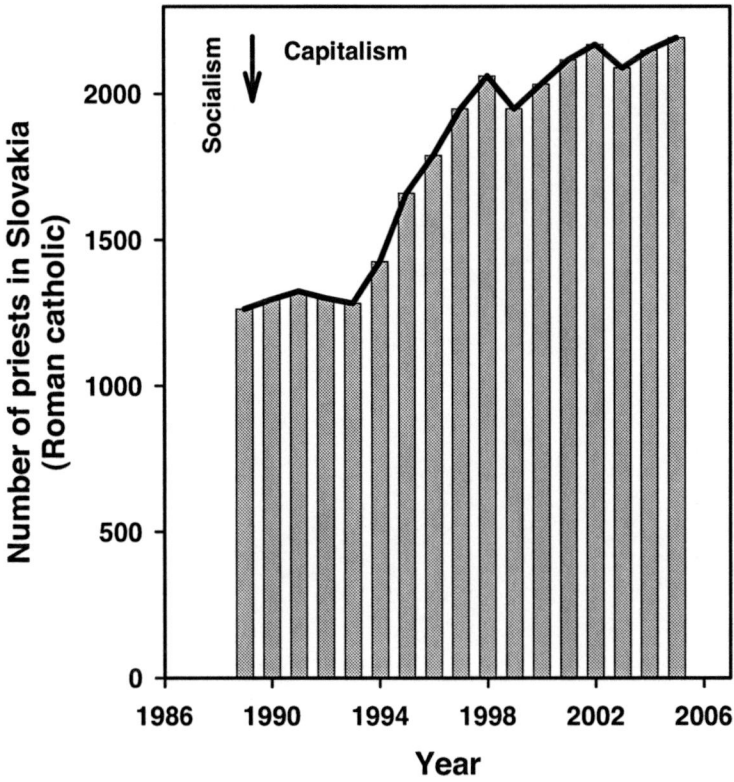

Statistical Yearbook of the Slovak Republic 1994-2006

Figure 68

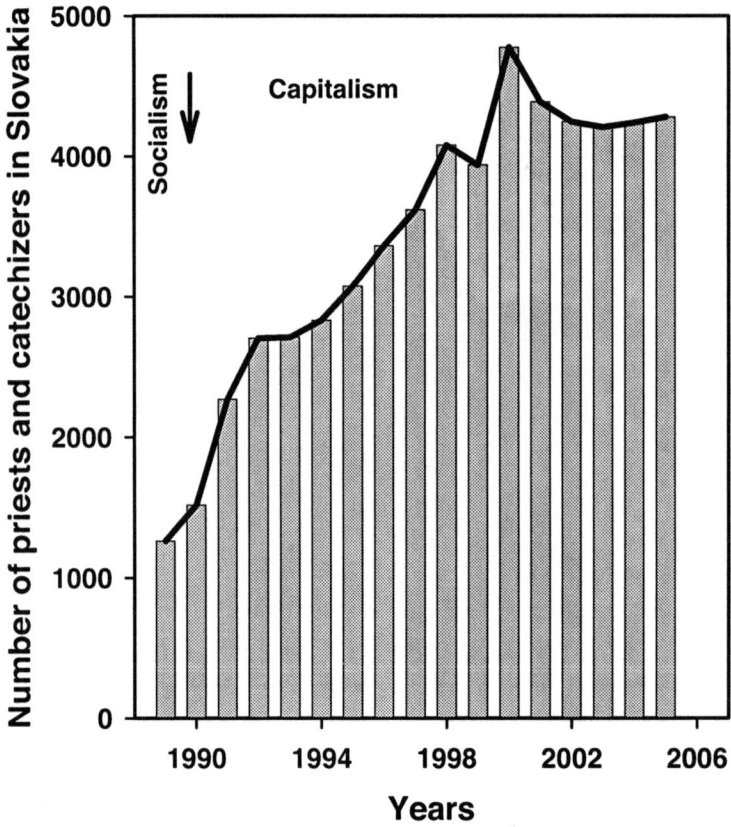

Statistical Yearbook of the Slovak Republic 1994-2006

Figure 69

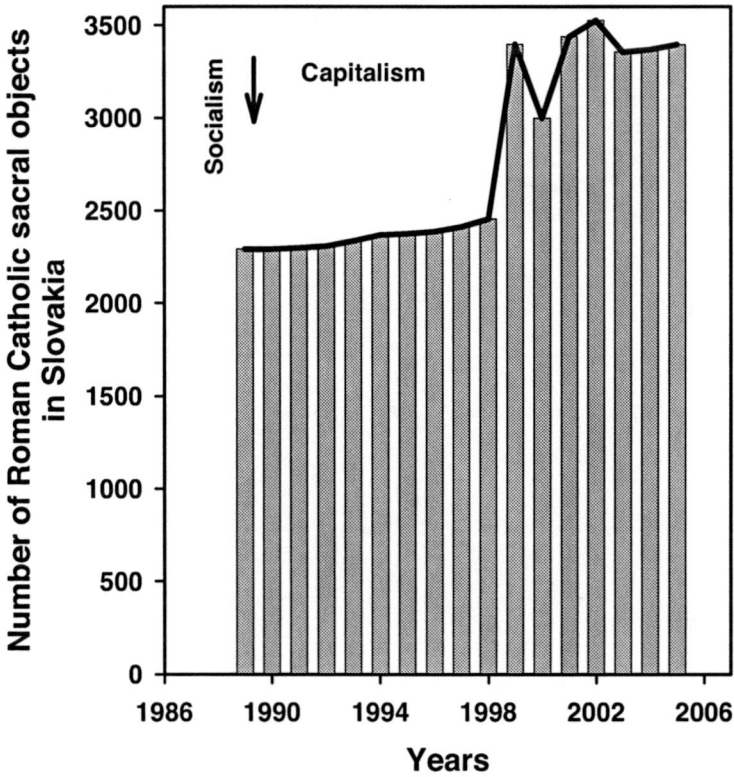

Statistical Yearbook of the Slovak Republic 1994-2006
(Only churches; > 1998 all sacral buildings)

Figure 70

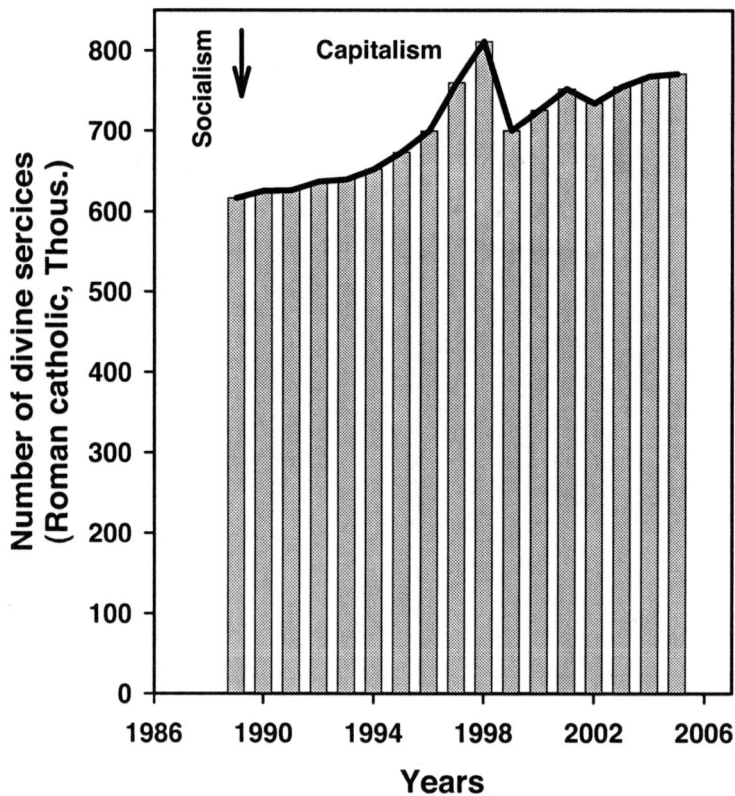

Statistical Yearbook of the Slovak Republic 1994-2006

Figure 71

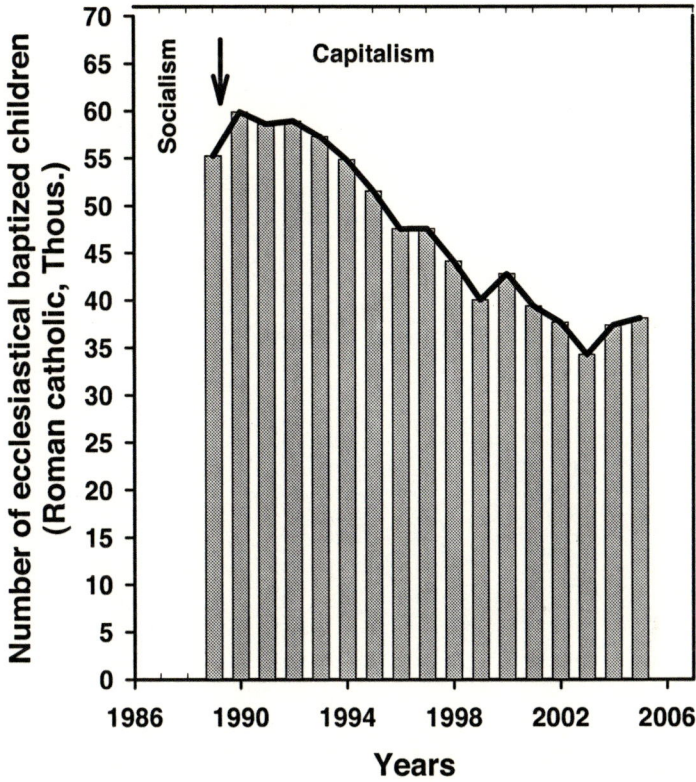

Statistical Yearbook of the Slovak Republic 1994-2006

Figure 72

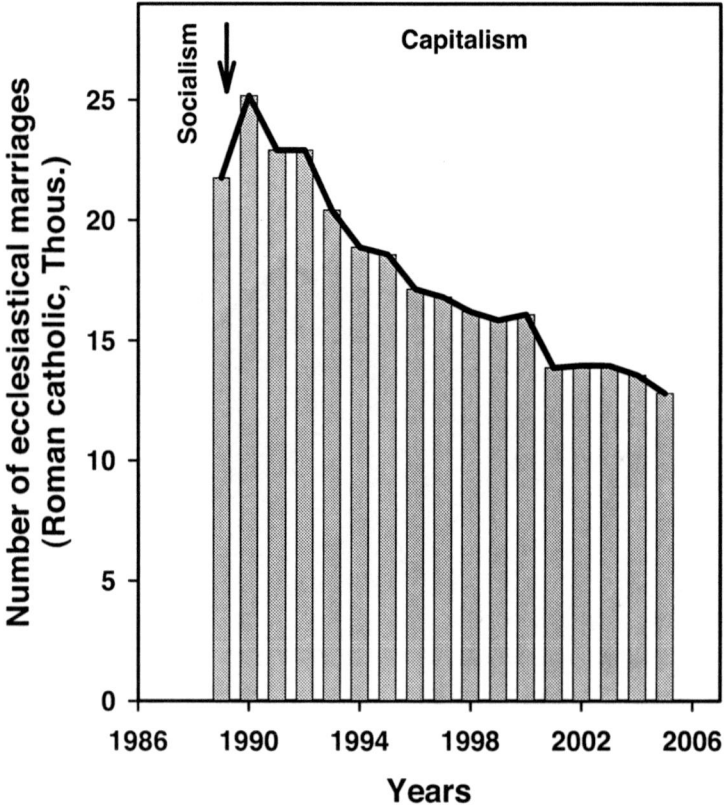

Statistical Yearbook of the Slovak Republic 1994-2006

Figure 73

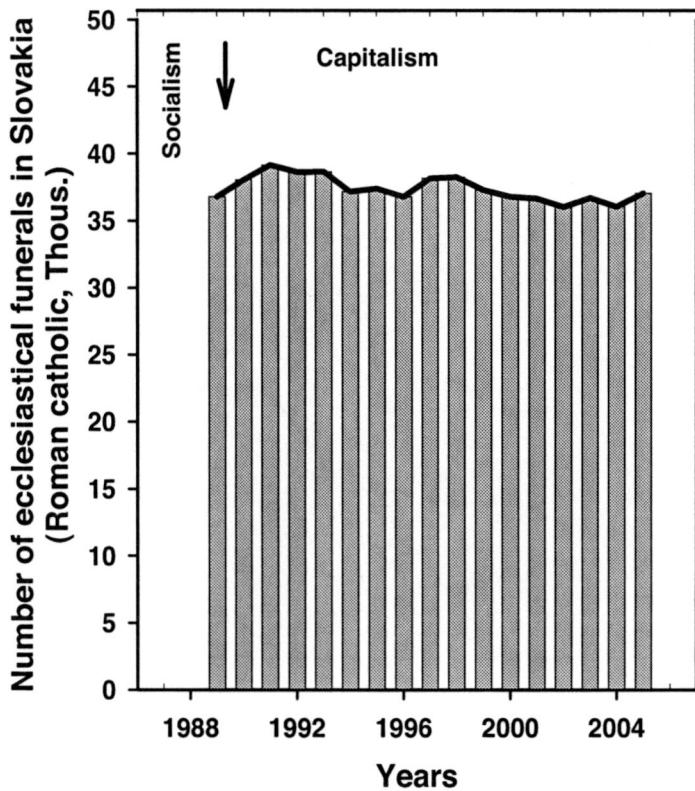

Statistical Yearbook of the Slovak Republic 1994-2006

Figure 74

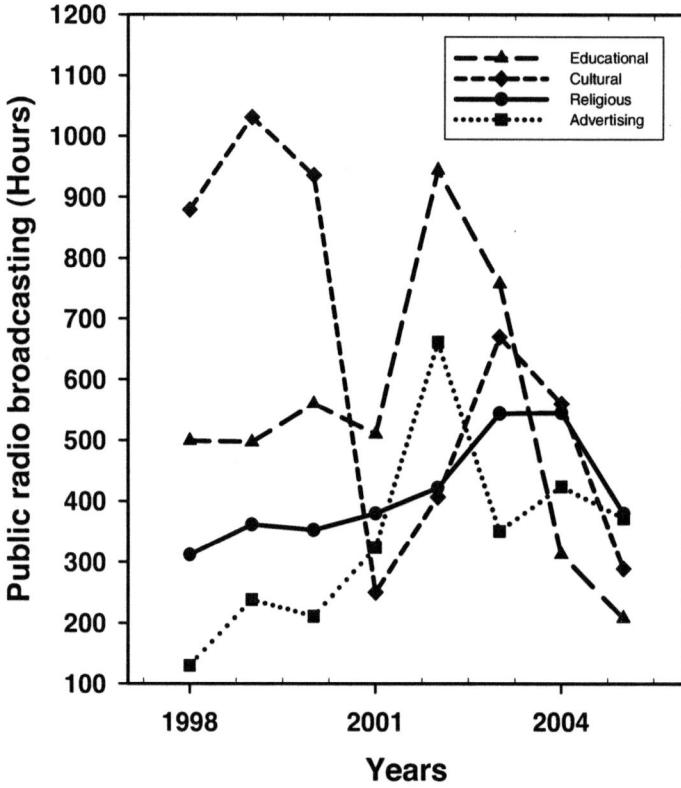

Statistical Yearbook of the Slovak Republic 1993-2006

Figure 75

2.8. A crime of communism - dependence on Moscow

The myths

Nearly everybody during socialism in Slovakia was convinced that Slovakia exported many products to the Soviet Union and was getting nothing valuable back. The brainwashing machine broadcasting from the west was so powerful that trade with the Soviet Union was considered to be very inconvenient for Slovakia. We were told that Slovakia was forced by Moscow into this trade. Therefore, after 1989, Slovakia voids most of the well-established commercial activities with the Soviet Union. Nearly everybody was convinced that our "bad living standard" was also the result of our economic cooperation in The Council for Mutual Economic Help (RVHP), which depended on Moscow, planned economy and the absence of free market forces. Many were convinced that Slovakia was colonized by Moscow.

The facts

Recently Slovakia has more or less balanced the trade deficit with all countries but Russia. The main trade deficit of Slovakia after 1989 is with Russia. It was €2.07 billion in 2003. Slovakia is largely dependent on imports of Russian fuel, energy and raw materials. These represent 90 percent of the imports from Russia.

Slovakia and other post-communist countries are very good samples for studying the impact of a free trade market and capitalistic democracy on their economy. The change of economic cooperation from RVHP to developed capitalist countries resulted in the situation described in the previous chapters. During socialism, all economic property was under state ownership and control. It was more or less a closed economy in comparison to the recent open free market economy and capitalist ownership. By a comparison of real GDP with real wages and pensions, one may estimate a colonization tax of the country as described in the Chapter: 1.4. Slovak's democratic colonization standard and the mysteries of liberation from communist totality. From all the data presented, it is clear that dependence on Moscow was economically positive with comparison to the dependence on the EU or countries with free market economies.

In May 2004 Slovakia joined the European Union. According to the Treaty of Accession to the European Union 2003, between Slovakia and the EU, Slovakia meets quotas for the total area of vineyards. The value of the quota is also shown in the Figure 6. It is only 72% of the area in the socialist year 1989. This means that, according to the agreement with EU, we are obliged to keep our total area of the vineyards in Slovakia to the area we have reached in 1968, 34 years back. According to the Treaty of Accession to the European Union 2003, Slovakia got quotas for the number of the sheep and goats. The number is shown in the Figure 7. This means that, according to the agreement with EU, we are obliged to keep the number of the sheep and goats similar to what we had already in 1948, which is less than Slovakia had in 1936. Similarly, according to the Treaty of Accession to the European Union 2003, the quota for milk production in Slovakia stabilizes our milk production at 58% of the values of 1989 (Figure 8).

Taking the European Union (EU) as the pattern of democracy, it was interesting to see, how the international democracy between the EU and Slovakia have influenced our agriculture after 1989. In spite of the fact that, according to EU rules and Slovak constitution both economies are based on the rule of free market economy, the international democratic interaction in the case of agriculture has not followed this much proclaimed rule. The state agricultural subsides in EU countries have been several times higher than the subsidies in Slovakia. Slovakia could not use economic tools to correct it. Of course, plummeting prices of EU agricultural products in Slovakia has had a negative influence on our agriculture. There is the mystery of, why, in this case, nobody from Slovakia or from EU countries pointed out the violation of the basic rule of EU democracy and Slovak constitution. On the other hand, any Slovak industrial products that were attempted to be sold at the EU market at dumping prices, were immediately stopped, arguing that it was not according to the rules of the free market economy.

The mystery

Why can Russia manage its economy now without our goods but we cannot manage our economy without imports from Russia? Why, in practice, is the opposite of what we were told by the capitalist propaganda true? The propaganda convinced us that the RVHP was a disaster of social economy. However, nobody analyzed what the economic development of RVHP countries was before WWII. How the economy increased during years of RVHP and how it performed after 1990 when RVHP was dissolved. Data about the living standard after the dissolution of RVHP (shown below), indicate that our dependence on western economies did not bring such positive development as did our dependence on Moscow.

2.9. A crimes of communism – not everybody hates communism

The myths

Recent democratically-totalitarian information systems are repeating the myths about how everybody in the former socialist country is happy to be liberated by capitalist democracy. That now everybody has freedom and democracy and hate to think of the time when they had to live under communist rule. Do they hate really communism?

The facts

According to official data from the Institute of Public Relation, Bratislava 1990 (a few months after the coup:
41% of the population preferred socialism,
3% of the population preferred capitalism,
52% of the population preferred something between the two.

According to the Research of Public Opinion (in Slovakia) organized by United States Information Agency in 1993, Economic Reform Today 1/1994:
- The recent economic situation in comparison to communism was better for 22% of people,
- The recent economic situation in comparison to communism was worse for 71% of people,
- 39% preferred private property to state controlled property.
- 53% preferred state controlled property to private property.

According to the publication [16]:
In the survey in Slovakia, the population responded that:
- In 1997 – 49% of the population lived a better life during socialism,
- In 1999 it was 56%,
- In 2001 it was 59%,
- In 2003 it was 66% and only 8% had the opposite opinion.

The mysteries

Why do many people still prefer socialism to capitalism in spite of every day's massive amount of anticommunist propaganda? Why did the new Communist Party of Slovakia, established in 1992, receive enough votes to get into the Slovak Parliament from 2002-2006? Why does everybody not hate communism? Why does anticommunist propaganda still exist, when communism was the "criminal, totalitarian, evil" society as everybody from the FSC proclaims?

I believe that the main crime of communism was the result of socialism in practice and therefore, the rulers over democracy are doing everything they can to wipe out the truth. The recent democratic capitalist oligarchs are afraid that the ideas of socialism will spread over the world and destroy their privileges.

2.10. Result of the real experiment: Capitalism won in the former socialist countries

In this book I described the positive aspects of socialism versus capitalism. When I look around, however, I see mostly capitalism. The results of the real experiment of the competition between socialism and capitalism in the twentieth century are very clear, socialism lost. I can see the unlimited power of money in private hands, based on the laws passed by democratically elected parliaments. I can see how the totalitarian democracy operates freely and nearly everywhere. Nearly all democratically elected governments prefer capitalism. Right orientated governments prefer recent neo-liberal capitalism; on the other hand, left oriented ones prefer recent neo-liberal capitalism with a capitalistic human face. Communist and worker parties, like the one we had during the socialist program, currently get less votes at election, than the parties offering some kind of capitalism. How come? It is not a goal of this book to evaluate the collapse of twentieth century socialism in the FSC, but I will mention some of the many possible reasons. For example:

- Capitalism had several times higher economic power than socialism.
- Socialism of the twentieth century was rigid and did not reflect changes of development of the society.
- Socialism restricted personal freedom.
- Total collective property is inconvenient for development of recent economy and society.
- Socialism was too ahead of the mental level of most of the population.
- Capitalism convinced more people by real facts or by propaganda.
- Totality of capitalism is more sophisticated than totality of communism.
- Totality of democracy is more efficient than totality of communism.
- Human beings are only programmable machines, using old programs by those that survived for the last 10 million years. The old programs are not (yet) compatible with socialism. To modify them it will take years.

I can use analogical reasoning for the results found in many other real experiments. There are even examples of new ideas and developments being destroyed by backward systems. We may ask the question of why for example, did democracy in ancient Greece not survive, why was Minoan civilization in Crete destroyed by barbaric invaders, why was the Roman Empire lost to barbarians, why were many developed kingdoms in

Mesopotamia regularly destroyed by primitive invaders for the last 3,000 years, why did Hitler defeat France in WWII?

There was a time when slavery and many Gods were generally accepted as the best base for society. It was similar in Buddhism or Hinduism. Later it was the worshipping of only one God in Christian and Islam religions. Colonialism was generally accepted as the best base for the colonial society. Today the neo-liberal capitalistic democracy plays the same role. And most likely, young socialism is knocking at the door.

3. Crimes of Democracy versus Crimes of Communism

Real experiment in the world - myths, facts and mysteries

3.1. The transition from socialism to capitalism in the former socialist countries - mysteries of the magical word 'democracy'

It is widely accepted that the grand experiment of scientific socialism (Communism) was a failure. The legacy of Communism isn't simply a small difference in the quality of living between the Communist and free economies. The legacy of Communism left killing fields stretching from Europe to Asia. There are large piles of corpses in South America and Africa as well. Communism didn't simply fail. In its brief moment in the sun, Communism managed to claim many of the worst atrocities committed in human history
http://crasscommercial.com/page.html?a=9

The myths

In late 1997 a leading French publishing house, Robert Laffont, published Le Livre Noir du Communisme (The Black Book of Communism), an 850-page book of scholarly essays that collectively provide a history of Communism in the 20th century. The contributors to the book include some of the finest scholars from both the East and West, who have drawn extensively on new archival findings. Every country that lived (or is still living) under Communism -- the Soviet Union, the Eastern European countries, China, Vietnam, North Korea, Cambodia, Laos, Cuba, Mongolia, and so forth -- is covered. The book also features many crucial, previously unpublished documents from the former Communist archives.... Stéphane Courtois in his introduction to the Black Book concludes, "the total approaches 100 million people killed." ONE HUNDRED MILLION! And that's just the number killed, which doesn't take into account of the millions more whose lives were disrupted and ruined.

The facts

It is very easy to compare the crimes of democracy against the crimes of communism, since we have many results of real experiments from former socialist countries. In the previous part of the book I described the crimes of democracy versus the crimes of communism in Slovakia. One can do a similar comparison in other former socialist countries. The results of the transition to capitalism in the former Soviet Union countries are more severe than in Slovakia. For example, in 11 former socialist countries the economy declined to less than 60% of what it was after the transition to democracy (Figure 76). In Slovakia it was to 80% only. According to my knowledge, there are no publicly known books comparing socialism and capitalism in the countries. Why? To be precise, there are many publicly known books comparing communism and capitalism, telling of criminal communist societies, describing non-efficient economy and violation of human rights. They, for the most part, do not show any important data or any important facts. There are some books describing the results after the transition to democracy and capitalism in the former socialist countries.

Another way to compare the crimes of democracy versus the crimes of communism is to compare the crimes of the policies of the leader of communism – the former Soviet Union, with the crimes of democracy of the policies of the leader of democracy – the USA. This comparison I am going to do later.

Proof of the decline of societies in the former socialist countries, after they abandoned real "totalitarian" socialism and established real democratic capitalism are published in many official reports, e.g. in the UN report [17]. When I read the statistical data in the report, I have a feeling that it was not capitalistic democracy that was established but genocide in former socialist countries after 1989 followed by general decline of society. The UNDP publication reports that after 'the transition' the biggest single 'cost of the transition' has undoubtedly been the loss of lives represented by the decline in life expectancy among young and middle-aged men. The decline in life expectancy has meant that several million people have not survived the 1990's, who would have done so if the life expectancy levels reached in the 1980's had been maintained. The number of missed men in the FSC after the transition from 1990-1999, reached 9.7 million. The cost of the transition has been the rise and persistently high level of morbidity, characterized by higher incidence of common illnesses and by the spread of such diseases as tuberculosis. It is also characterized by the extraordinary rise in poverty – both income and human poverty, the rise in income and wealth inequality, unemployment, drug addiction, homicide, suicide and so on. The costs of the transition across the whole region highlighted the dramatic and widespread deterioration of human security.

Recent UN publication, HDR 2005 p. 23, put it in seven stronger term: "Mortality crisis in the Russian Federation: 7 million 'missing' men. Life expectancy at birth in the Russian Federation is among the lowest for industrial countries: 65 years compared with 79 years in Western Europe. Since the early 1990s there has been a marked increase in male mortality over and above the historical trend. The number of additional deaths during 1992–2001 is estimated at 2.5–3 million. In the absence of war, famines or health epidemics there is no recent historical precedent for the scale of the loss. Mortality is higher among men than women, especially among single and less educated men. In 2003 life expectancy was 59 years for Russian men and 72 years for women, one of the widest gender gaps in the world. If normal mortality ratios prevailed, 7 million more men would be alive in Russia."

According to the World Bank, World Development Indicators 1999: Nowhere are these problems more evident than in the states of the former Soviet Union, where the numbers living in poverty increased from 14 million in 1989 to some 147 million by the middle of the decade, a ten-fold increase.

I will present other data obtained from HDRs and other sources, to show further results of the real experiment of the real capitalist democracy versus real "totalitarian" socialism in the FSC. The data are in agreement with the UNDP publications.

According to HDR 2003 (World Bank 2002, Figure 77) the annual per capita income growth in the 1990's was the worst in the FSC. After the transformation of socialism to the capitalistic democracy the average income decreased 1.9% each year, which was a higher decrease than in Sub-Saharan Africa countries (only 0.4% per year). According to the same report the poverty reduction in the 1990's was worst in the former socialist countries. After the transformation of socialism to capitalism and democracy poverty increased 13.5% each year, which was significantly higher than in Sub-Saharan Africa countries (poverty increase 1.6%) (Figure 78). Population living in poverty in some FSC countries increased more than 30% (Figure 79). Changes in the share and number of people living on $2 a day in the FSC were 6.8% or 31 mill. in 1990 and 20.3% or 97 mill. in 1999 (HDR 2003, p. 41). Time dependent data of income poverty in Europe and Central Asia show that after 1990 poverty significantly increased due to regression in the FSC (Figure 80).

It is unbelievable that the decrease in income and the increase of poverty in the FSC occurred in spite of the highly educated population, high quality of workers and industrial development, and high levels of scientific knowledge in the countries, particularly in comparison to the Sub-Saharan countries. These were unbelievable results from the introduction of capitalism and democracy into the FSC. Probably only a big war could produce similar results. Paradoxically, this situation is the result of the policy of democrats, humanists and fighters for human rights and freedom, the people who are celebrated by recent democracy.

Economic development of the world regions in different years is shown in Figures 81-82. The annual average compound growth rates of per capita growth in 1913-1950 were the highest in the former USSR in spite of damages caused by World War I and II and the civil war after the Bolshevik revolution in 1917 (Figure 81). Eastern Europe countries had lower development growth, about half that of the developed world. On the other hand, capitalist China had the worst performance. During 1950-1973 the rate of growth in the Eastern Europe countries, the former USSR and China was high when compared to developed countries (Figure 82). In 1973-1980 growth decreased significantly in the former USSR and increased significantly in China (Figure 83). During all these years, there was no negative growth as was seen in the FSC after the establishment of democracy and capitalism.

If we take Russia as an example of "communist totality", its agricultural, industrial and GDP productions increased during socialism and dramatically decreased after the introduction of democracy and capitalism (Figure 76, 84-86). The decrease of GDP and the deterioration of the society occurred in all countries in spite of different parties and religions having governed in the countries [18]. This demonstrates that the regression of society after the abandonment of socialism and acceptance of capitalistic democracy is a general law.

A very clear description of the results of the real experiment of the economic and social development of the former Soviet Union after the abandonment of socialism and introduction of democracy and capitalism one can find in [19]. To understand the shocking results of the introduction of democracy, I will quote the coauthor of the book [19], leading Russian economist Vladimir Popov: "By the end of the 1990's output (GDP, Soviet Union) fell by about 50% as compared to the highest pre-recession level of 1989, investment dropped even more, income inequalities rose greatly so that real incomes declined dramatically for the majority of the population, death rates increased by about 50%, whereas life expectancy declined markedly. In Russia output fell by 45% in 1989-98, death rates increased from 1% in the 1980s to 1.5% in 1994 and stayed at this high level thereafter, which was equivalent to over 700,000 additional deaths annually. Over the period of several years such population losses could be likened to the impact of a big war. By way of comparison, during WWII the national income in the USSR fell by only 20% in 1940-42, recovered to its 1940 level in 1944, fell again by 20% in 1944-46 during conversion of the defense industry, but already exceeded its 1940 level by nearly 20% in 1948.... in China and Vietnam there was no transformational recession at all – on the contrary, from the very outset of reforms economic growth accelerated."

More data from the results of the real experiment, in which violation of human rights increased after introducing democracy and capitalism are shown in the Figure 87. The crude mortality increased and the birth rate decreased significantly after the introduction democracy and capitalism in Russia. Similarly, HIV infection, drug-related convictions, and suicides increased after the introduction of real capitalism. A comparison of the incidence of tuberculosis, as a poverty index, clearly shows decline during socialism and increase during capitalism (Figure 88). Increase of alcoholism, homicides, violent crimes, drug addiction, HIV infection, suicides and other negative data of the society increased after the introduction of democracy and capitalism. These findings support the conclusion of significantly higher levels of crimes of democracy versus the crimes of communism (Figures 89-91). Simply, the FSC declined to the level of the old traditional democratic countries.

Other proof of the regression of the Russian society after the introduction of democracy and capitalism in also confirmed in a UN report [20]: "With a Human development index (HDI) of 0.862 in 1990, Russia ranked 37 out of a total of 173 countries, according to the Human Development Report, 1993. In 1998, however, with a HDI of 0.771, Russia dropped to a ranking of 62 out of 174 countries, according to the Human Development Report, 2000."

Many kinds of human rights violations unknown during socialism started flourishing after the introduction of democracy in the FSC. One of them is the trafficking of human beings. According to the report of E.V. Tiurukanova [21] "Trafficking occurs across state borders as well as within states, and in countries which have a long-established tradition of democracy, as well as in those with totalitarian systems of power. The total number of victims of cross-border trafficking is now estimated at 600,000 – 800,000 per annum, or 2 – 4 million, if victims of internal trafficking are included. International reports point out that 80 percent of the victims of cross-border trafficking are women and children, 70 percent of whom are sold to other countries for the purpose of sexual exploitation.... The Central and Eastern European countries, including the territory of the former Soviet Union, rank second after South-East Asia in regards to the scale of trafficking in human beings: 175,000 women are taken out of this area a year for the purpose of human trafficking. One third to one-fifth of this figure is comprised of women from the Russian Federation, i.e. roughly 57,750 to 35,000 women a year. Even if this estimate is high, these figures do not take into account the large flows of human trafficking of migrants for criminal purposes from the CIS Republics into Russia or between the CIS Republics".

The Russian Assembly of NGO's has announced (March 22, 2006) that the level of human trafficking within the country and out of the country is so high that it threatens national security and the country's gene pool. Two thousand cases of human trafficking were brought before the courts last year alone. Official statistics show that there are no less than 500,000 cases of women being sold in Russia.

Amounting to further atrocities of real democracy and real capitalism established in the former socialist countries are homeless street children. These atrocities are clearly described in the United Nations Children's Fund (UNICEF) reports [22], BBC news, general news and in reports of many human and democratic institutions. Paradoxically, as I mentioned many times, the organizations have not used the expression 'atrocities of democracy and capitalism', or 'crimes of capitalists' or the word 'socialism', or phrase 'after countries abandoned real socialism and have established real democracy and capitalism'. According to official Russian government estimations, UNICEF reports, and many other non-governmental organizations, there were about one million homeless children in Russia in the 1990's. A UNICEF report [22] has found that 18 million children in the FSC were living in conditions of extreme poverty. There were 1.5 million children in out-of-home care at the end of the 1990's, about 150,000 more than at the start of the decade, with the sharpest increase in the Baltic states. In Russia and the Ukraine, for example, one child in seven was undernourished, while in Albania, Uzbekistan and Tajikistan the figure rises to one in three. Kyrgyzstan, Kazakhstan and Romania were the worst affected by tuberculosis, while one 1999 study found that Estonia had the highest incidence of drug-resistant tuberculosis in the world. Eastern Europe and the former Soviet Union had the world's fastest growing rates of HIV infection (BBC News, Nov 29, 2001).

A recent report from a representative of UNICEF (Nov 15, 2005) estimates 150,000 homeless children in Russia, a figure that is much below than the official figures. This difference is due to the fact that UNICEF regards only those children who have lost their parents and there is no one to look after them as homeless. On the other hand the Russian government calls children who periodically run away from their home homeless and also takes into account the problems faced by those children who are not necessarily homeless.

On the other hand, the established democracy in Russia produced a very few very rich people and many poor in 1-5 years. Why are the rules of capitalistic democracy producing the few very rich people and the many poor? Where are the rulers of the capitalistic democracy introduced to the world as "democrats and humanists"?

However, somebody may say that there is not democracy in Russia. I do not agree. It is real democracy based on a multiparty system of regular free elections, similar to England, Iraq, Afghanistan and other African and Latin American countries.

The mysteries

When I read the publications mentioned above, I noticed at least two curiosities. Firstly, the authors did not use word - socialism. They did not say, "after the former socialist countries abandoned socialism and established democracy and capitalism", the society deteriorated significantly. Instead of this precise description, they used the expression, "after the transition" or "decade of transition". I do not know why, but my guess is that it is a result of the recent totalitarian information system we are living in. Secondly, the authors mostly showed what happened "after the transition". They rarely show trends of development of the society ten years before the transition and compared it with the ten years after the transition, as I did for Slovakia. If they published the data trends, the reader would have a complete picture and could easily compare the crimes of democracy versus the crimes of communism.

The official publications presented numerous examples of evidence of general regression and many cases of degeneration of the society after the transition (which means: after the abandonment of socialism and the introduction of real democracy and real capitalism). The comparison of the data of the 15 years before and the 15 years after "the transition" shows clear evidence that the crimes of democracy are several times higher than the crimes of communism in the FSC. I recommend to anybody who is interested in the crimes of democracy, and a comparison of the results of real capitalism versus real socialism, to study the above-mentioned official publications.

The atrocities of real democracy and capitalism in the FSC are clear and well documented. What is not clear is why many respected scholars, democrats and humanists do not call the data proof that recent democratic capitalism is a criminal, evil system that is killing people at the rate of a big war or epidemic. Why do students at school in democratic countries learn about communism in this way, "*In its brief moment in the sun, Communism managed to claim many of the worst atrocities committed in human history*". Is it a result of the decline of brain function of many respected scholars, democrats and humanists by capitalistic democracy? I assume yes, the presented data clearly show it.

In spite of the facts, nearly all rhetoric, as written in hundreds of books, by respected democratic capitalistic scholars is about the failure of socialist agriculture, industry, GDP, living standard, and human rights in the former Soviet Union. Their predictions on solving the problems include the abandonment of socialism, planned economy and introduction of democracy and capitalism. The results of real experiments are completely the opposite. Why is it not generally recognized?

Why is it forbidden to use the word "socialism", when respected democrats and humanists refer to the system before "the transition" in the former socialist countries? It is because the rulers over democracy would not only like to bury the truth about socialism, but even want the word socialism to be forgotten. This is a result of the democracy of free expression.

There are many books describing the crimes of Stalin, communists, and communism. There are many books describing the crimes of capitalist-democratic countries, but the capitalist crimes are not called the crimes of democracy or the crimes of liberal capitalism, or the crimes of capitalist freedom of expression. Why is it forbidden to use the expression "crimes of democracy, crimes of capitalists, crimes of democrats" or "crimes of capitalism", when respected democrats and humanists refer to crimes which happen in capitalist and democratic states?

I wonder, why there are not one million well known novels describing the misery of one million children in FSC living on the streets or in sewage canals as a result of capitalism and democracy. Why are there not thousands of movies showing thousands of people frozen to death, highlighting the results of the capitalistic democracy in FSC? Why there are not one million very good movies about one million girls democratically sold as animals for sex on the free market, highlighting that this was possible only after democracy was introduced in the FSC? Where are Aleksandr Solzhenitsyn, Milan Kundera or George Orwell? Is it possible that democracy also brought the degeneration of brain function making animal instincts prevail over humanity as a result of the practical function of democracy? I believe firmly that it must be so. I did not find any other reason except that the power of capitalistic democracy is so astonishing that, to produce such movies is not possible under the democratic rule of free expression.

Imagine there's no Stalin

It's easy if you try. Imagine that in the autumn 1941, when Hitler's army stopped in front of Moscow, Stalin got out and welcomed Hitler. Stalin would say to Hitler, "Yes, you won the war; I gave up. Please, my Red army, having 25 million soldiers, all military industry and all resources are available at your command. What would have happened if 70% of Hitler's army stopped fighting against the Red army and could have been used to fight in other fronts? What would have happened if Hitler had the Red army with all military resources at his disposal? The answer is very simple. He would have fulfilled his dreams. He would have won the war against England and very probably against the USA. Nobody could have beaten him. The consequences of that would be obvious. For example, Jews would not exist, as would be the case with many non-Aryans minorities. All "subhuman" Slavs, if any survived, would live somewhere behind Ural, and fed with vodka and tobacco. Frenchmen would proudly speak German. Certainly, the magical word "democracy" would have a different meaning and recent democrats and humanists would be in a different position. How would the European Union function if there were no Stalin? Of course, the European parliament would function on different rules, if any. What would be the suffering counts of Jews, Roma, Slavs and other non-Aryan populations if there were no Stalin?

It is clear for me that Stalin saved European civilization against Nazism – fascism. That Europe is a civilized democratic state and not Hitler's Third Reich. It is clear to me that Stalin saved more millions of Soviet Union citizens than he sacrificed.

I imagine that the role of Stalin in WWII is a dilemma for most European capitalistic democrats and humanists. For the Christian and capitalist European civilizations, it is unacceptable to tell the truth and present Stalin as the hero who saved European civilization, because he was atheist, communist and leader of the Communist party. Therefore, nearly each day we are bombarded by the presentation of Stalin as a criminal, mass-murder and totalitarian dictator. The rulers over democracy want to persuade us that because Stalin was a criminal it means that Marxism is a criminal theory.

In spite of many inhuman decisions Stalin made, I need to thank him because I am speaking Slovak in the middle of Europe and not behind Ural. I would also thank him because Slavs are still members of multicultural Europe. If I were a Jew, I would thank Stalin even more, and put his portrait in my private synagogue to remind me, 'thank you comrade Stalin that we exist'. If I were a member of the European Parliament I would make the suggestion to place Stalin's statue in front of the European Parliament, since the place belongs to him.

One of the many tricks of the brainwashing machine

The recent democratically-totalitarian system uses many tricks to keep demoserfdom alive. One of them is to use purposely cumulative data or instant data. For example, the atrocities of Stalin are cumulative data for 33 years. But when counting homeless children in Russia, (e.g. UNICEF (Nov 15, 2005) estimates 150,000 homeless children in Russia), it is an instant number. What would it be if we had cumulative data for 1990-2006? How many children combined were homeless for at least for 1 month during 1990-2006? Is it 1 million, 10 million or even more? How many beggars have accumulated during 1990-2006? I do not know. Why doesn't any social scientific institution present the results of these issues and cumulatively count children or people suffering?

Similarly in Slovakia the cumulative number of crimes of communism for 40 years is emphasized everyday. On the other hand, recent numbers of social pathologies in Slovakia are instant numbers for one year. Nobody asks how many homeless people, beggars or unemployed citizens we have had cumulatively for the last 16 democratic years. Paradoxically, we know how many chamois are living in the Slovakian mountains each year, but we do not know how many homeless people, beggars or overdose deaths we have for even one year. The numbers are not publicly known at least. The democratic freedom of information does not allow this.

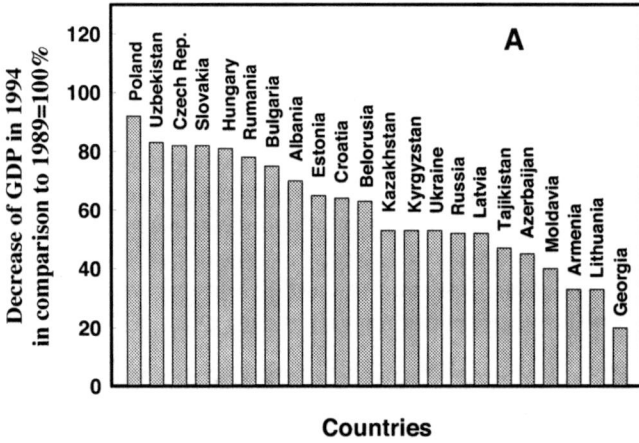

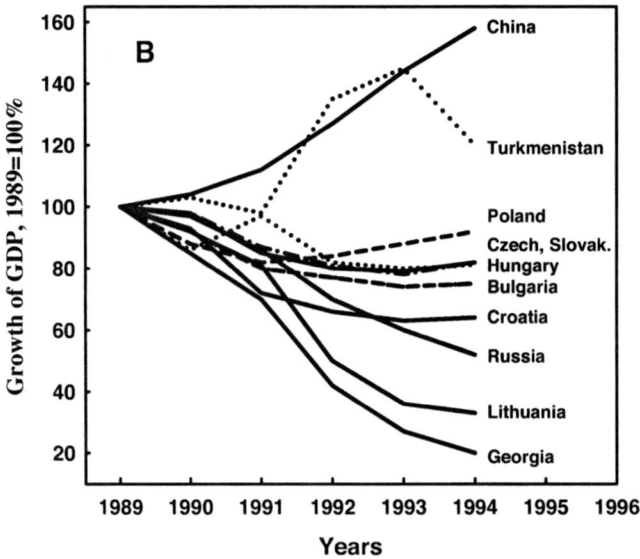

National statistics and direct communications
and from National statistical offices to UN/ECE secretariat, 1995

Figure 76

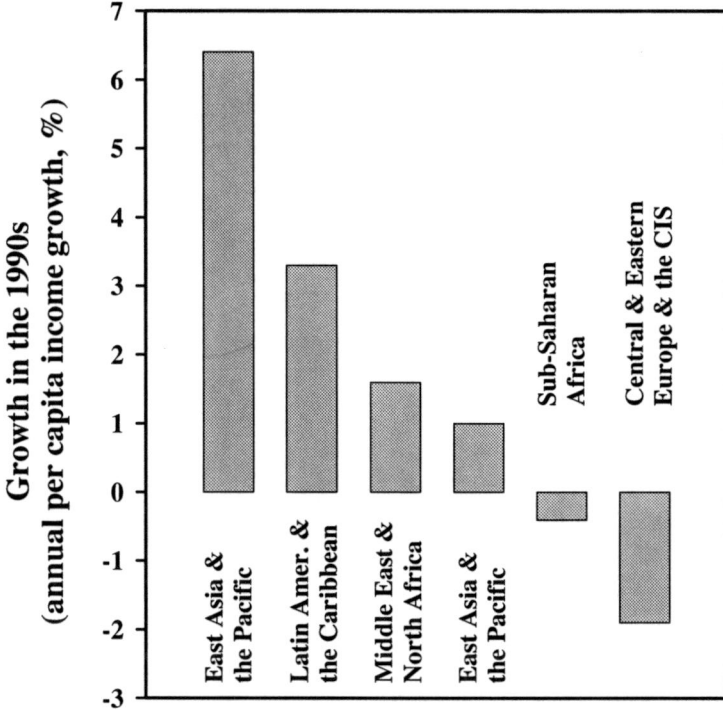

Human Development Report 2003, p. 53
(World Bank 2002)

Figure 77

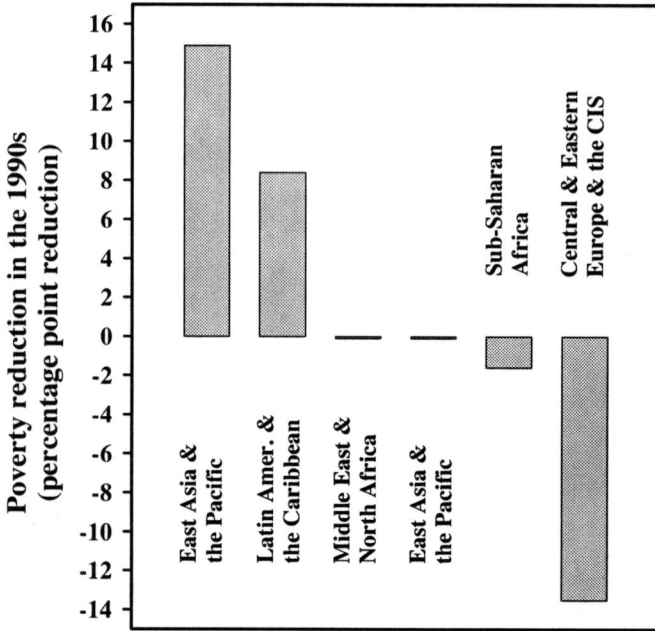

Human Development Report 2003, p. 53
(World Bank 2002)

Figure 78

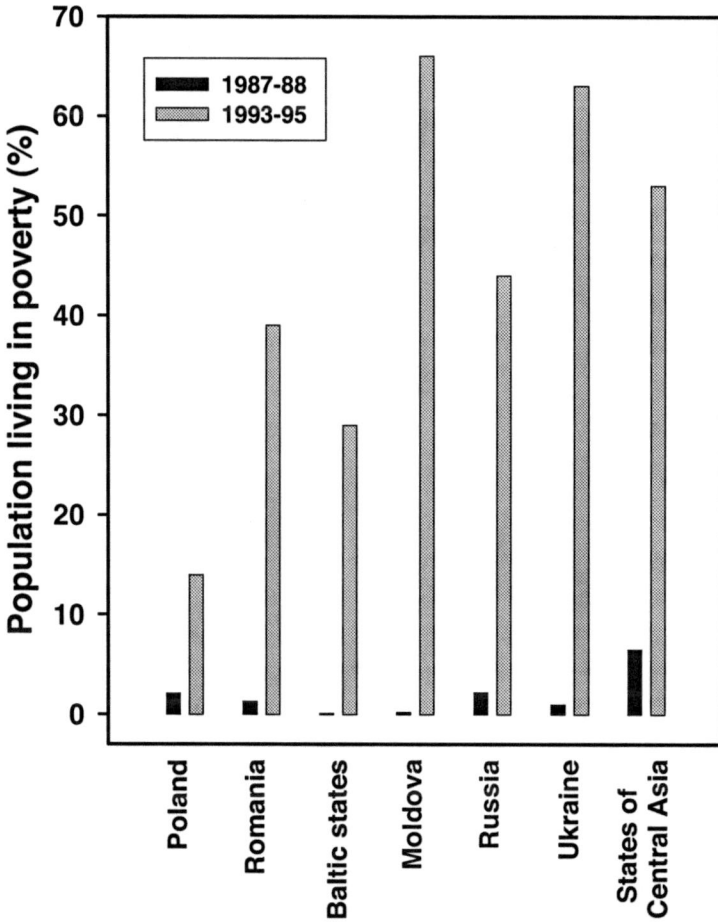

The World Bank report: World Development Indicators, 1999

Figure 79

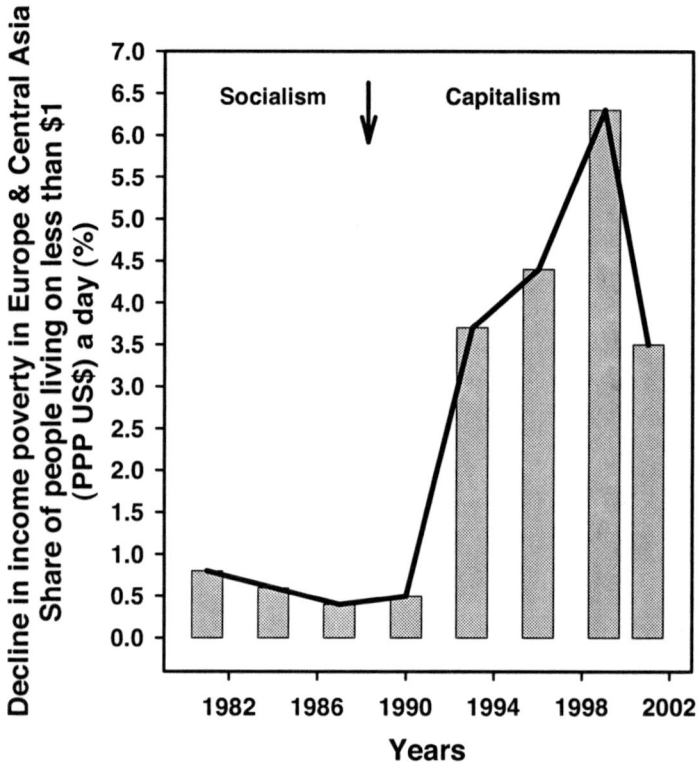

Human Development Report 2005
Source: World Bank 2005d

Figure 80

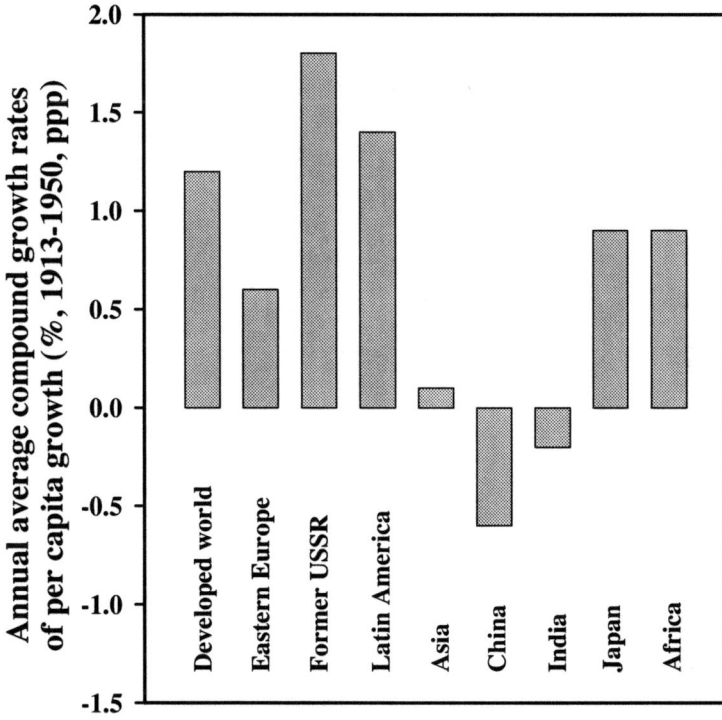

UN: World Economic and Social Survey 2006, p. 5.
Angus Maddison (2001): The World Economy:
A Millennial Perspective.

Figure 81

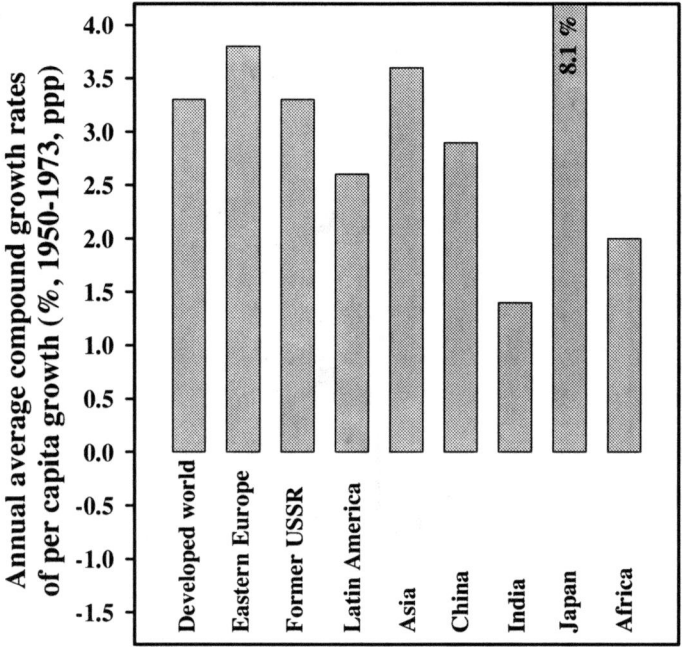

Annual average compound growth rates of per capita growth (%, 1950-1973, ppp)

Bars: Developed world, Eastern Europe, Former USSR, Latin America, Asia, China, India, Japan (8.1 %), Africa

UN: World Economic and Social Survey 2006, p. 5.
Angus Maddison (2001): The World Economy:
A Millennial Perspective.

Figure 82

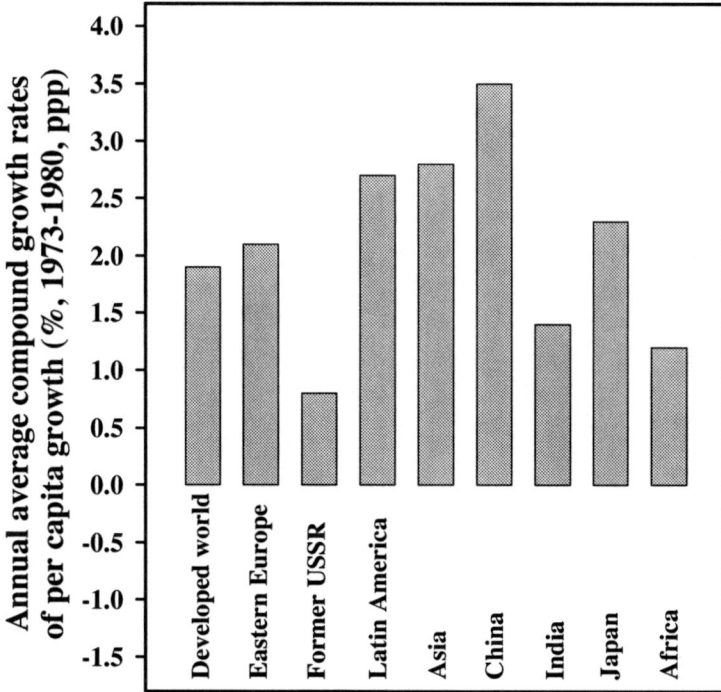

UN: World Economic and Social Survey 2006, p. 5.
Angus Maddison (2001): The World Economy:
A Millennial Perspective.

Figure 83

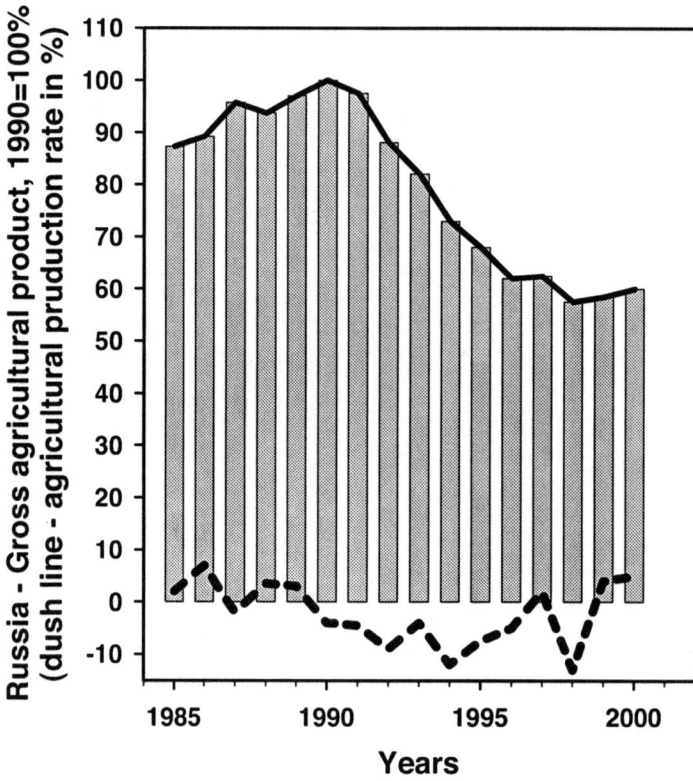

Human Development Report 2001, Russian Federation

Figure 84

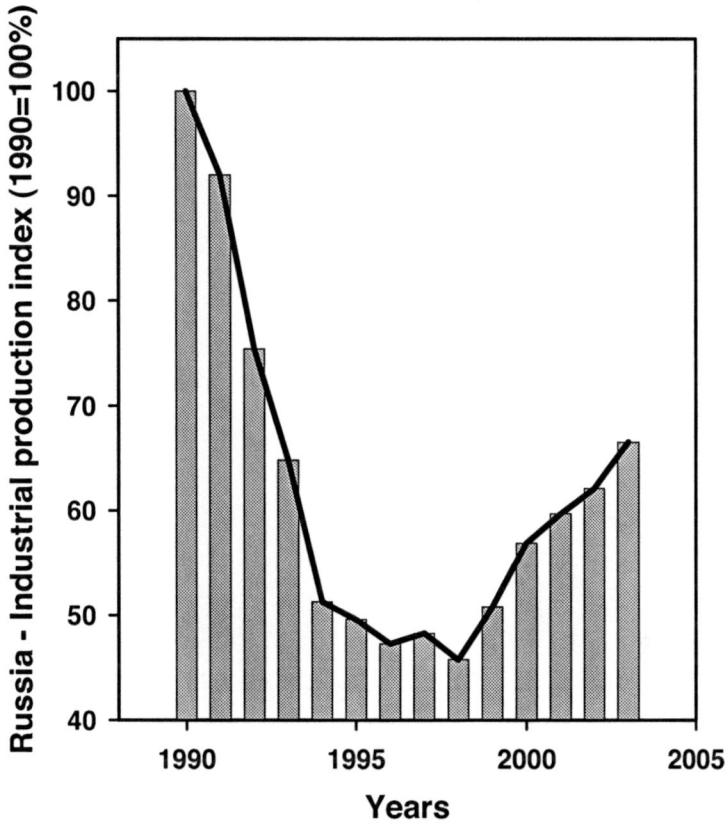

Human Development Report 2004, Russian Federation

Figure 85

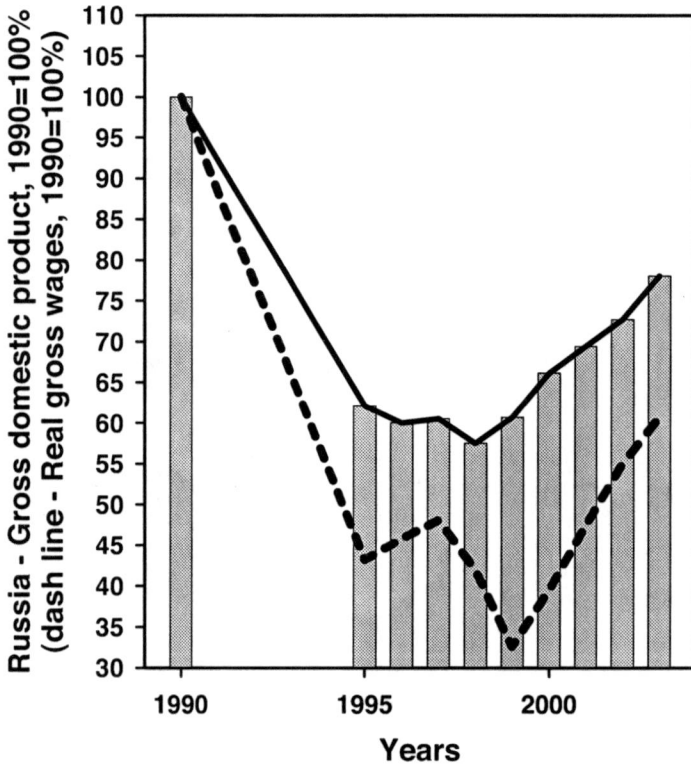

Human Development Report 2004, Russian Federation

Figure 86

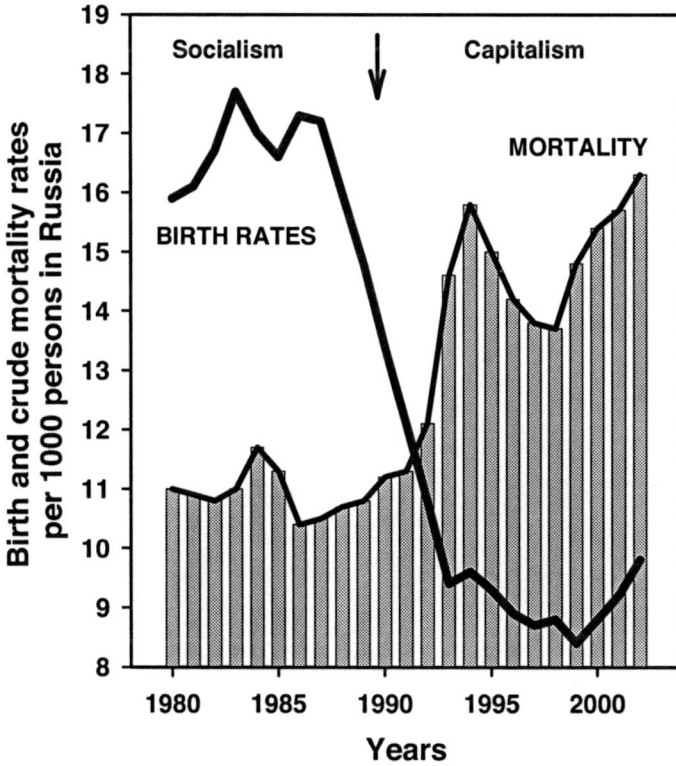

Human Development Report 2005, Russian Federation
Russia in 2015: Development goals and policy priorities

Figure 87

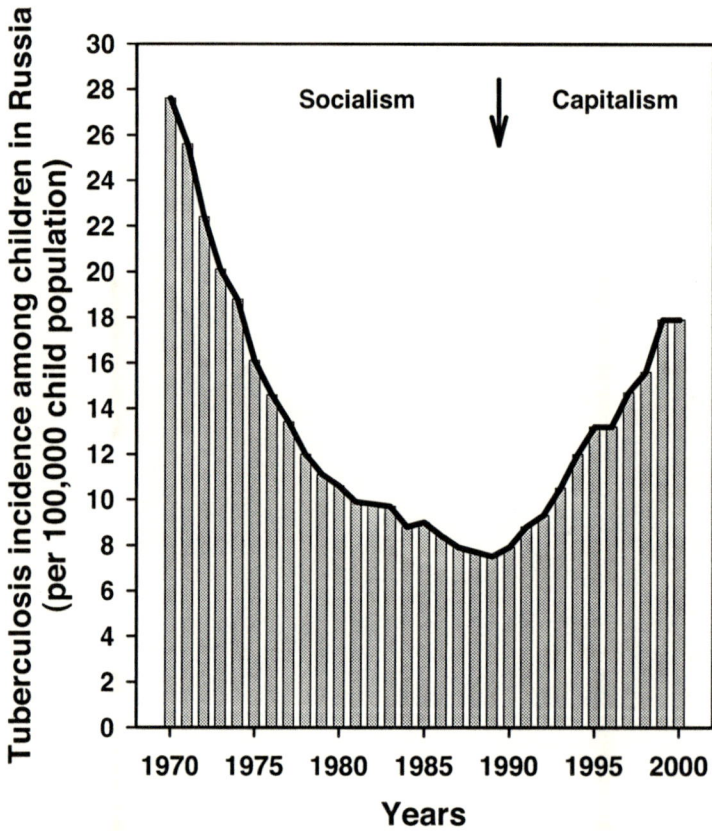

Human Development Report 2001, Russian Federation

Figure 88

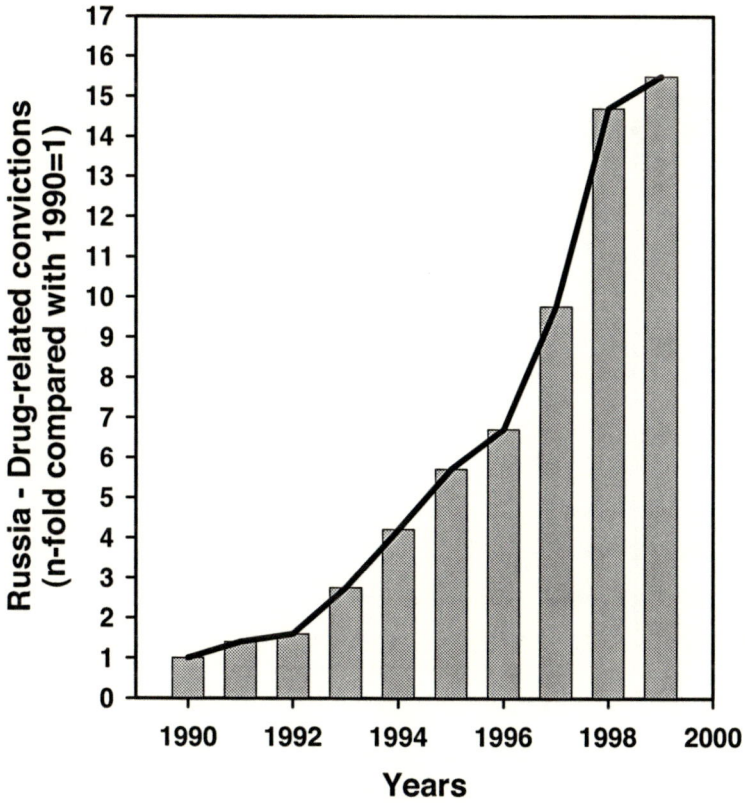

Human Development Report 2001, Russian Federation

Figure 89

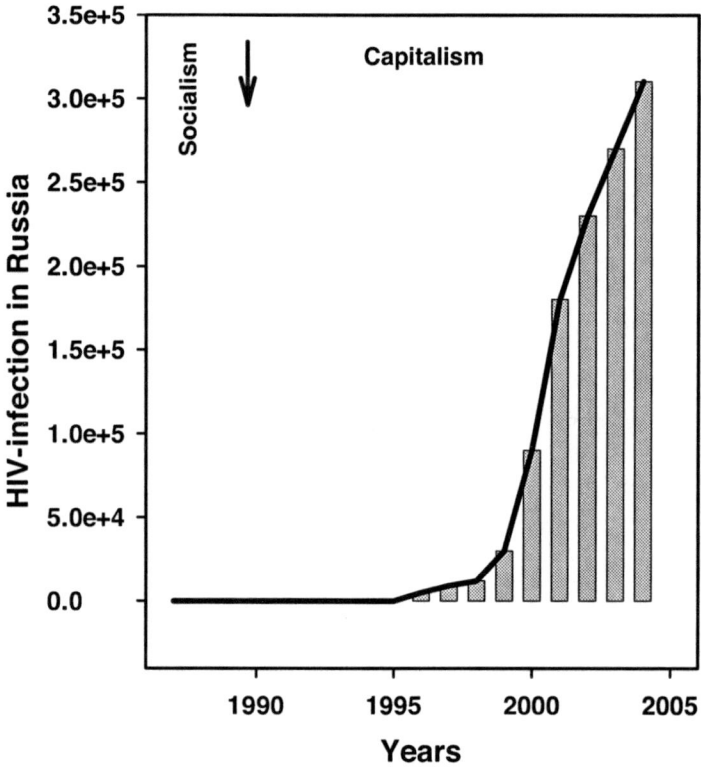

**Human Development Report 2005, Russian Federation
Russia in 2015: Development goals and policy priorities**

Figure 90

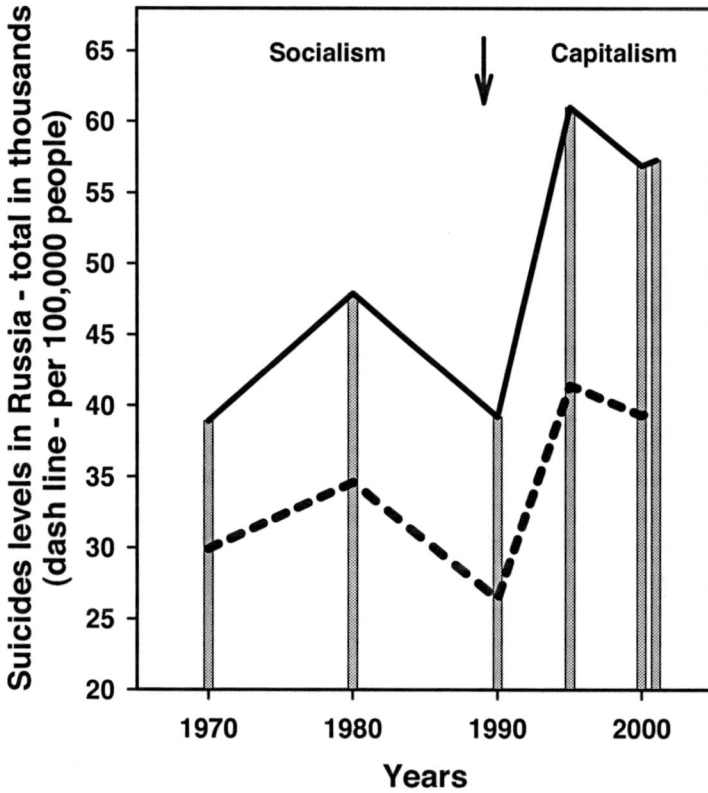

Human Development Report 2004, Russian Federation

Figure 91

3.2. Comparison of the "democratic" development of Russia and the "totalitarian" development of China

Capitalism is the only politico-economic system based on the doctrine of individual rights. This means that capitalism recognizes that each and every person is the owner of his own life, and has the right to live his life in any manner he chooses as long as he does not violate the rights of others

This website is created to explain the Superiority of Capitalism over Socialism.

http://www.srsd.org/search/studentprojects/2001/communism/

One can easily evaluate the crimes of democracy versus the crimes of communism in comparison to the development of the democratic capitalist Russia and the "totalitarian" communist China. There is a lot of evidence of decline in the democratic Russia and the general improvement of society in communist China. The next data were obtained from a real experiment and show clear results of the competition between democratic capitalism in Russia and "totalitarian" communism in China.

Comparison of the gross national income in purchasing power parity (PPP) in Russia and China is in Figure 92. The data show that income decreased in Russia after the abandonment of real socialism and the introduction of real democracy and capitalism. But, the income increased in China, who did not establish democracy and capitalism as was the case in Russia or developed capitalist countries. A similar trend is shown by the comparison of the growth of the GDP index of Russia, China and the USA. The GDP increased to 388% in China, 158% in the USA and decreased to 96% in Russia in 2005 with comparison to 1991=100% (Figure 93).

The regression of the society in Russia due to introduction of real democracy and real capitalism was followed by the violation of human rights – poverty. The opposite effect was observed in China, who did not followed the advice and pressure of world known democrats and humanists. As a UN publication remarks, "Much of the impressive reduction in global poverty has been driven by China's incredible economic growth of more than 9% a year in the 1990's, lifted 150 million people out of poverty", (HDR 2003, p. 41). The number of hungry people fell by nearly 20 million in the 1990s. But excluding China, the number of hungry people increased (HDR 2003, p. 20)...".

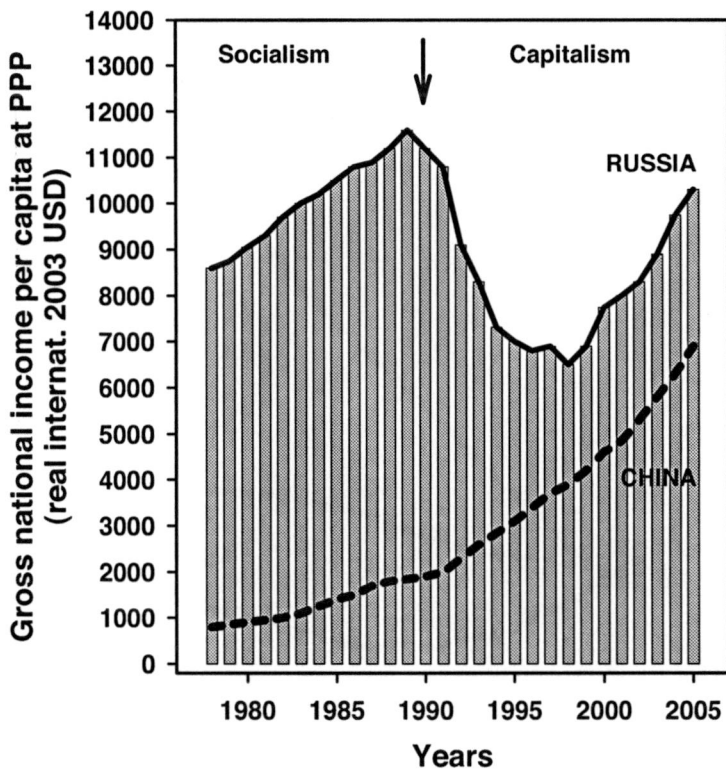

**The 2005 press release of the World Trade Organization (WTO)
http://www.wto.org/english/news_e/pres05_e/pr401_e.htm**

Figure 92

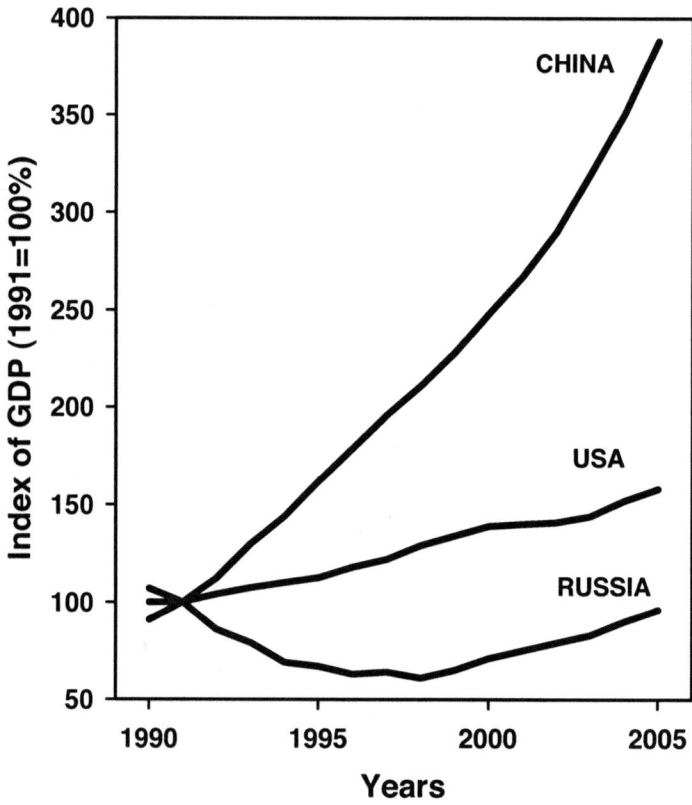

The 2005 press release of the World Trade Organization (WTO)
http://www.wto.org/english/news_e/pres05_e/pr401_e.htm

Figure 93

3.3. The on-line experiment of the competition between "totalitarian communism" in China and the democracy in India

And now the Internet is poised to narrow the gap (digital divide) that separates rich nations from poor nations even further in the decade to come (Engardio1). These points demonstrate how well capitalism works and how it has helped the world. These pieces of information are evidence of why capitalism is politically, economically, and socially superior to socialism.

This website is created to explain the Superiority of Capitalism over Socialism.

http://www.srsd.org/search/studentprojects/2001/communism/

Several reports show documentation that describes the general economic and social performance of China has been better than that of India for the last 25 years. It was not so in the past. According to the presentations of T. N. Srinivasan and S. Park [23]: "Maddison's historical analysis suggests that China and India had the same real per capita income in 1870. But by 1950, when the Communist regime took over, China's per capita income had declined by 17% while India's had increased by 16%. It took nearly two and a half decades, that is, from 1950 to 1973, for China to recover the lost ground with double India's rate of growth of per capita income. It is reasonable to presume that China and India again were roughly at the same level of per capita income in 1980, two years after Deng Xiao Ping abandoned the Maoist economic strategy that led to the death of 30 millions or more and initiated systemic reforms.... However, although both economies experienced acceleration in growth during 1980-2000 compared to the previous three decades, China's average growth rate of per capita income, at nearly 9% per year, far exceeded India's 4% per year, so that China's per capita income was nearly 70% higher than India's by 2000". An estimate of China's and India's per capita real incomes show that, starting from roughly equal levels in 1870, India forged ahead of China until the outbreak of the First World War. Though both experienced declines in their per capita incomes thereafter, China more so than India by 1950, India's per capita income was about 40% higher than China's and it took roughly the next three decades for China to catch up. Since 1980, China has forged much farther ahead" [24] (Figure 94).

According to Asia Times [25] China's GDP grew by an average of 9.7 percent during 1982-92, and by 9 percent during 1992-02. On the other hand, India grew by 5.6 percent and 6 percent in the same respective periods, still impressive by most developing countries' standards.

The human rights violations, mainly the violation of Article 1 of the Declaration of Human Rights "All human beings are born free and equal in dignity and rights…" in China and India are compared in many official institutions. According to the World Development Indicators 2005 [26]: mortality is under 5 (per 1000), under 5 malnutrition (%), and poverty ratio (% below 1 USD a day) for China/India are 37/87, 12.1/45.8, and 16.6/34.7 (Figure 95). The data documents that in human parameters China is ahead of India.

The debate whether China's communist dictatorship or India's democratic system will deliver and sustain rapid and equitable economic growth in the long run dates back to the early fifties, soon after India's independence in 1947 and China's communist victory in 1949 [27]. The experimental results are clear. After WWII, China and India started from similar levels of development. Some scholars estimate that in the 1950's India's per capita GNP was significantly higher than China's. The results of the ongoing experiments clearly show that the performance of China in most parameters is better than India. Communist ideology has helped China more than the cult of the magical word "democracy" to India.

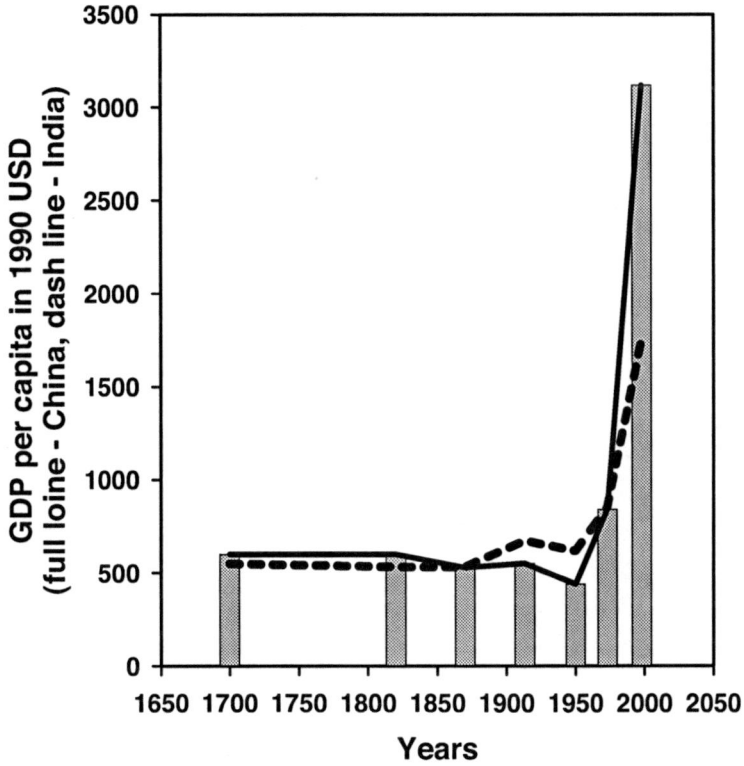

Maddison, Angus. 2002.
"Growth and Interaction in the World Economy:
The West and the Rest, 1000-2000 AD,"
paper presented at Harvard University, May 24, 2002.

Figure 94

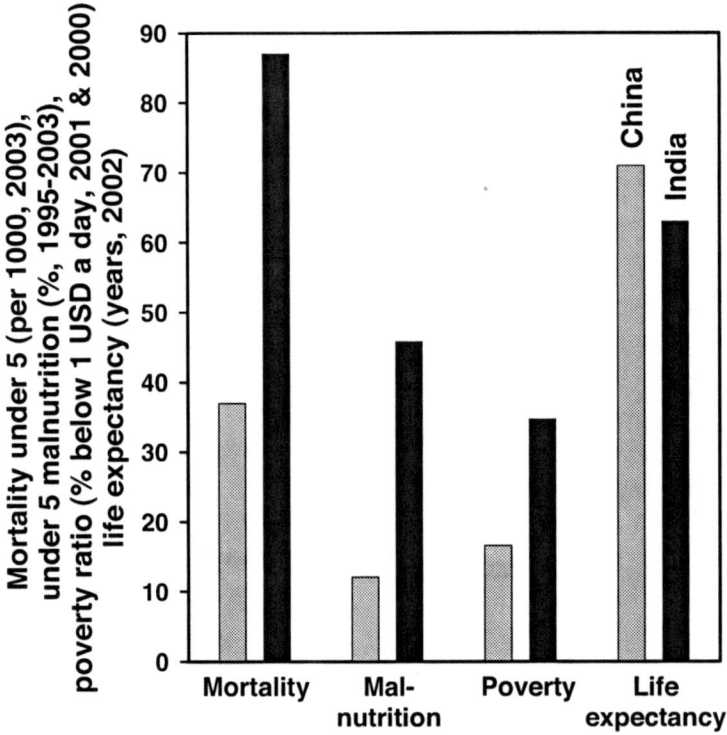

World Development Indicators (2005)
Institute of International Finance, RBI and CSO
(2004 data for India refer to the fiscal year 2004-05)
http://in.rediff.com/money/2005/sep/27china.htm

Figure 95

3.4. Comparison of "totalitarian" Cuba and the "freedom" countries around

As recent humanists and democrats in Slovakia and many others in the world used to say: There is only one totalitarian country in the Western hemisphere, where the communist regime of dictator Fidel Castro violates human rights. We need to do everything we can to remove the totalitarian regime in Cuba and install democracy and freedom for Cubans. Political leaders in the USA emphasize that Cuba is the only non-democratic country in the Western hemisphere. Nearly everyone compares the living standards and freedoms between Cuba and the USA.

How do we compare Cuba with the countries of the American continent? As it is seen from the figures below, real data show that the human and quality of life parameters for Cuba are better in comparison with most of the neighboring countries. Figure 96 shows that according to HDI, Cuba in 2001 was in tenth place of the 36 countries of the American continent. The HDI of Cuba is better than 25 democratic American countries. The quality of life in Cuba in literacy, infant mortality, mortality of children under 5 years, and life expectancy is very good in comparison to other neighbor countries (Figures 97-100).

After 1991, when the former Soviet Union stopped economic support to Cuba, quality of life in Cuba decreased (HDI from 60 to 85). After 1995 it increased again and in 2002, interestingly enough, it was better than it had been in 1988. It was also better than Russia (Figure 101). The figure also shows that quality of life in Russia decreased significantly after 1990.

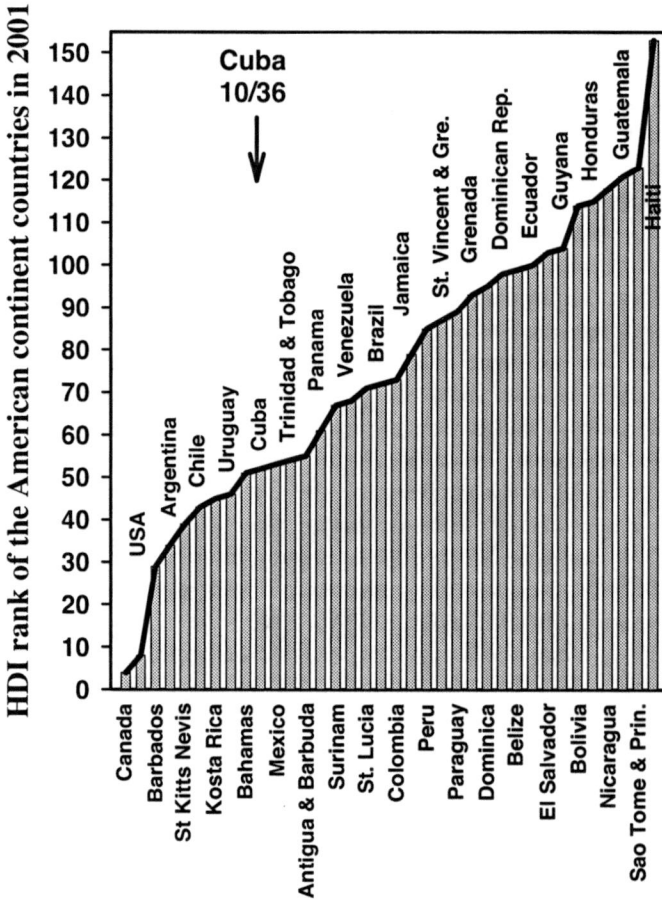

Human Development Report 2003

Figure 96

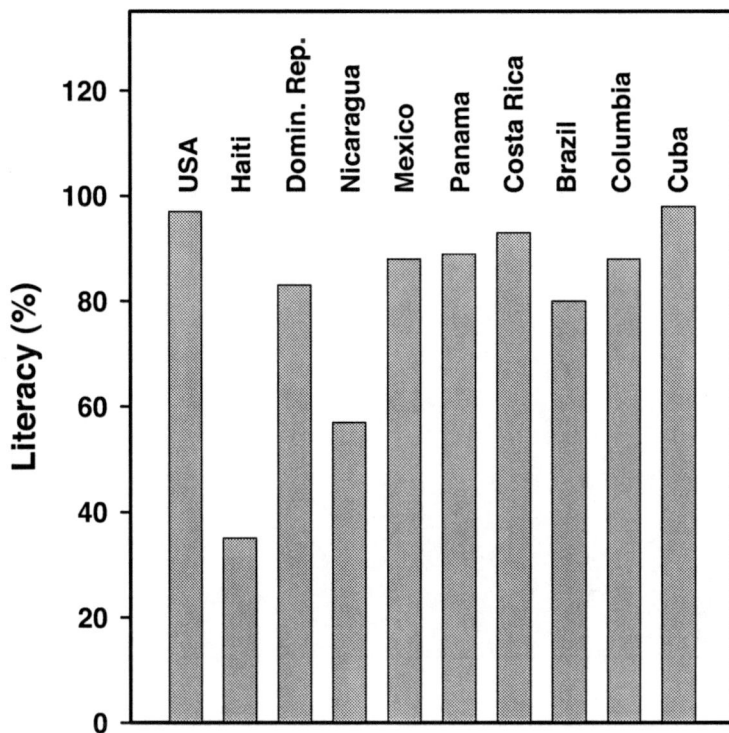

The World Factbook, 1996-1997
(CIA, Brassey's, Washington-London, 1996)

Figure 97

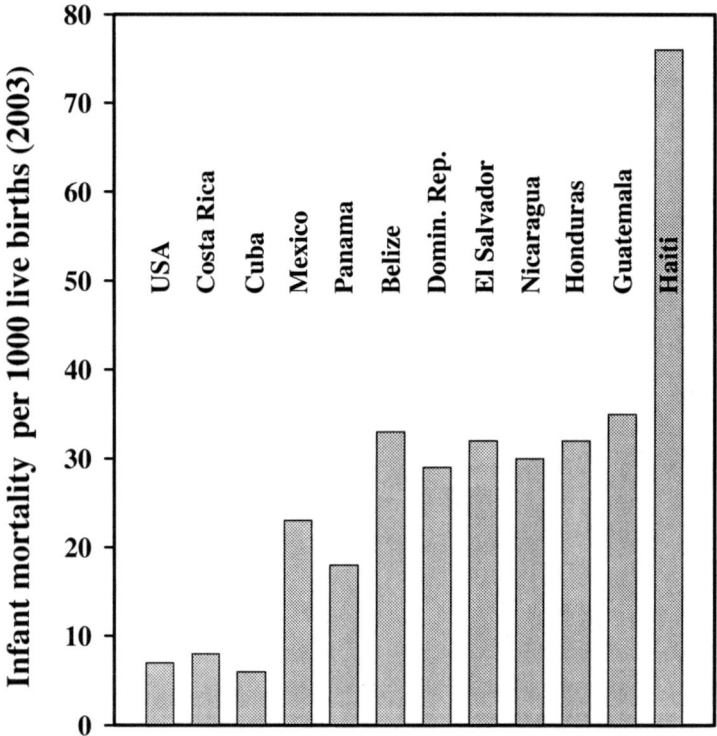

Human Development Report 2005

Figure 98

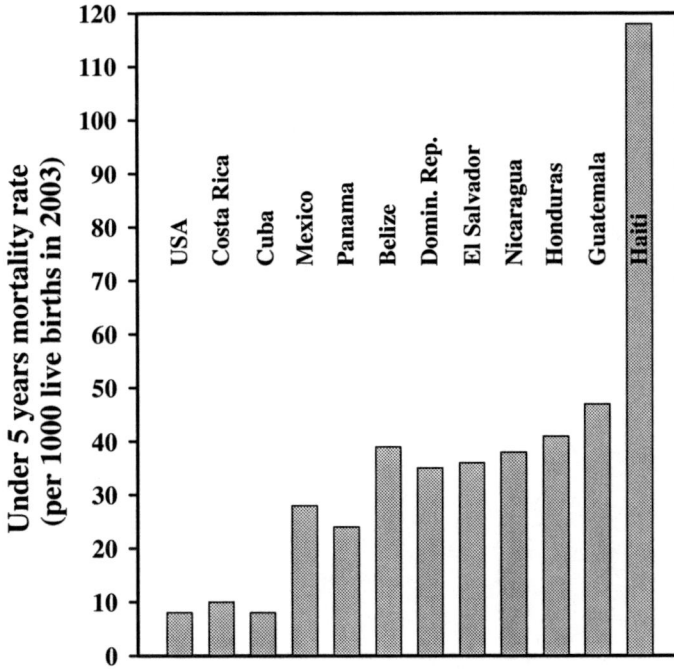

Human Development Report 2005

Figure 99

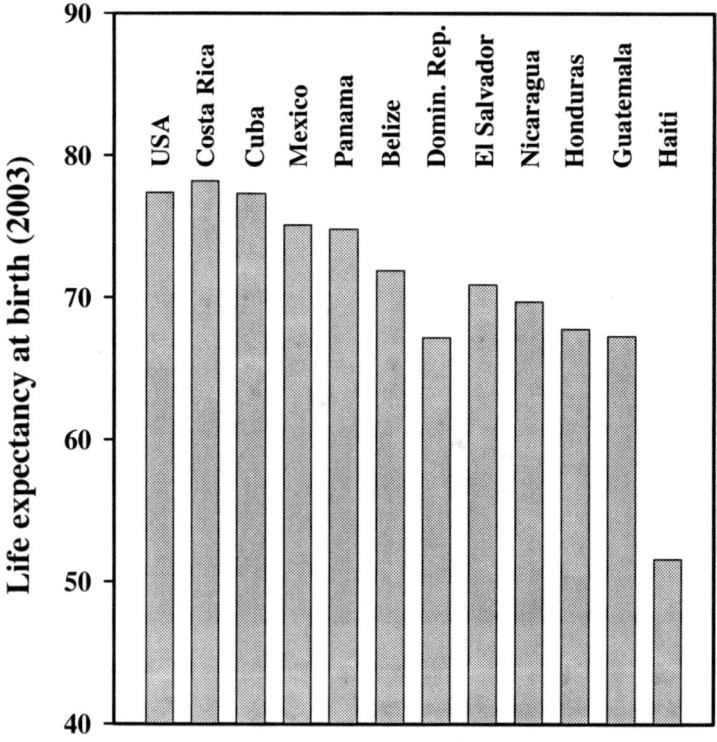

Human Development Report 2005

Figure 100

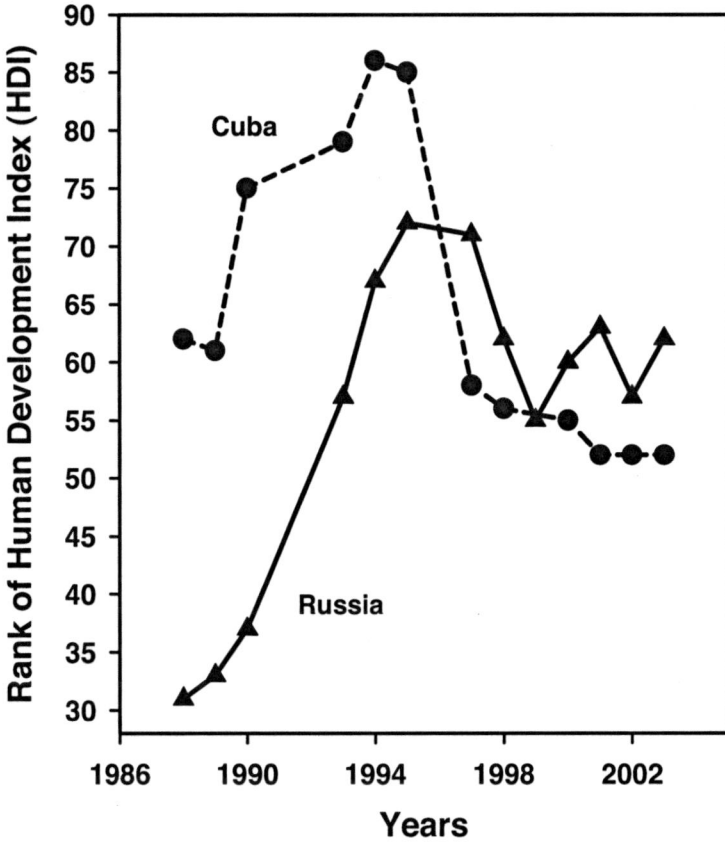

Human Development Report 1991-2003

Figure 101

3.5. The crimes of democracy vs. the crimes of communism: Body count

Crimes of Communism in Russia: My decision to compare the crimes of democracy with persecution during Stalin's era in Russia is not to apologize for Stalin's atrocities, but to have a good standard of comparison.

Body count as a rate of the crimes of communism is an old democratic tradition. It most likely started immediately after the Bolshevik revolution in Russia in 1917. There were more innocent deaths as a result of socialism, communism, Stalinism, more evidence against Marx, Marxism, communism, communists, socialism, and more evidence against planned economy and collective property.

After WWII, leaders of the body count claimed there to be more than 100 million victims of Communism in Russia. The number of the victims gradually decreased over time and in 2006, according to the Parliamentary Assembly of the Council of Europe, it was somehow only about 20 million deaths.

According to my knowledge, the first scientific body count of the persecution during Stalin's era, according to archived evidence of the Soviet secret police and judiciary was published in 1993 [28]. The obtained data were significantly lower than what had generally been presented for 60 years. The authors [28] concluded, "Mainstream published estimates of the total numbers of 'victims of repression' in the late 1930s have ranged from Dmitrii Volkogonov's 3.5 million to Olga Shatunovskaia's nearly 20 million. The basis for these assessments are unclear in most cases and seem to have come from guesses, rumors, or extrapolations from isolated local observations. As the table shows, the documental numbers of victims are much smaller". They also found that the secret police were not involved in the persecution as was generally presented. The author concluded: "we can conclude that, on the whole, only about 8.4 percent of the sentences of courts and extra-judicial bodies were rendered 'on cases of the secret police' and for alleged political reasons between 1933 and 1953". The generally presented opinion that the prisoners in GULAG were mostly political was also not true. According to a publication, "offenses of GULAG population sentenced for 'Counterrevolutionary offenses' were in 1934 - 26.5%, 1936 - 12.6%, and in 1940-33.1%." Unfortunately, the authors of this publication could not find information about how many of the counterrevolutionary offenses were really counterrevolutionary, i.e. the same as terrorists in recent understanding and how many were really innocent political opponents.

According to the scientific publication [28] between 1930 and 1952-1953, 786,098 were executed in the USSR (i.e. an average of 34,178 per year). However, the scientific publication did not clearly distinguish how many were real political prisoners, how many were real counterrevolutionaries, and how many were criminals. The total number of victims was 2.3 million (again I do not know how many real criminals are included in the number and how many were really political prisoners). Between 1934 and 1953, 1,053,829 people died in the camps of GULAG. I do not know the rate of mortality in GULAG in comparison to the mortality in the civil sector. I may assume that the mortality in the civil sector was also very high (maybe even higher that in GULAG?). Anyway, I will use this data and consider all of the deaths of the prisoners at GULAG as the deaths of innocent people.

Crimes of the capitalistic democracy in Russia after 1990: According to leading Russian economist Vladimir Popov [19]: "death rates increased (after introduction of capitalism and democracy in Russia)... and stayed at this high level thereafter, which was equivalent to over 700,000 additional deaths annually". Comparing this with the number of communist atrocities, the execution of on average 34,178 "counter-revolutionaries" per year,, the democracy in Russia is killing people 20 times more efficiently than Stalin's execution guards. However, the killing efficiency of democracy is even higher, since I do not think that all "counter-revolutionaries" were political prisoners.

According to HDR 2005, there are 7 million "missing" men since 1990 in democratic Russia. Comparing this number with the communist execution of the "counter-revolutionaries", democracy is killing people 15 times more efficiently than Stalin's execution guards.

According to HDR 2005, the number of additional deaths during 1992–2001 is estimated at 2.5–3 million. Comparing this number with the communist execution of the "counter-revolutionaries", democracy is killing people 8 times more efficiently than Stalin's execution guards.

Similarly, the total number of GULAG victims of Stalin's communism was 2.3 million people over 33 years with an average of 70,000 victims per year. The rate of Stalin's killing was 10 times less than the rate of the recent capitalistic democracy. It was 7 times less than "missing" men in Russia due to the crimes of recent democracy. It was 4 times less than the additional deaths during 1992–2001 in Russia (I repeat again, I do not know how many people of the 2.3 million were innocent).

The comparisons clearly show that it does not matter what kind of comparison one uses, the conclusion is the same: the recent capitalistic democracy in Russia is killing innocent people significantly more efficiently than communists did.

Of course, the crimes of democracy would be more pronounced if we compared the 15 years of democracy in the former socialist countries after 1990 and 15 years of totalitarian communism before 1990. This comparison would be more real. The crimes of democracy would be even more pronounced if we compared the crimes of communism for 15 years before 1990 and the crimes of democracy during The First World War and WWII.

When I normalized the number of the "contra-revolutionaries" [28] who died in GULAG to the recent Slovak population, I came to about 500 dead "counter-revolutionaries" per year in GULAG, per 5 million people. This number is similar to the number of innocent people, who were recently murdered, lost, or found dead in the street per year in Slovakia (I did not include suicides). Can I say that the recent capitalistic democracy in Slovakia is killing innocent people at a similar rate as Stalin at GULAG?

The mystery

Why is the real killing rate by Stalin in GULAG and by recent capitalistic democracy overlooked by respected scholars? Why are the data of the crimes of democracy and the conclusions from the data not presented in textbooks? Many times I have heard that Pope John Paul II contributed he most to the break-up of the communist regime in the FSC and that he fought against poverty. According to the UN report [17], the break-up of the communist regime in the FSC caused millions of deaths and significantly increased poverty. I wonder whether somebody in the Vatican connected these two pieces of information. Why are people, including democratic politicians, head of state, and artists, who contributed to 700,000 innocent victims per year in Russia, which is significantly more than Stalin's crimes, celebrated as liberators, humanists, democrats and fighters for freedom? Who decides whom to celebrate and whom to burn to death? This decision is probably made by anyone who can influence our mental decisions based on the rules of the recent capitalistic democracy.

Why have the respected democratic humanists and political leaders who are convincing us of the crimes of communism not lodged a claim about it to the international courts? If they did, why were communists not judged or sentenced?

What kind of rules guarantied that, after establishing capitalist democracy in the FSC, it only took 1-5 years for a few to get extremely rich and for very many to become extremely poor? Why are these rules celebrated by humanists, democrats and fighters for human rights?

For the last million years if somebody wanted to become rich quickly, he or she had to take wealth from another. Mostly, they had to rob or even kill many people. The result of this practice was that a very few became rich and many were miserable. This is similar to the result of the recent capitalistic democracy in the FSC. The only difference is that the robbery in the FSC was supported by all united humanists and democrats as a fight for freedom and democracy, whereas robbery in the long past was simply supported by looters. During those long past times looting was not necessary presented as a fight for democracy and freedom.

3.6. Democratic India and "totalitarian" communist China: Body count

I must say at the beginning that I recognize the positive achievement of humanity in India in the last 50 years. I chose India to compare with China due to some similarities between the two counties.

According to Jean Bricmont: "The economists Jean Dreze and Amartya Sen estimate that, departing from a similar base, China and India have followed different development paths and that the difference between the social systems of these two countries results in about 3.9 million extra deaths in India every year" [29].

According to UNICEF data for India [30]:
Under-5 mortality rate (2004)=85
   Annual number of births (2004)=26 million
   Annual number of under-5 deaths (2004)=2.21 million
   Total population (2004)=1087.124 million

According to UNICEF data for China [31]:
   Under-5 mortality rate (2004)=31
   Annual number of births (2004)=17.372 million
   Annual number of under-5 deaths (2004)=0.539 million
   Total population (2004)=1308 million

According to the 2004 data, in India 2.21 million children died who were under the age of five. If India had an under 5 mortality rate as China had, 31 out of 1,000 live births, only 806,000 children would die. It means that in the real experiment, democratic capitalism in India killed 1.4 million more children in one year than "totalitarian" communism in China. How many killed children were there over 50 years? Why is the crime of democracy versus the crime of communism so high in this case? Why is it not publicized and generally recognized by our democratic and humanistic leaders?

Imagine that communist China killed 1.4 million innocent children under five in 2004, to have a similar mortality rate as in India. If they hypothetically did it, it would be an unprecedented atrocity and an extreme violation of human rights. China's leaders would be called criminals, charged with crimes against humanity and tried in an international court. China's communist system would be called criminal, fascist, totalitarian, inhumane and in violation of human rights. Probably all democratic political leaders and all human organizations would call to overthrow China's government. Some democratic leaders would immediately call for an embargo; some democrats would call for democratic bombardment of China with an international military invasion in order to establish democracy in China, which includes freedom, free market economy, capitalism, and respect for human rights. Paradoxically, in reality they try to establish the same rules in China, which are used in the real experiment in India, and kill 1.4 million more children per year than in China.

Using the body counts of children under five only, the crimes of democracy in India produce an extra 1.4 million children dead in comparison to the crimes of communism in China. The results are very clear; the crime of democracy is significantly higher than the crime of communism.

If I use other comparisons, e.g. HDR report 2005, "Currently, 4.8 million children in Sub-Saharan Africa die before the age of 5 every year" – that is 9 deaths every minute, the comparison would be even more severe.

3.7. Democratic Haiti and "totalitarian" communist Cuba: Body count

I chose to compare Haiti with Cuba because it is in the same region, has a similar climate, has a partially similar history, and mainly, because Haiti was "liberated" by the USA many times. It was liberated directly by military invasion in 1888, 1891, 1914, 1915, 1934, and indirectly in 1959-1963, 1986-1994 [3]. Cuba was not "liberated" after 1960. In Latin America 285,000 lives would be saved each year if Cuban health and food policies were applied [29].

According to UNICEF data for Haiti [32]:
    Under-5 mortality rate (2004)=117
    Annual number. of births (2004)=253,000
    Annual number of under-5 deaths (2004)=30,000
    Total population (2004)=8.407 million

According to UNICEF data for Cuba [33]:
    Under-5 mortality rate (2004)=7
    Annual number of births (2004)=136,000
    Annual number of under-5 deaths (2004)=1,000
    Total population (2004)=11.245 million

Using the similar approach as above for India versus China, if Haiti had the same under 5 mortality rate as Cuba, 7 out of 1,000 live births, only 1794 children would have died in 2004. It means that in the real experiment, in 2004, democratic capitalism in Haiti killed 28,205 more children than "totalitarian" communist Cuba (calculated on equal population).

Imagine that communist Cuba decided to kill 28,205 innocent children under five during 2004, to be at similar mortality rate as Haiti. If they would have, hypothetically, done it, it would be an unprecedented atrocity, an extreme violation of human rights and genocide. Cuba's leadership would be called criminals, charged with genocide and tried in an international court. Cuba's communist system would be called criminal, fascist, totalitarian, very inhumane and in volition of human rights. Most likely, all democratic political leaders and human organizations would call to overthrow Cuba's government. Some democratic leaders would immediately call for an embargo and the democratic bombardment of Cuba by an international military invasion would begin. This would happen in order to establish democracy, freedom, a free market economy, capitalism, and a respect for human rights. Paradoxically, they would try to establish the same rules, which are used in the real experiment in Haiti, and kill 28,205 more children per year than Cuba. Even more paradoxically, some democratic leaders call to overthrow Cuba's government now, in spite of the fact that it saves the innocent lives of 28,205 children annually. Nobody calls to overthrow Haiti's government.

The paradox of the paradoxes is that these are the results of the functioning of the real capitalistic democracy we are living in.

3.8. The crimes of democracy vs. the crimes of communism: Suffering count

It is not easy to evaluate suffering counts, but it is very easy to manipulate them. Watching a 60 minute TV program about the suffering of one man under communism contributes more to the public opinion about suffering counts than hearing a 10 second long sentence in the news about the increase of 310,000 HIV positive people in the former socialist countries.

Suffering of innocent people in Stalin's Gulags was serious. The suffering of innocent people in colonies and developing countries in 18th, 19th and 20th centuries under capitalism were serious. Suffering of innocent people during the fight for private property in hundreds of wars, based on a free market economy, was also serious.

What about the suffering count of people as a result of establishing real capitalistic democracy in the FSC? Data on the deterioration of society after the introduction of democracy clearly indicate that the suffering significantly increased. The dramatic increase of violent crimes in Slovakia (Figure 36) and in all FSC after the abandonment of socialism and establishment of capitalism is proof of the increased suffering. The crimes of democracy — significant increase of poverty, alcoholism, drug addiction, homelessness, beggars, homicides, and violent crimes are proof of the suffering documented in many official publications. The suffering of 1 million innocent homeless children in 15 democratic years in Russia is serious in comparison to communism 15 years before 1990. The suffering of 18 million children in the former socialist countries, living in conditions of extreme democratic poverty, is serious. The suffering of no less than 500,000 women being sold in democratic Russia is serious. Similarly, the democratic results of 310,000 HIV positive people, hundreds of thousands of addicts and alcoholics or the 2.5-3 million innocent people who democratically lost their lives in former socialist countries, is serious.

But, there is one big difference between the suffering count caused by "totalitarian" communism and capitalistic democracy. The suffering during communism in the FSC, which was relatively innocent in comparison to recent capitalism, is regularly publicized in the media The suffering is emphasized to be connected with totalitarian communism, with evil communists, Marxists and with the political and economic socialist system. There are many films, documentaries and books that underline this connection that we had to watch and hear and read everyday.

On the other hand, suffering caused by capitalism, or by established capitalistic democracy in the FSC is rarely mentioned, if mentioned at all. It is not connected with established democracy in the FSC, the capitalist system or capitalists, democrats, capitalistic freedom or head leaders. Why is this so? I assume because it is an integral part of our demoserfdom.

Who decides how the suffering count of communism and capitalism are presented in the media? I do not know namely who, but I know that it is the real experimental result of the media practice based on the real rules of the capitalist democracy we are living in.

3.9. The crimes of democracy vs. the crimes of communism: USA vs. Soviet Union

The most data one can easily obtain to compare the crimes of democracy vs. the crimes of communism, are the results of the real policies of the leader of democracy – the USA, and the policies of the leader of communism – the former Soviet Union. I will estimate the body count of the policies of the USA and the Soviet Union after WWII only. This is since I have already mentioned the atrocities of the Soviet Union before 1945 and because this would be a very heavy book if I did a body count of the USA as a result of colonial policy and the many military interventions before 1945.

The crimes of the capitalistic democracy, as the results of American policy, are well documented in many books and official statistics. I will not discuss them, but as an example I will compare the intervention of the USA in Panama in 1989 and the intervention of the Soviet Union with its allies in Czechoslovakia in 1968.

Most of the democratic atrocities of the USA were military interventions into foreign sovereign states, those that did not obey democracy and freedom as the USA thinks they should. "The Federation of American Scientists has compiled a list of over 201 overseas military operations from the end of WWII until September 11, 2001 in which the USA was involved and normally struck the first blow. The current wars in Afghanistan and Iraq are not included. In no instance did democratic governments come about as a direct result of any of these military activities" [34].

The body counts of the USA's military interventions after 1945 are estimated by various sources. For example, the data from William Blum's books [35,36], supplemented by data from various sources, estimates 10-16 million dead from democratic capitalism, with most of them being caused by the USA's military interventions [37]. According to other sources, since WWII, the US government has bombed 21 countries: China in 1945-46 and again in 1950-53, Korea in 1950-53, Guatemala in 1954, 1960, and 1967-69, Indonesia in 1958, Vietnam in 1961-73, Congo in 1964, Laos in 1964-73, Peru in 1965, Cambodia in 1969-70, El Salvador throughout the 1980s, Nicaragua throughout the 1980s, Lebanon in 1983-84, Grenada in 1983, Bosnia in 1985, Libya in 1986, Panama in 1989, Iraq in 1991-20??, Sudan in 1998, Former Yugoslavia in 1999, and Afghanistan in 1998 and 2002 [38].

What about the atrocities of the Soviet Union after WWII? The Soviet Union invaded 4-5 countries. Besides Afghanistan, it invaded countries associated in the military Warsaw Pact. It was difficult for me to find any relevant numbers of deaths caused by the Soviet military interventions, since even the general bible of anticommunists [39] is not giving the number of deaths. The military interventions of the Soviet Union to Hungary, Czechoslovakia or Poland, counting 3,000-20,000 deaths, were relatively peaceful operations in comparison to the USA's military interventions. Only the military intervention of Soviet Union into Afghanistan was comparable to the interventions of the USA. The Soviet Union bombed only in Afghanistan. Its military atrocities might have caused between 30,000 and one million deaths, more or less, I could not find any relevant numbers.

Using the body counts of the military interventions, the crimes of democracy of the USA is more than 10 times higher than the crimes of communism of the Soviet Union. Paradoxically, the atrocities of the USA are not called the crimes of democracy, crimes of capitalism or crimes of capitalists. They are often called "fighting for freedom and democracy". On the other hand, the atrocities of the former Soviet Union are always called the crimes of communism or crimes of communists. This is to persuade us that it was the communist system that produced such atrocities. I agree that they are right. Similarly however, the atrocities of the USA are the results of capitalism, capitalists, and the capitalist democratic system.

The democratic capitalist military interventions vs. the totalitarian communist military interventions. As an example, I will compare the democratic USA's intervention in Panama in 1989 with the totalitarian Warsaw Pact's (lead by the Soviet Union) intervention in Czechoslovakia in 1968. I can do this partially, since I lived in Czechoslovakia during the Soviet invasion (I was 16), and in the USA during the USA invasion in 1989. (If some democrats think that I did not choose the right comparison, I can compare the USA's intervention in Vietnam with the totalitarian Soviet Union's intervention in Afghanistan. I could also use the democratic USA's bombardment of Cambodia with the totalitarian Soviet Union's intervention in Hungary).

An example of the democratic intervention of the USA to Panama in 1989. On December 19, 1989, U.S. President George Bush ordered operation "Just Cause". This caused12,000 troops to invade Panama (12,000 were in already), with the subsequently announced goals of: seizing Noriega to face drug charges in the United States, protecting American lives and property, and restoring Panamanian liberties. The USA, UK and France vetoed a United Nations resolution condemning the invasion. The USA bombed 27 targets, mostly in densely-populated areas in Panama. Political offices, newspaper offices and radio stations were searched and looted; opposition and union leaders and staff from the Embassy of Cuba were detained. The residence of the ambassador of Nicaragua was ransacked by USA troops.... Noriega took refuge in the Vatican nunciature (embassy) in Panama until he surrendered to U.S. authorities on January 3, 1990, and was then transported to Miami, Florida. There he stood trial, was convicted on a host of charges, and was sentenced to a U.S. prison. Noriega was imprisoned in the USA after having worked for the CIA since the early 1950's. He had spied on fellow students, instructors and officers at the Military Academy for the CIA. He had monitored union activity against the American company United Fruit and helped support anti left forces in Latin America. During the 1980's he had been receiving $ 100,000-200,000 per year from the USA for his activities. According to USA sources, the number of Panamanians killed in the operation was estimated at 200-300 combatants (soldiers and paramilitaries) and some 300 civilians. Twenty three U.S. soldiers were also killed and hundreds from both nations were wounded. According to other sources, over 4,000 Panamanians were killed in the operation with unknown numbers buried in mass graves or incinerated.

The reasons for the democratic military invasion according to The Columbia Encyclopedia, the fifth edition, 1993, under the label of Manuel Noriega reads: "...A one-time operative for the U.S. Central Intelligence Agency, he was implicated in drug trafficking, the sale of U.S. secrets to Cuba, and other illegal activities. U.S. officials urged him to step down (Jan., 1988), but he refused. Following the murder of a U.S. marine on the streets of Panama City, President George Bush ordered troops to Panama (Dec., 1989). Noriega was captured and brought to the United States to stand trial..." It is my feeling that the very democratic reasons for the military invasion – involvement in drug trafficking and the killing of an unarmed U.S. Marine officer dressed in civilian clothes was generally and democratically accepted.

When I was in the USA and saw the beginning of the Panama invasion (later it was not seen) and later the documentary video of the invasion 'The Panama Deception' [40], I had the feeling that I had seen similar scenes many years before. It reminded me of some documentary videos about the German invasion of Poland or the Soviet Union in World War II. The USA's intervention was a real atrocity and it has been well documented.

An example of the totalitarian intervention of the Soviet Union (Warsaw Pact) to Czechoslovakia (CSSR) in 1968. In 1968 the Communist Party of the CSSR started political reforms of socialism, which were independent of the Soviet Union model. The result was that the armies of the Warsaw pact (according to Warsaw treaty) lead by the Soviet Union invaded the CSSR on August 21, 1968 with 100,000-600,000 soldiers, 2,300-7,000 tanks, and 700 aircraft. The armies crossed borders and were moving by road to places of future military camps. Leaders of the CSSR government were detained and taken to Moscow where all except one signed an agreement with the Soviet Union to follow socialism. The result of the invasion was that most of the reforms were abolished, many citizens lost their convenient jobs and had to take less convenient ones, and censorship increased. Paradoxically, nobody was charged or put in jail due to activities against the Warsaw Army invasion.

It must be mentioned that the CSSR was a member of the Warsaw pact and the invasion of the CSSR was according to the Warsaw pact treaty signed by the CSSR to defend socialism. So, the Warsaw pact invasion might have had some justification. On the other hand, the USA's invasion into Panama was the invasion of a sovereign country.

According to [12] the number of people killed by the armies that invaded the CSSR was about 80, and 20 in Slovakia (from August 21st to October 10th, 1968). As I remember from my own experience and from many documentaries still showing on TV, people were angry and shouted at the Russian soldiers, even jumped at the tanks. Some of them threw stones at the soldiers. Such behavior provoked some soldiers to fire and kill some people in Slovakia. According to the book [12], the total amount of damage by the invasion of the CSSR was 16 million USD, this is including the damage caused by death (I do not know how they calculated this) and damage to the health of the people.

I have remarked on the 20 victims of the Soviet Union invasion in the CSSR in Slovakia. I will compare this number with the victims of the established capitalistic democracy in Slovakia after 1989, when we abandoned socialism. As it is described in Chapter: '1.5. Development of the crimes of democracy in Slovakia' extra deaths in Slovakia due to the increase of homicides, lost people and people found dead in the street are about 25 victims per month. One can calculate that the rate of people killed by the invasion of the Warsaw army into the CSSR was only 50% of the rate of people kill by recent democracy. The other difference is that the killing by the invasion of the Warsaw army was for only two months, while the killing by capitalistic democracy has been taking place for more than 15 years, and it is not known when it will stop.

How do common people judge and compare these two military invasions? They judge them according to the information they are getting from books and media. How did some respected scholars judge the invasions? They should compare the basic data. What do historical books and encyclopedias print about these events?

I will give you a few examples. In the historical book [41] at Chapter 71, under the title "Central America in Revolution: Costa Rica, Nicaragua,

Honduras, El Salvador, Guatemala, Panama and Mexico" on p. 731 is written: "On 20 December 1989, President Bush cut the Gordian knot and 24,000 US troops descended on Panama City to arrest and overthrow Noriega. He fled to the Embassy of the Vatican but gave himself up in January 1990. He was tried and sent to prison." On page 731 is a photograph of Noriega (9x7 cm) standing in front of a wall carrying a prison identification number in a Miami prison. The text under the photograph reads "The drug-trafficking leader of Panama, General Manuel Noriega, is captured and arraigned in Miami, Florida." The reader can see that Noriega was the criminal, not the USA. In Chapter 81 "The United States: Reagan and Bush" on page 839 it is written: "Finally on 20 December 1989, a large US military force descended on Panama City, causing some loss of life and destruction. Noriega was cornered, captured and brought to the United States for trial....". There is no photography about this event.

The invasion of the Warsaw pact into the CSSR in the same historical book is described more dramatically than the invasion of the USA into Panama. It is mentioned even in the title of Chapter 77: "The Soviet Union and the Wider World: Crushing the Prague Spring" and shows a photograph of unhappy and angry people (7x8cm). The text under the picture reads, "Tearful crowds holding flowers congregate in Prague to confront the Russian invaders who seek to terminate the 'Prague Spring' in August 1968." The Warsaw pact invasion is described on nearly half of page 798 emphasizing that "The Prague Spring was crushed by Soviet tanks on 20 August 1968". The suppression of the Prague Spring is mentioned again in the book on a figure on page 844 showing students on a street with papers in their hands. The text under the figure reads, "Students distributing underground literature in Wenceslas Square after the suppression of the Prague Spring".

When I compared the description of the two invasions in another historical book [42] I came to the same conclusion. The book mentions the Warsaw pact invasion on page 879 in two sentences: "After a series of attempts to bring her to heel, Czechoslovakia was invaded in August 1968 by Warsaw Pact forces. To avoid a repetition of what had happened in Hungary in 1956, the Czech government did not resist and a brief attempt to provide an example of 'socialism with a human face', as a Czech politician had put it, was obliterated." Interestingly much of page 880 is photography (13x9cm) of an armored military vehicle with a soldier in it and angry people around shouting. The text under the photography reads, "A dramatic confrontation in Prague during the Russian invasion in 1968". On the other hand, I was not able to find any mention of the USA's invasion of Panama.

I was surprised by the description of these two military interventions. Why were there no photographs of bombed cities in Panama or dead civilians on the street and other atrocities of the USA in the books, but photographs of the Soviet invasion? Why is the relatively peaceful operation of the Soviet intervention described in more detail and more dramatically than the USA atrocities? It is because of the result of free speech and the freedom of information of the recent capitalistic democracy based on privately owned media. Why can't the truth be generally known? I assume that totalitarian democracy does not allow it.

The response of the general public to these military interventions was also different. After invasion of Warsaw Pact into the CSSR in 1968 there were massive demonstrations in many cities condemning the invasion, the crimes of communism, and the barbaric act of communism. Some documentary films were produced about the invasion and showed many times on TV.

What was the reaction of the public after the USA invasion of Panama? It was not so massive, in many countries there was none at all. My guess is that the condemnation of the American invasion was not so big because it was something common in the world. The Warsaw Pact invasion was very rare however, so it must be remembered.

Democratic conclusions

The first conclusion of the comparison of the interventions is that the totalitarian intervention into the CSSR was a relatively peaceful operation in comparison to the democratic invasion of Panama. Seems to me, the invasion by the USA was a barbaric act of a super-human versus a sub-human, and the invasion of the totalitarian Soviet Union was a careful operation causing minimal damage to people or property. The Soviet Union did not use the intervention to test new weapons in the CSSR as the USA did in Panama, Yugoslavia, Afghanistan or Iraq. As far as I know, during the CSSR invasion, there wasn't any fire from tanks or canons of armored vehicle. No bomb was dropped by the Warsaw army, there was only the fire of Kalashnikov.

The second conclusion results from the citizen support of the interventions. The criminal act of the USA invasion into a sovereign country was supported by most of the USA's population. According to Newsweek (Jan 1, 1990), 75-85% of the USA population supported the invasion, and only 8-18% were against it.

How much of the population of the former communist countries supported the criminal act of the Warsaw pact invasion into the CSSR? The totalitarian communist system did not ask the citizens for support, and did not ask about their opinions. The population probably did not support the invasion, but that was not allowed to be publicized.

Concerning the popular support of the Warsaw pact invasion, we know why it was such. It was a totalitarian system. But how are democracy, free elections and freedom of speech working when most of the USA's population supported the criminal act of the mass murder, which violated all local and international laws? The results show that the free and democratic information system is very well organized so that anybody who democratically owns it can manipulate public opinion to such an extent that most of the population supports the criminal-terrorist act.

The totalitarian system of the Soviet Union used state owned media for the same goal. But the difference is that the crimes of the democratic USA military interventions is at least 10 times more severe than the crimes of the totalitarian Soviet Union military interventions. Why did the Soviet Union not use military intervention in more countries, since it did not need to ask the opinion of its citizens, as the USA has to? Why have democratically elected leaders produced more criminal acts and killed several times more innocent people than the leaders elected by non-democratic communist rules?

Democratic mysteries: Imagine if a Slovak military commander or local mafia boss ordered his army to invade a sovereign neighboring country, bombed it, and explained that somebody there killed one of his soldiers and smuggle drugs into Slovakia. Imagine that the result of the invasion would be 1,000 dead innocent people. What would happen? Certainly, according to local and international laws, the military commander or mafia boss would be charged and sentenced to prison for many years. The Slovakian system, which allowed the order and performed the military invasion would be called criminal, fascist, inhumane and undemocratic.

Why were the commanders of the invasions of Panama and the CSSR not brought to justice? Why is the democratic system of USA, which allowed the order and performed many military invasions, not generally called by democratic leaders as criminal, fascist, inhumane and undemocratic, as the communist system is often called? Why is the capitalistic democracy not called a criminal-totalitarian system? The reason is simple; the practical function of recent democracy does not allow it. This conclusion is based on the results of the real experiments we are living in today. The recent practical rules of democracy created the conditions and allows someone to kill 1,000 or 1 million innocent people without any consequences. What are these rules? They are, after all, the rules of the recent democracy, as everyone knows it.

I repeat. What do the results of the real democratic experiments concerning USA military interventions show? The results show that the rules of democracy are used by democratic countries to perform criminal acts without consequences. There are many published examples of it.

Imagine that there is no recent capitalistic democracy on the top and anybody can use the justice system, state or international laws to punish any criminals. Imagine that law is above democracy.

Why hasn't totalitarian communist China's military invaded 50 sovereign countries to increase its economic or political power? Because, the capitalistic democracy is restricted in China, it is not so powerful as in the USA.

3.10. Divine Comedy

From the real experiments of the communistic totality and the capitalistic democracy in the former socialist countries and from the results of the USA and former Soviet Union's military interventions, it is evident that the recent capitalist democracy is a better matrix for legal criminal military interventions than communist totality was.

I would like to answer the following questions of this divine democratic comedy:
-Why have the policies of democratically elected governments produced significantly more criminal military interventions and significantly more innocent deaths than totalitarian communism?
-Why does democracy allow democratically elected governments to commit more severe crimes against humanity than totalitarian communists did?
-Why is it not possible, under the recent democratic rules, to punish democratically elected governments for well-known crimes against humanity and international law violation?
-Why do people repeatedly elect politicians who performed acts against humanity and violated international law?
-Why does democracy allow some democratic states to openly behave as well organized mafia or terrorist organizations?

I can answer this very simply, because real capitalistic democracy produces and secures such conditions. This conclusion is based on the practical results of recent capitalistic democracy. What we have in reality are the results of a practice based on the rules of the recent capitalistic democracy. This is the main reason that powerful democratic countries demand the respect of democracy and they punish anybody, or any state, who tries to protect itself against the totality of capitalistic democracy. The result of today's (Oct 25, 2006) situation in Afghanistan and Iraq is the result of democracy after multi-party free elections with the combination of capitalism, free market economy and unlimited private property.

4. Capitalistic democracy as a base for modern democratic serfdom – demoserfdom

4.1. Product of the recent capitalistic democracy – inequality

The Myth?

World Economic and Social Survey 2006, p. 4, reads: "Nobel Prize winner Robert Lucas (2000) has estimated that the diffusion of technology and ideas will allow income distribution across nations to narrow and make everyone "equally rich and growing" by the year 2100. Using sophisticated economic analysis, others have strengthened this claim with similar estimates showing that convergence can be expected to take place when the forces of the global market are left free to act."

The facts

According to the Universal Declaration of Human Rights, the first article reads: "All human beings are born free and equal in dignity and rights…". Based on the rules of democracy, free market economy and freedom, everybody expects that inequality between people or states should decrease gradually. Also that democracy is a guarantee of the equality and observation of the Universal Declaration of Human Rights.

How does democracy rate in regard to this first article? What do official UN publications report? The UN publication, *World Economic and Social Survey 2006* concludes: "Broadly speaking, the income gap between the industrialized economies and developing countries was already very high in 1960 and has continued to widen since then….during the 1980's and 1990's, international inequality increased sharply between developed countries and all developing-country regions, except for East and South Asia."

According to HDR 2005 [43]: "Income inequality is increasing in countries that account for more than 80% of the world's population… The gap between rich and poor countries is widening, most spectacularly between rich countries and countries in Africa but also for other regions. In 1980 child death rates in Sub-Saharan Africa were 13 times higher than in rich countries. They are now 29 times higher… Absolute income inequalities between rich and poor countries are increasing even when developing countries have higher growth rates - precisely because the initial income gaps are so large. If average incomes grow by 3% in Sub-Saharan Africa and in high-income Europe, for example, the absolute change will be an extra $51 per person in Africa and an extra $854 per person in Europe …. Income inequality is exceptionally high however it is measured and regardless of whether it is rising or falling. On the (conservative) assumption that the world's 500 richest people listed by *Forbes* magazine have an income equivalent to no more than 5% of their assets, their income exceeds that of the poorest 416 million people... the 2.5 billion people living on less than $2 a day – 40% of the world's population – account for 5% of global income. The richest 10%, almost all of whom live in high-income countries, account for 54%. Global income distribution resembles a champagne glass... At the top, where the glass is widest, the richest 20% of the population hold three-quarters of world income. At the bottom of the stem, where the glass is narrowest, the poorest 40% hold 5% of world income and the poorest 20% hold just 1.5%. The poorest 40% roughly corresponds to the 2 billion people living on less than $2 a day."

According to HDR 2003, p. 39: "The richest 5% of the world's people receive 114 times the income of the poorest 5%. The richest 1% receive as much as the poorest 57%. The 25 million richest Americans have as much income as almost 2 billion of the world's poorest people". According to the House of Commons Library [44]: "The richest one-tenth of the population of Latin America and the Caribbean earn 48 percent of total income, while the poorest tenth earn only 1.6 percent, the research team found. In industrialized countries, by contrast, the top tenth receive 29.1 percent, while the bottom tenth earn 2.5 percent. Using the 'Gini Index' of inequality in the distribution of income and consumption, the researchers found that Latin America and the Caribbean, from the 1970s through the 1990s, measured nearly 10 points more unequal than Asia, 17.5 points more unequal than the 30 countries in the Organization for Economic Cooperation and Development, and 20.4 points more unequal than Eastern Europe."

Even the issue of whether income inequality increases or does not increase, is still under discussion. Paradoxically, if one includes communist China, the inequality decreased, but without China the inequality increased. Why does "totalitarian" communist China decrease the inequality and not others in the democratic world? Published sources confirm the fact that in the last 25 years the difference between the income of the poorest and the richest in the population in most countries is high and, in many, are on the increase. For example, in the USA between 1979 and 1998, the top fifth of American families gained 38 percent, and the top 5 percent gained 64 percent, while the bottom fifth lost 5 percent in real income [45]. For example, in Brazil the ratio of the income of the poorest 10% of the population to the richest 10% is 1 to 94 (HDR 2005, p. 38). According to HDR 2005, p. 4: "Using a global income distribution database, we estimate a cost of $300 billion for lifting 1 billion people living on less than $1 a day above the extreme poverty line threshold. That amount represents 1.6% of the income of the richest 10% of the world's population."

As it is shown in Figure 102, the ratio of GDP per capita in the poor regions and poor countries in comparison to the developed countries was about 0.5 in 1820. Later, the divergence increased (Figure 103), and in 2001 the ratio was about 0.1-0.2 (Figure 104). The data clearly show that after spreading of the free market economy and capitalistic democracy, the inequality increased. Capitalistic democracy with free market economy secures higher inequality than the colonial system in 1820. Similarly, from the comparison of the crimes of democracy versus the crimes of communism in the former socialist countries it is evident that after the introduction of capitalistic democracy the inequality in the FSC increased significantly. The increase of inequality is evident also from the comparison of the GDP of the five richest and five poorest countries (Figure 105), and from the comparison of the increase of the income of the poor and rich populations (Figure 106) or countries (Figure 107, 108).

The presented data show that the capitalistic democracy does not respect the First article of the Universal Declaration of Human Rights: "All human beings are born free and equal in dignity and rights...", as did "communist totality". From the published results and from the results of the real experiment in the FSC, it is evident that recent capitalistic democracy is a significantly better matrix for inequality than the communist "totality".

According to Forbes (March 10, 2005) a number of the world's billionaires increased from 476 in 2003 to 691 in 2005. Their aggregate net worth has grown from $1.4 trillion to $2.2 trillion (in 2004 it was $1.9 trillion). When I compared the growth of their net worth in one year with HDP production of poor world regions I was surprised. GDP production in the least developed countries (50 countries, 723 million population) was $221.4 bill. in 2003. This means that all the income produced in 2003 by the 723 million poorest, was only 74% of the combined income of 691 richest. Similarly in Sub-Saharan Africa (45 countries, 674 mill. population, GDP $418 bill. in 2003), total GDP production of 483 million people was equal to the combined income of 691 billionaires. In Central and Eastern Europe and CIS (27 countries, 406 mill. population, GDP $1190 bill. in 2003) was the GDP of 102 million people and in the developing countries (137 countries, 5 mill. population, GDP 6982 Bill. USD in 2003) was the GDP of 215 million. Who produces the income of the 691 billionaires?

According to Forbes, the number of the world's billionaires on March 9, 2006 increased to 793 and their net worth has grown to 2.6 trillion. In 1986 there were only 140 billionaires. Why has the rate of the number of billionaires increased? Is it an integral part of demoserfdom?

Mystery

The data shows very clearly that the developed colonization system in 1820 did not have the power to increase inequality to such an extent as the recent neo-liberal capitalistic democracy has. To say it in other words, the neo-liberal capitalistic democracy is able to rob people legally and more efficiently than colonialism did. The global neo-liberal capitalism is using the new technology and ideology of the capitalistic democracy to increase inequality and create a neo-liberal democratic aristocracy. As development of technology goes on, inequality, based on democracy, may increase. It is possible that a few families will own everything. It is also possible that we will not know that a few rich families own and control everything. We will not know names of the few rich families. This may be the legal dream of democrats spreading neo-liberal capitalistic democracy everywhere. The power of private property over democracy increases as a result of increased inequality. The increased inequality increases the power of private property. So far, this mutual relationship is working well. But where is the limit?

Why hasn't capitalism, liberalism and capitalistic democracy not been making everyone "equally rich and growing" for the last 200 years? Why has the opposite so far been true? Will the capitalistic democracy create equality as the communists did according to the first article of the Universal Declaration of Human Rights: "All human beings are born free and equal in dignity and rights…"?

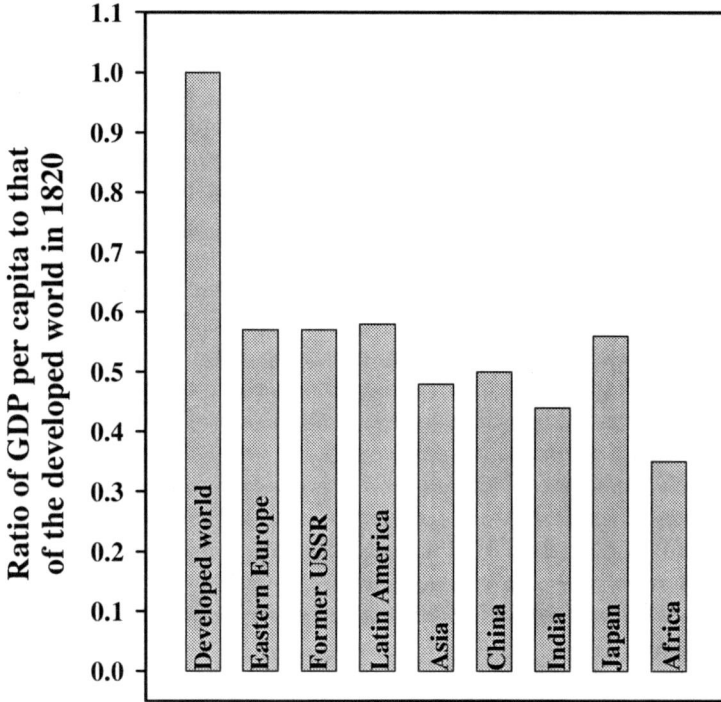

UN: World Economic and Social Survey 2006, p. 5.
Angus Maddison (2001): The World Economy:
A Millennial Perspective.

Figure 102

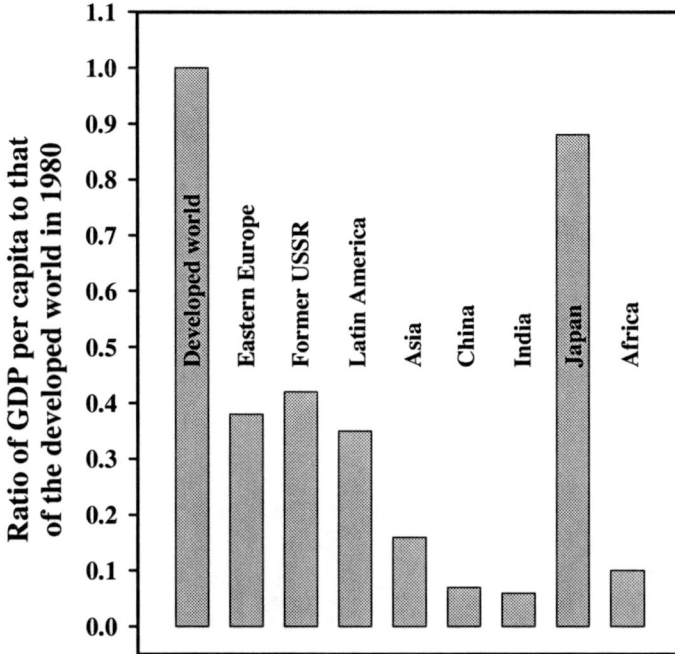

UN: World Economic and Social Survey 2006, p. 5.
Angus Maddison (2001): The World Economy:
A Millennial Perspective.

Figure 103

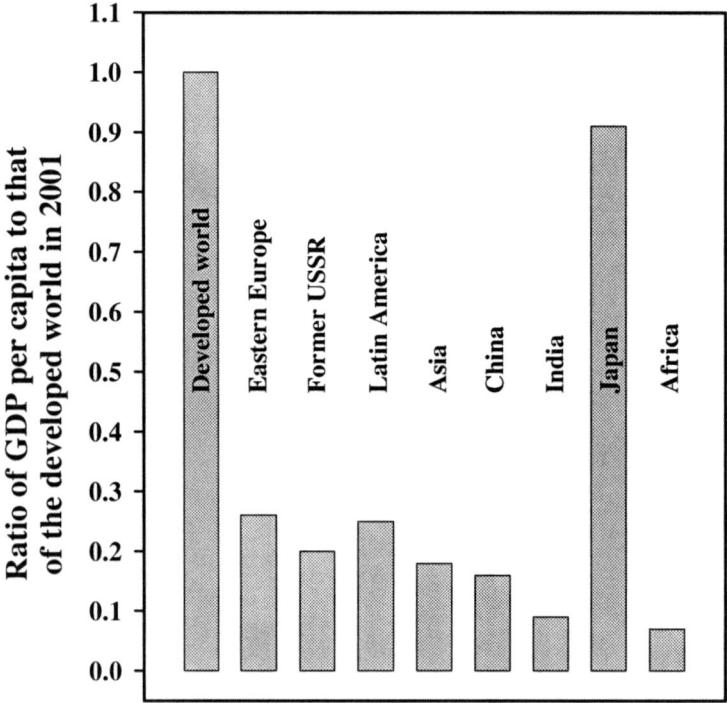

UN: World Economic and Social Survey 2006, p. 5.
Angus Maddison (2001): The World Economy:
A Millennial Perspective.

Figure 104

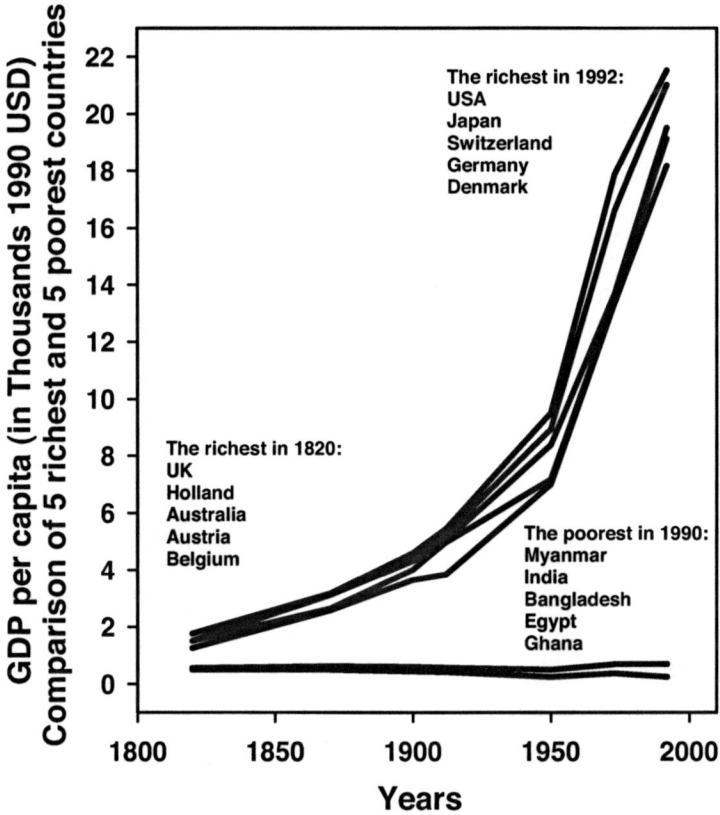

GDP per capita (in Thousands 1990 USD)
Comparison of 5 richest and 5 poorest countries

The richest in 1992:
USA
Japan
Switzerland
Germany
Denmark

The richest in 1820:
UK
Holland
Australia
Austria
Belgium

The poorest in 1990:
Myanmar
India
Bangladesh
Egypt
Ghana

Years

UN: Human development report 1999, p. 38
Sorce: Maddison 1995

Figure 105

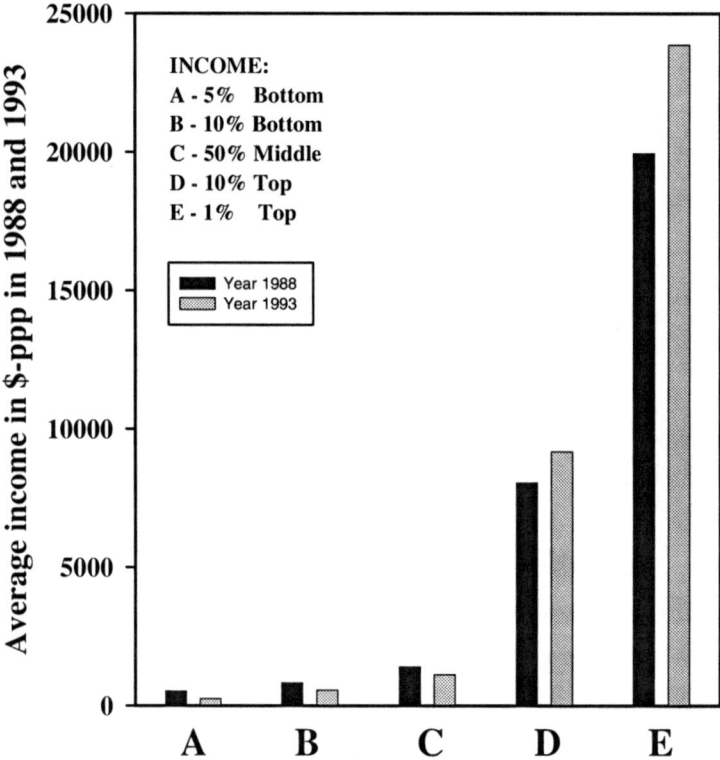

Economic Journal, January 2002

Figure 106

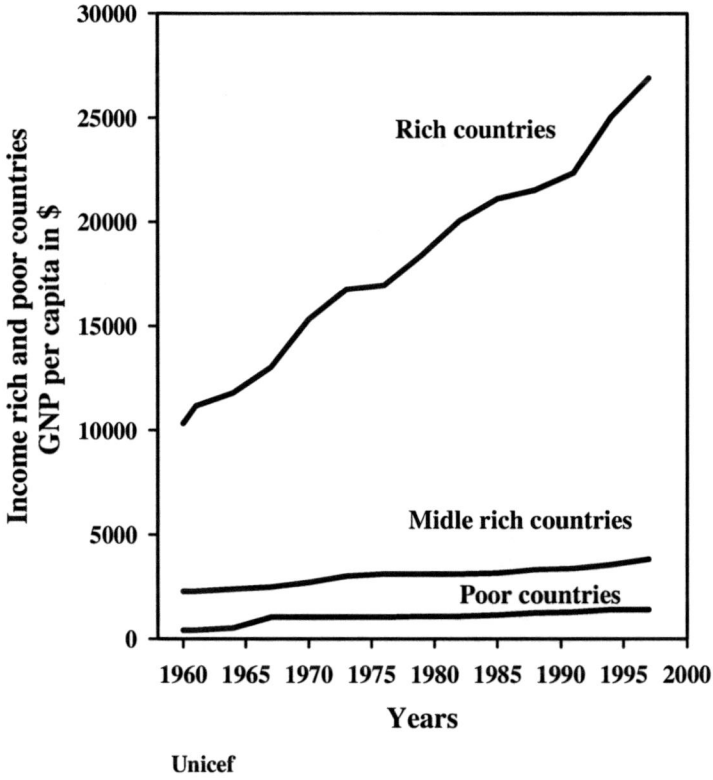

Unicef

Figure 107

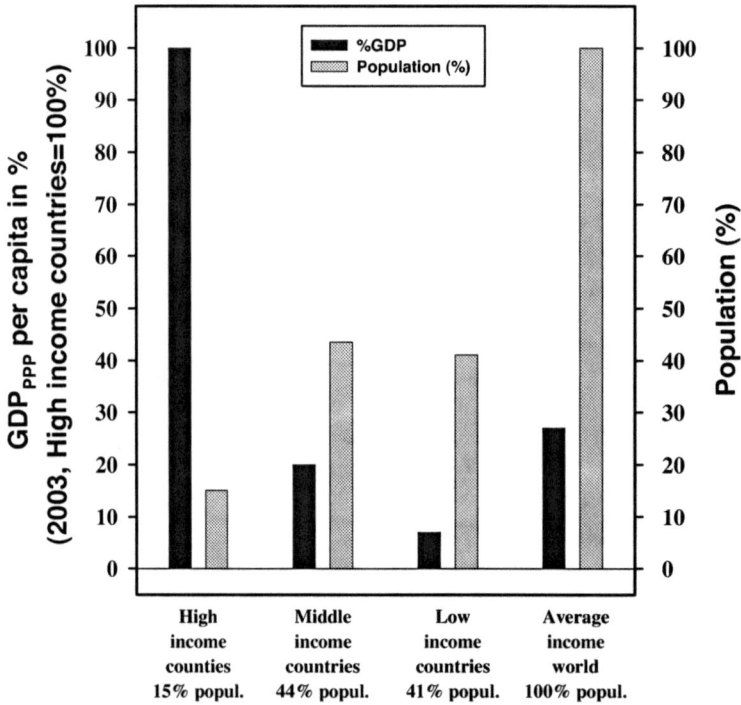

HDR 2005, p. 269

Figure 108

4.2. Modern democratic serfdom of capitalistic democracy – demoserfdom

There is one practical problem with democratic freedom. Every human being needs to eat, have a place to dwell, have clothes, and would like to reproduce. It means that he or she has to produce or buy food, produce or buy a dwelling, produce or buy clothes and so on. Under the recent industrial development of the free market economy, it is difficult for most people to produce food, dwellings or clothes by themselves. They have to buy them. They have to interact with private companies, in which the leaders are not democratically elected. Therefore, they do not have freedom; they have to be involved in, and accept, the political and economic rules of recent capitalist democracy. They must work for money as a part of the system. They interact more with issues that are under the rules of private unelected leaders than with issues that are under the rules of a democratically elected leader. They have no other option if they want to live a normal, dignified life. The results of the acceptance of the rules of capitalistic democracy are high: inequality, very uneven income, bombardment for profit, preemptive wars, and preemptive murders, as was described previously and will be described later.

During the last 200 years of the influence of capitalism, and later democracy and freedom, the world has been divided into 10-50 very wealthy countries on the one hand, and on the other hand 50-100 impoverished nations. For example, Figure 109 shows the GDP_{ppp} per capita of different countries divided into groups. The GDP_{ppp} per capita in OECD countries (1.2 billion population) is five times higher than in other parts of the world (5.1 billion population).

There are many possibilities about how to scientifically describe differences between the rich and the poor countries or between the rich and the poor people. One can describe them as differences of GDP, GDP_{ppp} (real income per capita), as a possible bond-service of the people living in the poor countries to the people living in the rich countries, as a possible bond-service of poor people to the rich people, and so on. There are many examples in which workers in poor countries have a salary less than 10% of the workers in developed countries for the same work. When I compared the real GDP production and the real income in Slovakia after the establishment of capitalistic democracy, the ratio of the real income to the real GDP decreased significantly (Figures 19,20,22). After 1989 Slovak's started to pay colonization tax to somebody. Some of them have become demoserfs. According to HDR 2005, p. 36: "The average income of the top

20% of the world's population is about 50 times the average income of the bottom 20%." This is a very high difference based on recent capitalistic democracy, free market economy and liberal globalization. The difference would be somehow justified if the real GDP of the top 20% of the world's population is 50 times the average GDP of the bottom 20%. Or, if the top 20% work 8 hours a day and the bottom 20% only 10 minutes a day of the same work. Is it the case? It is most likely not.

It is difficult to account for the real production of the top 20% (at least for me). I do not know how to calculate the real production of the GDP, for example, of the 793 billionaires (0.000013% population), since I do not know how many hours they work per year, and what they actually produce. Each of them has an average combined income of ~1.2 million USD per day. On the other hand, each of the bottom 2 billion people is living on less than $2 a day. Of course, each of the 793 billionaires would probably argue that his or her work is even more efficient than 1 million times the work of the bottom 2 billion, and that they should earn even more than a million times the average salary of the bottom 2 billion people. I only assume that one billionaire does not work one million times harder, longer or more efficiently than the bottom 2 billion people. Similarly, I do not know how to estimate the GDP of mediaeval kings in Europe or rulers in Mesopotamia or Latin America from 1,000-3,000 years ago. I do not know how many hours they worked per day and what they practically produced.

From the data, the bottom 20% receives 1/50 income of the top 20%. From the data above, it is highly probable that the bottom 20% produce more than 1/50 of the GDP. This means that the bottom 20% provides a bond-service to the top 20%. For example, according to the National Labor Committee, in Bangladesh contractors providing clothing for Hanes, Wal-Mart and J.C. Penney employ children, making them work shifts as long as 20 hours. These children are paid 6.5 cents an hour.

From the presented results, from the high inequality after the spread of capitalistic democracy, from the evidence that for the same work many are paid less than 10% of what others are, we may define a democratic serfdom of capitalistic democracy. To distinguish it from the middle age serfdom, I will call it "democratic serfdom", or "demoserfdom" for short, I will label those who receive for their work less than the actual value of their production - demoserfs. I used the abbreviation "demo", because many of us have practically only demo from the democracy.

It would be nice to know exact fees and taxes paid by the demoserfs to a democratic aristocracy, but it is not easy to calculate. It is not even yet included in official UN and World Bank publications. If I take Slovakia as an example and use the data discussed in Chapter 1.4. (Slovak democratic colonization standard and the mysteries of liberation from communist totality), one may estimate that the combined fees paid by Slovak's demoserfs might be ~36% of their production in 2005.

The colonization of the FSC in 1989 changed the world distribution of demoserfs. As seen from the values of the Dow index (Figures 110, 111), they increased significantly after the collapse of the FSC. This was during the years of the robbing of the FSC from 1990-2000. The unprecedented increase of Dow was the highest in its history, whether one uses nominal values (Figure 110) or the values corrected for inflation (Figure 111). People who drew the time dependence of the Dow Index even put a remark on it, as I repeated in Figure 110: "The longest economical boom in history ends its 107th month of expansion". It was on January 4, 2000, when the Dow=11,722.98. The high increase of the Dow after 1990 may indicate not only the quality of non-living resources, which new democratic owners got, but also the quality of the demoserfs.

There are many differences between the middle age and the modern serfdoms. I will stress only a few. In the middle ages, serfs paid fees to a local ruler or a local owner. The serfs knew exactly how much to pay to whom and also who to kill during rebellion. Since they paid it to the local owner, some of the fees were distributed back into the local area. On the other hand, most of today's demoserfs do not even know that they pay fees, and nobody knows to whom. There is high probability that in the case of a rebellion the demoserfs may kill the wrong people. The problem is also that demoserfs mostly pay the fees to somebody that does not live locally, so the fees are not distributed back into the community but are mostly collected somewhere very far away.

An important part of demoserfdom is that money, capital and people from the capital, media and members of the media or aids can cross the borders without passports or visas. Usually, according to recent liberal capitalistic democracy, they are free to do business without restriction anywhere. On the other hand, demoserfs, according to the rules of the recent capitalistic democracy, need a passport and visa and usually are not free to work or to do business anywhere without restriction. Of course, they have right to do it as illegal immigrants. This recent democratic bondage has not yet been abolished by the capitalistic democracy.

If all people, including demoserfs, have the same rights as money, capital or people from the capital have, to cross any border without restriction and to do business without discrimination, the inequality might gradually decrease. Why is this not possible? Because it would be against the rules of capitalistic democracy. To say it exactly, it would be against the wish of the world aristocracy who rules over the capitalistic democracy. It would decrease their profit and unsecure their convenient positions.

How many rulers over democracy do we have? I do not know. I can only estimate the number. For example, if I know how many hotels rooms are selling for >$990 per night, I can estimate how many people do not need to care about money, and so on. Similarly, I do not know how many goods and services are produced to satisfy the extra needs of richest 1% and what percentage of population is working to produce those goods.

I can see the problems produced by the high inequality of income or GDP production described in the figures. In a crude estimation, if 20% of the population has a GDPppp production five times higher than the rest of the 80%, the poorest 80% of the population must increase production at least five times to be in the same living standard of the richest 20%. Could our planet sustain it, when richest 20% would like to increase production each year by a few percent also? Our planet probably could not sustain it. How will the neo-liberal capitalistic democracy solve this problem on our planet? There are at least three possibilities: i.- to keep the poor population as poor as possible for as long as possible, ii.- to decrease the population somehow, iii. - to rationalize production and consumption. What will they choose?

How could we solve the problem if the bottom 20%, having 1/50 of the income of the top 20%, would like to increase their income 50 times? What approach would the totalitarian democracy choose?

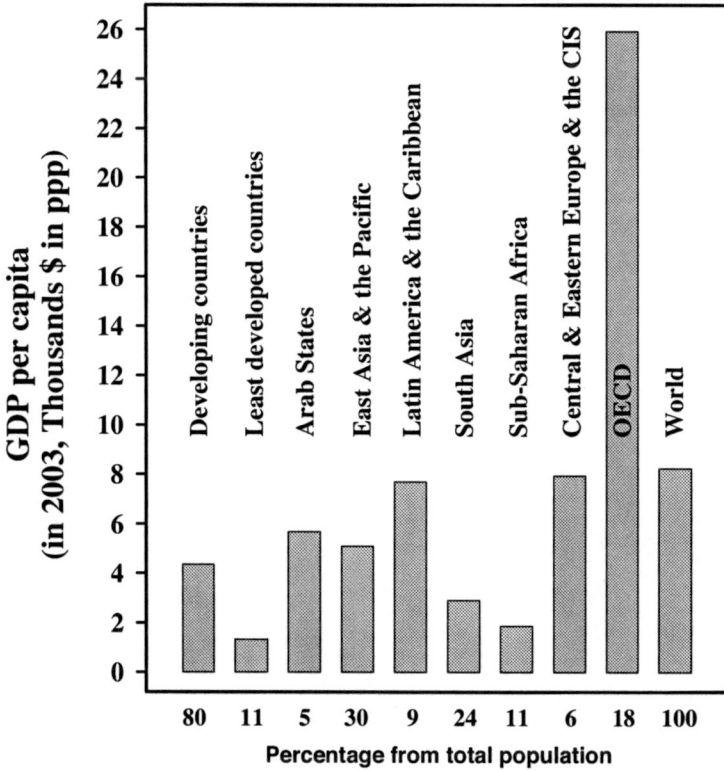

Human development report 2005

Figure 109

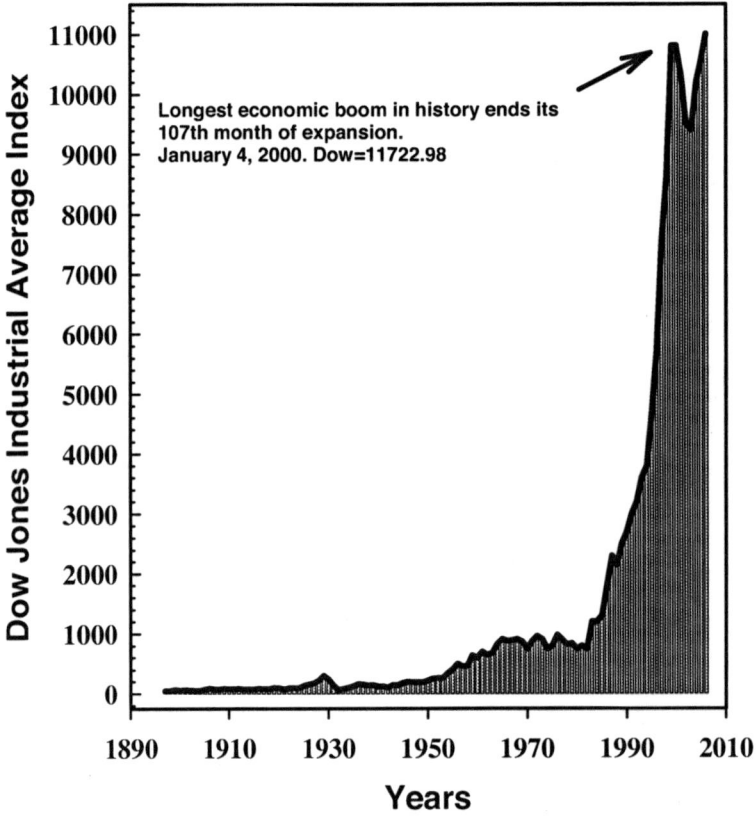

Longest economic boom in history ends its
107th month of expansion.
January 4, 2000. Dow=11722.98

Source: Http://averages.dowjones.com/

Figure 110

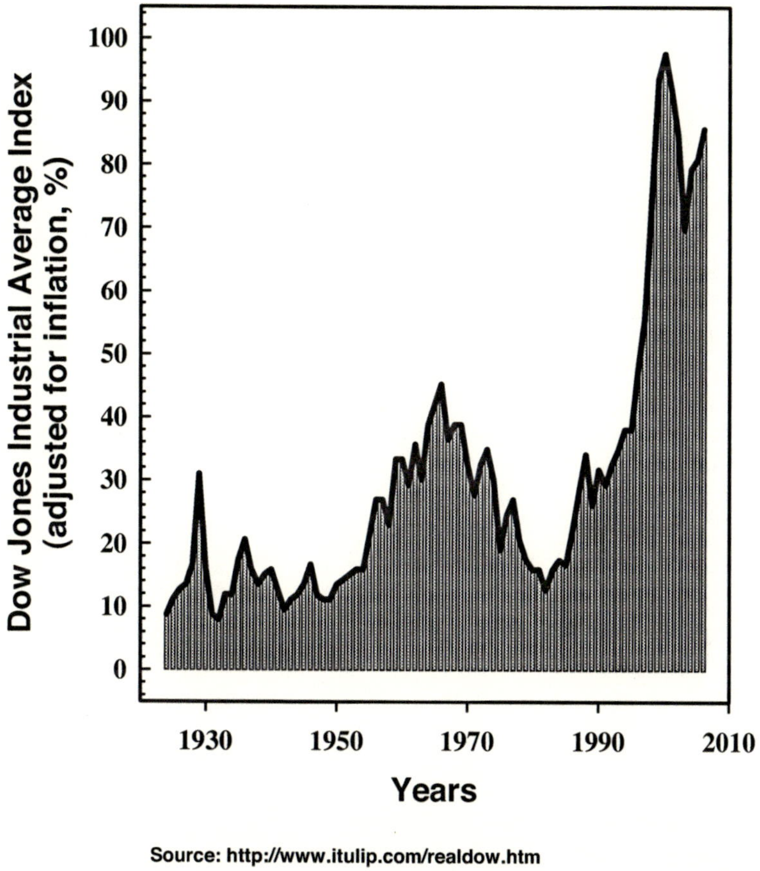
Dow Jones Industrial Average Index
(adjusted for inflation, %)
100
90
80
70
60
50
40
30
20
10
0
1930
1950
1970
1990
2010
Years
Source: http://www.itulip.com/realdow.htm

Figure 111

4.3. The capitalistic totalitarian democracy as a base of demoserfdom

The presented and published data show positive development, but also the high inequality of demoserfdom, the unpunished criminal acts of the leaders of democratic countries and freedom of economic, political and mental colonization in our globalized world. Why is this so? It is the result of the rules we are living under. It is the result of the rules of global capitalism, free market economy, free election, plurality of political parties, private property, freedom of expression, private media ownership and so on. Simply, it is the results of the rules of the global neo-liberal capitalistic democracy.

Who is responsible for the present situation? The rulers over the global neo-liberal capitalistic democracy. Who are the rulers? Anybody, who has enough money to take advantage in recent democracy.

Paradoxically, the main rule that secures the high inequality of demoserfdom and unpunished criminal acts is the freedom of expression. As everybody knows, when the media can manipulate 80% of the population, it is enough to only use the media. Anybody, who has enough money can own media, and can thereby, manipulate the opinion of 80% of the population. In a free election, the vote of the manipulated voter is equal to the vote of the non-manipulated voter.

The freedom of expression in the capitalistic system can not work and is not working because the recent democracy is based on unlimited private property. The freedom of expression is incompatible with unlimited private property. Democracy is incompatible with unlimited private property. Therefore I call the recent democracy – capitalistic democracy. Capitalistic democracy means that the owners of the unlimited property have power to govern through the democratically elected representatives.

In all human history for the last thousands of years, there were rulers, kings, and nobility, to whom servants paid fees. The rulers, kings, and nobility had to secure their position somehow. They used many tools to secure their convenient positions. They had gods, voodoos, body guards, army, religion, and so on. Mostly they were not secure, the gods were changed, the body guards were bought over and they were killed and substituted by other rulers.

The recent rulers over democracy are in a different position. They use only one tool – capitalistic democracy, to secure their convenient positions forever. They are more secure than any rulers before. This is the reason why the recent capitalistic democracy is so popular with them. This is the reason why the rulers over democracy fight against communism, Marxism, and anybody who restricts unlimited private property or prefers state ownership. The rulers are afraid to lose power over democracy; they are afraid to not have enough money to rule over democracy.

4.4. An astonishing power of the recent totalitarian capitalistic democracy

Fighting for oil fields. On June 28th, 1942 during WWII, Hitler ordered the Army Group South (Army Group A) 1st Panzer Armies, the 17th Army, and later the 4th Panzer Army, to continue advancing south towards the Caucasus to capture the vital Soviet oil fields. After long and heavy fighting they captured only part of the Maikop oil fields, but never even got 1 liter of oil from it, and never reached Grozny and Baku oil fields. After several months of bitter fighting against the Red Army, using hundreds or thousands of tanks, planes, artilleries and soldiers, Hitler's army was defeated.

Paradoxically, after 1990 when capitalistic democracy in the Caucasus region was established, the oil rich fields were occupied by the rulers of democracy, without the use of any soldiers, tanks or military planes. It was enough to adhere to the rules of democracy and punish anybody who tries to avoid it. The power of democracy is astonishing. It could substitute soldiers, tanks, bombs or planes. It did not kill anyone as Hitler's army did, besides the 9.7 million missing men in the FSC during 1990-1999. But, these missing men are not counted by the historians studying the spread of freedom and democracy.

Slovakia is a similar example. The Slovak state, as a puppet regime of Hitler's Germany, was established in 1938. During 6 years of the shared regime, the German capital in Slovakia increased from 4% to 52%. This situation was repeated after democracy was established in Slovakia in 1989. The share of foreign capital in Slovakia increased significantly from the zero it started as. Most of the banks, insurance, industry, and media were taken by foreign companies without any fire from machineguns or bombardment, but by using democratic fire and bombardment from foreign owned media.

Bombardment of Cambodia. During 1969-1973 the USA bombed Cambodia to kill Vietnam's soldiers and its military installations. However, from the cockpit of a B-52 it was not easy to distinguish between a Vietnamese soldier and a Cambodian peasant. B-52's dropped 240,000 tons of bombs for 160 days in 1973 only (500,000 tons in total, more than they dropped on Japan in WWII). The USA's soldiers murdered nearly all humans, animals and fish in the Laotian Plain of the Jurs region. A Finnish government report estimates 600,000 innocent killed by the bombardment [46]. The power of totalitarian democracy was so strong that not only was nobody tried for this criminal act of the mass murder, but also most of the population did not know about this crime of democracy. Not one democratically elected leader officially accused representatives of the USA for crimes or genocide in Cambodia. Not one of them presented it in international court. Why? I assume because they recognized the power of the totalitarian democracy from the first hand.

Liberation of Iraq from totality. In 2003, coalition forces invited Iraq to remove their "totality and establish democracy". They even claimed many other reasons. The fact is that the military intervention was illegal. The UN Security Council resolution 1546 (2004) reads: "The Security Council, Welcoming the beginning of a new phase in Iraq's transition to a democratically elected government, and looking forward to the end of the occupation"... "2. Welcomes that, also by 30 June 2004, the occupation will end and the Coalition Provisional Authority will cease to exist, and that Iraq will reassert its full sovereignty;". The resolution clearly says that it was occupation in Iraq, not liberation. The UN Secretary General, Kofi Annan (BBC news, Sept 6, 2004) believes the American-led invasion of Iraq last year was illegal. He said it directly in the interview:

Q: So you don't think there was legal authority for the war?
A: I have stated clearly that it was not in conformity with the Security Council - with the UN Charter.
Q: It was illegal?
A: Yes, if you wish.
Q: It was illegal?
A: Yes, I have indicated it is not in conformity with the UN Charter, from our point of view and from the Charter point of view it was illegal.

If Iraq's occupation was illegal, it means that anyone who sent the troops to Iraq committed a criminal act and, according to democracy they must be brought to justice. Not one democratically elected leader officially accused representatives of the USA and its allies of crimes or genocide in Iraq. Not one of them presented it in international court. Why? I assume again, because they have recognized the power of the totalitarian democracy. Paradoxically, the criminal act of the military invasion to Iraq was condemned by leaders of communist and other countries These countries are mostly those that were not democratically elected and, according to a democratic tradition they belong to axis of evil.

Concentration camp to protect freedom and democracy. When Hitler's army invaded Eastern Europe during WWII, its commanders had the right to capture anybody without accusation and trial and bring him to a concentration camp. The democratic version of this tradition is recently publicized by the USA at Guantánamo Bay in Cuba. Anybody who is suspected of fighting against the military promotion of freedom and democracy can be detained at the democratic concentration camp at Guantánamo Bay. Of course, there is a difference between Hitler's and America's concentration camps. Hitler tried to hide his concentration camp practice, whereas the USA does not – because of the power of totalitarian democracy.

If terrorists or the mafia kidnap someone, everything is done to find them, try them and punish them. If capitalistic democracy does the same, not one democratically elected leader has officially accused democracy for criminal practice at Guantánamo Bay. Not one of them presented it in international court. Why? Because, they again recognize the power of the totalitarian democracy. Paradoxically again, the criminal practice at Guantánamo Bay was officially condemned by most leaders of communist and other countries, those that were not democratically elected.

Preemptive murder. In a CNN interview former president of the USA, Bill Clinton said that during his presidency he signed an order to physically liquidate Bin Ladin. He emphasized that unfortunately it was not successful. I remark that Bin Ladin was unknown to the general public at the time of the Clinton's presidency (as I am and many of us are now aware). Before I saw the interview on CNN, I did not know that preemptive murder also belongs to the rules of capitalistic democracy, similarly as preventive war or multiparty free elections do. No respected elected democratic leaders have officially condemned the preemptive murder, as they have not condemned the preemptive war. Not one of them presented it in international court. Why? Because they recognize the astonishing power of the totalitarian democracy we are living in. It means that the preemptive murder and the preemptive wars are generally legalized by recent capitalistic democracy.

Democratic power of money: The U.S. Federal Reserve, which is privately-owned by mostly unknown owners, has the right to print or issue money. Before the Great Depression, the quantity of M2-money supplied increased each year. After the stock market crashed at the New York stock exchange in 1929 the M2 supply gradually decreased (Figure 112). Many economists believe that because of the lack of available money after the crash, enterprises bankrupted and the stock market collapsed. The banks and enterprises that had collapsed were bought up and giant holding companies were created [47]. According to E. Mullins [47], these holding companies included those developed by some of the owners of the Federal Reserve, including the Marine Midland Corporation, the Lehman Corporation, and the Equity Corporation. The rulers over democracy enlarged and consolidated their holdings. Is it a democratic tradition? Was it repeated during the East Asian financial crisis in 1997 or when the Russian market collapsed in 1998? How many people died from poverty and how many holders enlarged and consolidated their holdings? What was the ratio? Is a traditional collection of the scalps of Indians a substitute for the democratic collection of shares by holders?

Another new rule of the capitalistic democracy. On August 5, 2004, the White House created the Office of the Coordinator for Reconstruction and Stabilization headed by former U.S. Ambassador to the Ukraine Carlos Pascual. Its mandate is to draw up elaborate "post-conflict" plans for the twenty-five countries that are not, as of yet, in conflict. According to Pascual, it will also be able to coordinate three full-scale reconstruction operations in different countries "at the same time," each lasting "five to seven years". Fittingly, a government devoted to perpetual pre-emptive deconstruction now has a standing office for perpetual pre-emptive reconstruction (Naomi Klein: The Rise of Disaster Capitalism). Unfortunately I could not find the list of the twenty-five countries. Since the leaders of the old Western European democratic countries have not objected to it, I assume that they are not on the list. I hope Slovakia or our neighbors are not on it neither. If we are, we will probably have to plan to use a nuclear power for civilian purposes only. I recognize that to use a perpetual mobile approach of destruction/reconstruction can secure the main goal of capitalism - to have maximum profit. The destruction-reconstruction industry was legalized and introduced into the rules of capitalistic democracy without any objection. The astonishing power of our democracy increased again.

These are only a few examples of the astonishing power of the recent totalitarian neo-liberal capitalistic democracy. There is more proof published in many books, and debates in many discussions all without positive effect so far. This is also poof that the power of the totalitarian capitalistic democracy is astonishing.

The practical position of most of the common citizens and all democratically elected leaders of the democratic developed countries to the killing in Cambodia and Guantanamo Bay or the preemptive wars is the same as they have to local or international mafia – most of them are afraid to touch it, some of them are terrorized by mafia and some of them belong to the mafia. Democratically legalized mass murder or genocide is an astonishing power of totalitarian capitalistic democracy. Paradoxically, the criminal rules of the totalitarian democracy are mostly condemned by leaders of communist countries, those were not democratically elected.

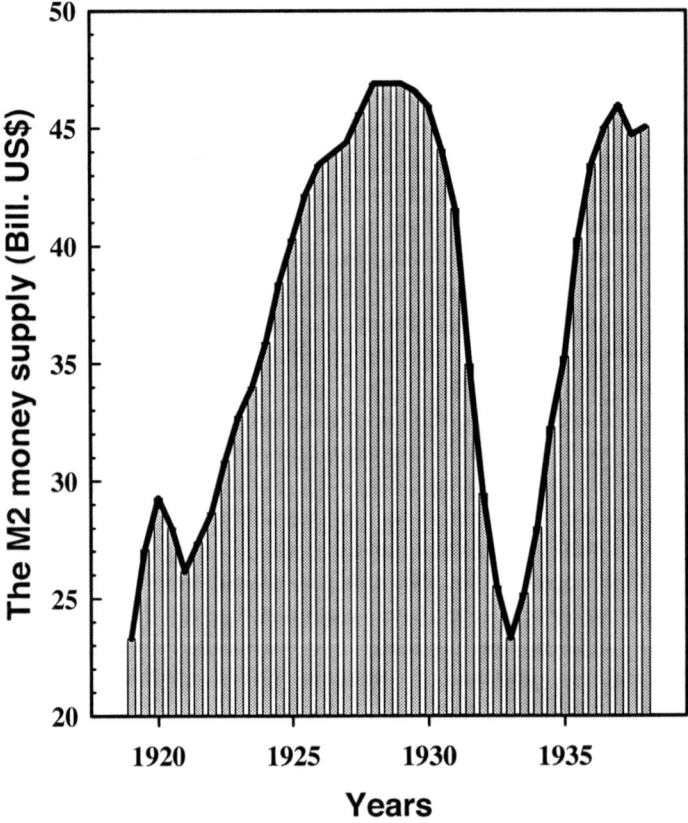

David C. Wheelock: Monetary Policy in the Great Depression:
What the Fed Did, and Why

Figure 112

5. Cult of ancient and our gods

5.1. Slavery and unlimited private property

How many states or what percent of the population would like to own slaves? I do not know; I do not even remember if any public opinion research has asked such a direct question. In the present-day it would be strange, and generally unacceptable for a state to own slaves. Similarly in our day it is unacceptable, and would be morally unacceptable for a family or individuals to own slaves, or for each free citizen to be allowed to buy slaves in the shopping-centre or at the market in cash or by leasing them. However it is not so long ago, maybe 300 years, that slavery was a normal phenomenon. For example, in the middle of the 19th century almost 50% of the Cuban population were slaves. In 1825 in the Southern part of the USA, private owners possessed about 1,750,000 slaves. 42% of New York homes owned at least one slave in 1703.

From the oldest written news from the times of the empires in Mesopotamia and Old Testament Moses to the end of the 17th century, a period of thousands of years, each statesman, philosopher, author, theologian, contemporary humanists and democrat accepted the existence and the legitimacy of slavery as a normal part of their world. Slavery was taken as something natural, organically belonging to the scheme of the functioning of the world. Aristotle's truth was legitimate: From the first hour after birth some are marked to be subordinate and others that they may rule. In the far past, slavery was so far spread and famous that people could not imagine the world without slaves. The democrat Socrates could not imagine the functioning of a democratic state without slaves. The humanist Thomas More even placed slaves into his vision of the world in the future in his booklet "Utopia", which was published in the 16th century. Christianity, which proclaimed equality of men before God, accepted slavery as a normal and essential thing. Saint Paul said that slaves and slave masters should accept their position because the Kingdom of the world would not survive if some people were not slaves and others free. Christianity "rationally" solved the problem of slavery. It divided the slave into two compartments: body and soul. In the spiritual eternal kingdom, where the soul belongs, all people are equal before God. In our temporary world slavery is natural because it is part of the sin of the world. The Catholic religion not only rationalized the ownership of slaves but even possessed slaves and supported the importation of African slaves to the American continent.

The contemporary fathers of democracy regarded slavery as normal. The Declaration of the Independence of the USA accepted in 1776 says: "that all men are created equal, that they are endowed by their Creator with certain unalienable Rights, that among these are Life, Liberty and the pursuit of Happiness". It is interesting that Thomas Jefferson, the chief author of the Declaration of Independence, at the time of its implementation owned about a hundred slaves. The Preamble of the U.S. Constitution states: "promote the general Wellfare, and secure the Blessing of Liberty to ourselves and our Posterity". The First Amendment of the US constitution reads: "Congress shall make no law respecting an establishment of religion, or prohibiting the free exercise thereof; or abridging the freedom of speech, or of the press; or the right of the people peaceably to assemble, and to petition the Government for a redress of grievances". It is again interesting, that five out of the first seven American presidents, who swore to the Constitution, were slave masters.

At the end of the 17th and the beginning of the 18th century, religious world radicals started to condemn the practice of slavery as a gross sin of greed, corruption and immorality in the society.

In the world today there is a generally accepted axiom that unlimited private ownership is the foundation of life and of successful development of the entire society and civilization. The trial to establish a society of limitations of the ownership of private resources failed. It is presented as an example of the inability of such a system to compete with the system of private ownership. The ability to own unlimited amounts of property is presented as an attribute of general justice, as the driving force of individuals and the society moving the development of the world the most optimal and quickest way forward.

Interesting, only a very few mention that the possibility to own an unlimited amount of property was mostly the driving motor behind individual's and the society to murder and wage war, in which they enslaved and murdered whole nations. Nobody reminds us that most of the bloody history of the human race is based on the right of the private ownership, on the possibility to own and use unlimited amounts of private property. The driving motor is ignited more by private property than collective property.

The benefits of private ownership are presented mainly by people who possess private property. The more of it they have, the more they propagate and gain more resources and the better their opportunities to propagate it become. They may increase their private property only in the case where other private property exists, which they can buy. The free market – free and unlimited purchase of property, factories, land, raw materials – is the modern analogy of the military occupation of a territory in the past, when sale-purchase agreements had no guarantee.

Unlimited ownership is likewise ingrained in the present world, as was slavery in the past. After some millennia, slavery was regarded as an inseparable part of the functioning of the world. I am curious to know when the human race will mature in its development; when it will make a step forward and start to regard private ownership of an unlimited amount of wealth as a great sin. When greed, corruption and immorality, will be seen as the main obstacles to the development of the society. I am curious. Will it make the step before the use of weapons of mass destruction for the increase or protection of private property?

How many states or what percentage of the population would like to own unlimited private property and rule over democracy? I do not know, even I do not remember if any public opinion research asked such a direct question. But I assume that this question is asked periodically during meetings of IMF, World Bank, WTO, NATO, UN, EU and many other institutions, as common citizen are asked it during democratic election.

5.2. Cult of the free election

During each democratic free election I am surprised by how relatively easy it is to choose someone who will have the right to make decisions about our life. As I described above, freely elected representatives in the FSC after 1989 managed to decrease living standards and caused a regression of society. Why was this so?

When we look at present-day politics, we see a very complicated giant. It requires talented, well-educated professional politicians, who devote more than 8 hours every day, who competently handle the synthesis and the analysis of information of complex internal and international relations (at least they are supposed to do so). Their decisions are exacting and very important for our life. Many ordinary people with their everyday worries do not have the time, capability, talent, or even the desire to devote time to politics. Therefore, most people are political layman – even when most have their personal views on it. Just as most people have their views on if there is other life in our galaxy. In politics, in relation to elections, it is also important to realize that many of the results of the most important meetings of highly placed politicians, financiers, industrial, military or broadcasting functionaries are held in secret from the most voters. The voters get to know of them sometime after 10-30 years, if at all. Hence, most of the voters do not have adequate information about the quality of the candidates.

Analogically we can implement the prescribed political patterns in directing an atomic power station. The directing of such a power plant requires talented, educated and professional experts to understand the complex processes in the power station. The decisions of the leaders of the power stations must be professional and very accurate. Ordinary people with their day-to-day worries do not have the time, the capability, the talent and not even the desire to understand the complexity of the atomic power station. Therefore most people are layman in the question of the power station complexity.

Now let us assume that "democracy of free elections" of the present type was introduced into an atomic power station and the voters would choose the leaders of the political parties to manage the atomic power station. In the election campaign the presidents of the parties would not explain to the people how the atomic power station would be best run (for most people would not understand it). They would convince them that they are fantastic in the running of an atomic power station. And the people, laymen in the running of an atomic power station would vote them into power. The essential component to such free elections would be the fact that the leader of the power station would be elected mostly by nonprofessionals.

Why is the leadership of atomic power plants not elected in free elections, in spite of the proclamation that free election is the best approach to run our civilization? Because mistakes made by the leadership of an atomic station could be immediate disaster for everybody around, and everybody would realize it immediately. Why is the leadership of a state democratically elected in free elections by laymen? Because possible mistakes are not immediately known for the most part and many people would not realize them for a long time. This is an advantage for the rulers over democracy using the laymen in free elections.

Why do most people suppose that the best situation is when laymen elect state rulers? Why is a state government of professional political experts, who would be chosen by competition on the basis of their references and professionalism, not being propagated? I assume that because it could be a disadvantage for the rulers over democracy. The recent democratic free election cannot work properly because free election is not compatible with unlimited private property.

Bowing down to trust and respect the present-day free democratic elections, based on capitalist democracy and unlimited private property, is the modern analogy of the faith and worship of the ancient societies to the gods of wind, trees or sun. It is a modern analogy of the orthodoxy, undoubtingness and truthfulness to which our developed brain is accustomed.

5.3. The magical world of the free market economy

Another pillar of capitalistic democracy we worship at is free market economy, even if it exists only in limited cases. The free market economy in many areas is not free, since it depends on many parameters of the parties involved. For example it depends on the number of nuclear weapons each party possesses, number and efficiency of military bases, professional soldiers, intelligence, owners of media, many local and international laws and agreements under unequal conditions. The free market economy has its own role in the recent system of the capitalist democracy.

In the past, even up to ten thousand years ago, a part of the generally accepted principle of politics was that when a group of people, tribe, nation, or state found out that they were physically or militarily stronger than another group of people, tribe, nation or state, they then used their superiority. The militarily stronger attacked the weaker. The stronger group often challenged the weaker group to meet on the battle field, where the victor takes everything. Each participant admitted that this working principle of the relationship of the stronger to the weaker, as a generally accepted principle of the then democracy.

Because development in every area progresses, in the present-day the ancient principle of democracy, the stronger invades the weaker is replaced by the modern democratic principle of the free market economy. The principle of the free market economy enables groups of people, tribes, nations, states, or multinational groups to realize that they are economically stronger than another group of people, tribe, nation, state or multinational group effectively and easily use its predominance. The economically stronger besieges the one who is economically weaker. In the present-day democracy the economically stronger group challenges the weaker group to sign treaties on the free market economy. The economically weaker is forced to meet in an economic battle in which the stronger takes everything. In the present-day each economic subject is forced to accept this principle of economic relations: the rights of the economically stronger to the property and products of the economically weaker. This is the generally accepted principle of the free market economy based on capitalist democracy and unlimited private property. The examples of the free market economic battle was seen in the FSC, after they accepted the principle of the free market economy, in Latin America, Africa and East Asia.

5.4. History has many years

In July 14, 1989, many of us watched on TV a pompous celebration of the 200th jubilee of the capture of Bastille in Paris. The French and many others are very proud of the French revolution, which shaped a new positive way for our civilization. Interestingly, the French revolution was drowning in blood, more than 20,000 revolutionaries were shot to death. I ask myself, did any of the military commanders ordering the execution of the communards think of the possibly that the capture of Bastille and thoughts of the executed communards would in the future be proudly celebrated by the French as a very significant positive step in human civilization? My guess is not any of them.

Thoughts of Christianity at the beginning of A.D. were very epochal and advanced. But at that time they were funny and considered to be potentially dangerous to the Roman Empire based on a slavery system. I wonder if any of the nobilities of the Roman Empire ~2000 years ago, sitting in the Coliseum and recreating in the Christians deadly struggle with wild animals, imagined that the thoughts and faith of the mocked and poor Christians would spread to all continents and live for more than 2,000 years, long after the Roman Empire lay in ruins? I would guess that nobody from the nobilities imagined such a development.

I am thinking about a parallel history with the future of socialism compared to the capture of Bastille and the humiliation of Christian ideas in the Roman Empire. Will our civilization proudly celebrate the capture of the Winter palace during the Bolshevik socialist revolution in 1917 as the French and many others proudly celebrate the capture of the Bastille in 1789?

I am very proud to say, yes.

References

[1] K. Ondrias: My, motroci XXI. storocia, takto prisahame (Agentura IQ+, Bratislava, 2000)

[2] K. Ondrias: Vseobecne kecy, fakty a nezodpovedane otazky (Agentura IQ+, Bratislava, 2001)

[3] K. Ondrias: Socializmus versus kapiatlizmus, Hry sex a terorizmus (Agentura IQ+, Bratislava, 2005)

[4] D. Caplovic, Viliam Cicaj, Lubomir Liptak, Jan Lukacka: Dejiny Slovenska (AEPress, Bratislava, 2000)

[5] Human Development Report 2001, Tab. 20, p. 208

[6] Human Development Report 2004, Tab. 23, p. 215

[7] M. Kollar, G. Meseznikov (eds): Slovensko 2003 – Suhrnna sprava o stave spolocnosti (IVO, Bratislava, 2003)

[8] http://www.fbi.gov/ucr/05cius/offenses/violent_crimes/murder_homicide.html
http://www.fbi.gov/ucr/05cius/data/table_16.html

[9] http://www.fbi.gov/ucr/05cius/offenses/violent_crimes/murder_homicide.html
http://www.fbi.gov/ucr/05cius/data/table_16.html

[10] Statisticka rocenka Ceskoslovensko 1930

[11] F. Gebauer, K. Kaplan, F. Koudelka, R. Vyhnalek: Soudni perzekuce politicke povahy v Ceskoslovensku 1948–1989 (Ustav pro soudobe dejiny AV CR. Praha, 1993)

[12] F. Miklosko, G. Smolikova, P. Smolik (eds.): Zlociny komunizmu na Slovensku 1948 – 1989, Vol. l., Vol. 2. (Michal Vasek, Presov, 2001)

[13] http://www.heise.de/tp/r4/artikel/5/5263/1.html

[14] M. E. Herman-Giddens et al.: Secondary Sexual Characteristics and Menses in Young Girls Seen in Office Practice: A Study from the Pediatric Research in Office Settings Network. PEDIATRICS Vol. 99, No. 4 (April 1997), pgs. 505-512.

[15] Psychology Today: Jul/Aug 2001.
http://www.ourstolenfuture.org/NewScience/reproduction/Puberty/potentialcauses.htm

[16] G. Meseznikov: Slovakia after Election (Institute for public questions, 2003, pp 10)

[17] UNDP: TRANSITION 1999: Human Development Report for Central and Eastern Europe and the CIS

[18] http://www.wider.unu.edu/pressrelease/press-release-2001-4.pdf

[19] G. A. Cornia, V. Popov (eds.): Where do we Stand a Decade After the Collapse of the USSR? Transition and Institutions: The Experience of

Late Reformers (Oxford University Press, 2001). http://www.wider.unu.edu/pressrelease/press-release-2001-4.pdf

[20] Executive Board of the UN, Development Programme and of the United Nations Population Fund: Second Country cooperation framework for the Russian Federation (2001–2003), First regular session 2001, Country cooperation frameworks and related matters.

[21] E.V. Tiurukanova: Human Trafficking in the Russian, Federation Inventory and Analysis of the Current Situation and Responses (Institute for Urban Economics for the UN/IOM Working Group on Trafficking in Human Beings, Moscow, 2006)

[22] UNICEF: A Decade of Transition, The MONEE Project CEE/CIS/Baltics REGIONAL MONITORING REPORT No. 8 – 2001
www.unicef-icdc.org/publications/pdf/monee8/eng/5.pdf

[23] T. N. Srinivasan, S. Park: China and India: Growth and Poverty, 1980-2000, China and India: Economic Performance, Competition and Cooperation, An Update.

[24] Growth and Interaction in the World Economy: The West and the Rest, 1000-2000 AD (paper presented at Harvard University, May 24, 2002, Maddison, Angus. 2002)

[25] Asia Times (Apr 30,2004), (http://www.atimes.com/atimes/China/FD30Ad04.html.)

[26] World Development Indicators 2005; Institute of International Finance, RBI and CSO: (http://in.rediff.com/money/2005/sep/27china.htm).

[27] T.N. Srinivasan: China, India and the World Economy. Working Paper No. 286. Stanford Center for International Development (July 2006).

[28] J. Arch Getty, Gabor Rittersporn, Victor Zemskov: Victims of the Soviet Penal System in the Pre-War Years: A First Approach on the Basis of Archival Evidence (American Historical Review, 98, October 1993, 1017-1049)

[29] Znet: Humanitarian imperialism, January 11, 2006

[30] http://www.unicef.org/infobycountry/india_india_statistics.html

[31] http://www.unicef.org/infobycountry/china.html

[32] http://www.unicef.org/infobycountry/haiti.html

[33] http://www.unicef.org/infobycountry/cuba.html

[34] C. Johnson: Exporting the American Model Markets and Democracy, (Znet 3.5.2006), http://www.zmag.org/content/showarticle.cfm?SectionID=72&ItemID=10197

[35] W. Blum: Killing Hope. U.S. Military and CIA Interventions Since World War II. (Common Courage Press, Monroe, Maine, 1995)

[36] W. Blum: Rogue State, A Guide to the World's Only Superpower (Common Courage Press, 2000)

[37] http://nottheenemy.com/index_files/Death%20Counts/Death %20 Counts.htm,
http://academic.evergreen.edu/g/grossmaz/interventions.html

[38] http://www.xs4all.nl/~stgvisie/VISIE/interventielijst.html

[39] S. Courtois, N. Werth, J.-L. Panne, A. Paczkowski, K. Bartosek, J.-L. Margolin: The Black Book of Communism: Crimes, Terror, Repression (Harvard University Press, 1999)

[40] B. Trent: The Panama Deception (DVD).
http://www.informationclearinghouse.info/article4078.htm)

[41] J.A.S. Grenville: A History of the World in the Twentieth Century. (The Belknap University Press, Cambridge, Massachusetts. 1994)

[42] J.M. Roberts: History of the World (Oxford University Press, New York 1993)

[43] Human Development Report 2005, pp. 4, 6, 28, 36 and 37

[44] House of Commons Library, Research Paper 04/70, Sept 15, 2004

[45] http://www.zmag.org/zmag/articles/march2000sklar.htm.

[46] J. B. Quigley: The Ruses for War: American Interventionism since World War II. (Prometheus Book, 1992)

[47] E. Mullins: The Secrets of the Federal Reserve (Bankers Research Institute, 1985)

Printed in the United Kingdom
by Lightning Source UK Ltd.
125694UK00001B/190/A